MW01406139

Verse by Verse Commentary on

JUDGES & RUTH

*Enduring Word Commentary Series
By David Guzik*

*The grass withers, the flower fades,
but the word of our God stands forever.*
Isaiah 40:8

Commentary on Judges & Ruth

Copyright ©1996 - 2024 by David Guzik

Printed in the United States of America or in the United Kingdom

Print Edition ISBN: 978-1-939466-85-3

Enduring Word

5662 Calle Real #184

Goleta, CA 93117

Electronic Mail: ewm@enduringword.com

Internet Home Page: www.enduringword.com

All rights reserved. No portion of this book may be reproduced in any form (except for quotations in reviews) without the written permission of the publisher.

Scripture references, unless noted, are from the New King James Version of the Bible, copyright ©1979, 1980, 1982, Thomas Nelson, Inc., Publisher.

Table of Contents

Judges 1 – Victory and Defeat in the Promised Land 7
Judges 2 – Israel's Failure, God's Mercy 20
Judges 3 – The First Three Judges 30
Judges 4 – Deborah and Barak 40
Judges 5 – The Song of Deborah 48
Judges 6 – The Call of Gideon 55
Judges 7 – The Battle Against Midian 66
Judges 8 – Pursuing After Midian 73
Judges 9 – The Rise and Fall of Abimelech 81
Judges 10 – Two Minor Judges and More Oppression 92
Judges 11 – Jephthah and the Ammonites 97
Judges 12 – Jephthah and the Ephraimites; Three Minor Judges 106
Judges 13 – The Birth of Samson 110
Judges 14 – Samson's First Failed Marriage 116
Judges 15 – Samson Against the Philistines 124
Judges 16 – Samson's Disgrace and Death 130
Judges 17 – Micah's Idolatry 139
Judges 18 – Micah's Idolatry and the Migration of the Tribe of Dan 144
Judges 19 – Gibeah's Crime 150
Judges 20 – Israel's War with Benjamin and Gibeah 156
Judges 21 – Wives for the Remnant of Benjamin 163

Ruth 1 – Ruth's Journey 168
Ruth 2 – Ruth's Work as a Gleaner 176
Ruth 3 – Ruth Makes an Appeal 184
Ruth 4 – The Marriage of Boaz and Ruth 192

Bibliography 201
Author's Remarks 203

Judges 1 – Victory and Defeat in the Promised Land

A. Continuing victory in Israel.

1. (1a) After the death of Joshua.

Now after the death of Joshua

> a. **Now after the death of Joshua**: In this period of the judges, Israel lost the critical next link in its godly leadership. Moses was the great leader used by God to bring them out of Egypt; Joshua was Moses' assistant and the great leader used by God to bring them into the land of promise. But Joshua appointed no leader after him to guide the whole nation. They were in a critical place where they had to trust God more intensely than they ever had before.
>
>> i. God gives wonderful human leaders to His work on this earth, and it is always difficult for God's people when those human leaders pass from the scene. In such a situation, it is possible to live in the past, wishing that leader was still present.
>
> b. **After the death of Joshua**: During this period of the judges (lasting some 340 years), there was no standing "office" of national leadership. Israel had no king, no president, and no prime minister on earth – only God in heaven. Yet at the necessary and appropriate times God called a leader for Israel. For the most part these leaders would rise, do his (or her) job, and then return to their obscurity. This required that the people of Israel maintain a real, abiding trust in God.
>
>> i. These national deliverers were not elected, and they didn't come to leadership through royal succession. They were specially gifted by God for leadership in their times, and the people of God recognized and respected that gifting.

ii. When this book uses the term *judge*, it doesn't mean someone who sits in a court and decides legal issues; the Hebrew word *shaphat* has more the idea of a *heroic leader*. "The Hebrew word *Shophetim* is derived from a word meaning to put right, and so to rule, and this is exactly what these men did." (Morgan)

iii. The people of Israel faced great obstacles. They were surrounded by people who lived in the most terrible immorality and idolatry, making a constant temptation to the same sins. The idolatrous lives of the Canaanites who lived around Israel were focused mainly on three things: money, sex, and having a relationship with their gods on their own terms.

c. **After the death of Joshua**: The book of Judges shows us a time that is sometimes confusing, difficult, and dark. For this reason, many neglect Judges and regard this period as a "dark age" of Israel's history. Yet if Judges is neglected, one passes over a wonderful account of the love and graciousness of God, and how He lovingly corrects His people.

i. What is revealed about *man* in Judges is depressing but what is shown about *God* in Judges is wonderful. "On the human side, it is a story of disobedience and disaster; and on the Divine side, of continued direction and deliverance." (Morgan)

ii. "There is, however, one light in which the whole book may be viewed, which renders it invaluable; it is a most remarkable history of the long-suffering of God towards the Israelites, in which we find the most signal instances of his *justice* and *mercy* alternately displayed; the people *sinned*, and were *punished*; they *repented*, and found *mercy*. Something of this kind we meet with in every page. And these things are written for our warning. None should *presume*, for God is JUST; none need *despair*, for God is MERCIFUL." (Clarke)

2. (1b-2) After Joshua's death, Israel seeks the LORD.

It came to pass that the children of Israel asked the LORD, saying, "Who shall be first to go up for us against the Canaanites to fight against them?"

And the LORD said, "Judah shall go up. Indeed I have delivered the land into his hand."

a. **The children of Israel asked the LORD**: Here they did the *right* thing – the thing Joshua would have wanted them to do. With Joshua gone, they were not left without a leader; they were simply called to a renewed trust in God.

b. **And the LORD said**: When Israel sought the LORD, He guided them. This is a consistent pattern throughout the book of Judges. God never failed to deliver and help His people when they sought Him.

i. Jesus expressed the same idea in Luke 11:9: *"So I say to you, ask, and it will be given to you; seek, and you will find; knock, and it will be opened to you."* When believers ask of God and seek Him in sincerity, they should expect that He will answer. His response may come in an unexpected way, but believers should expect that it will come.

c. **Judah shall go up**: God directed that the tribe of Judah – the tribe that the Messiah would come from – should lead the way in this fight. Judah was also the largest and strongest tribe. In this case, God's plan made obvious military sense as well.

i. Under the leadership of Joshua Israel had broken the back of the Canaanite military strength, yet it remained for each individual tribe to go in and possess what God had given them.

3. (3-7) Judah (with the tribe of Simeon) defeats Bezek and their king.

So Judah said to Simeon his brother, "Come up with me to my allotted territory, that we may fight against the Canaanites; and I will likewise go with you to your allotted territory." And Simeon went with him. Then Judah went up, and the LORD delivered the Canaanites and the Perizzites into their hand; and they killed ten thousand men at Bezek. And they found Adoni-Bezek in Bezek, and fought against him; and they defeated the Canaanites and the Perizzites. Then Adoni-Bezek fled, and they pursued him and caught him and cut off his thumbs and big toes. And Adoni-Bezek said, "Seventy kings with their thumbs and big toes cut off used to gather *scraps* under my table; as I have done, so God has repaid me." Then they brought him to Jerusalem, and there he died.

a. **Judah said to Simeon his brother, "Come up with me"**: The leaders of the tribe of Judah acted wisely here. By partnering with another tribe, the work was much easier. Here, the tribes functioned in the same way that God wants the church to function – as a body, with each part of the body helping other parts of the body.

i. "The tribes of Judah and Simeon were blood-brothers (Genesis 29:33-35) and are uniformly depicted as acting in the closest relationship." (Cundall)

b. **The LORD delivered the Canaanites and the Perizzites into their hand**: Seeking the LORD, obeying His guidance, and working together as a community always produces helpful results. Their success was plain to see: the LORD **delivered** all their enemies into their hands.

c. **They killed ten thousand men at Bezek**: This place that they conquered was called **Bezek** and the leader of this city was **Adoni-Bezek**, which means "lord of lightning." This was an enemy with a fearful name, but Judah and Simeon defeated him nonetheless.

> i. **And they found Adoni-Bezek in Bezek**: The word **found** in this verse expresses a hostile encounter. The armies of Judah and Simeon didn't just stumble over **Adoni-Bezek**.
>
> ii. Their punishment of **Adoni-Bezek** may seem cruel, yet it was simply justice in its truest sense. He had done this same thing to **seventy kings**; so now he had his own toes and fingers cut off.
>
> iii. The punishment made Adoni-Bezek worthless as a warrior; he could trouble Israel no more as a military man. "It was a custom among those Romans who did not like a military life, to cut off their own thumbs, that they might not be called into the army. Sometimes the parents cut off the thumbs of their children, that they might not be called into the army." (Clarke)
>
> iv. Judah and Simeon acted in an unselfish manner. They fought a battle in territory that did not directly belong to them. The city of Bezek was far to the north of Judah's tribal lands.

4. (8-11) The victories won by the tribe of Judah in the south.

Now the children of Judah fought against Jerusalem and took it; they struck it with the edge of the sword and set the city on fire. And afterward the children of Judah went down to fight against the Canaanites who dwelt in the mountains, in the South, and in the lowland. Then Judah went against the Canaanites who dwelt in Hebron. (Now the name of Hebron *was* formerly Kirjath Arba.) And they killed Sheshai, Ahiman, and Talmai.

From there they went against the inhabitants of Debir. (The name of Debir *was* formerly Kirjath Sepher.)

> a. **Judah fought against Jerusalem and took it**: Here it is recorded that the city of Jerusalem fell to Judah. According to the division of land to the tribes Jerusalem was on the border between Judah and Benjamin (Joshua 15:2, 18:28). It was occupied for a time (Adoni-Bezek was taken there and died there), but later fell back to the Jebusites (Judges 1:21). Under the leadership of King David Israel conquered the city again some 400 years later (2 Samuel 5:6-10).

i. "The city of Jerusalem is one of the oldest cities in the world, having been occupied almost continually for a period of 5,000 years." (Cundall)

b. **Then Judah went against the Canaanites who dwelt in Hebron**: Judah also conquered Hebron, and the city was given to faithful Caleb and his family (see Joshua 15:13-19).

i. Hebron was the ancient city of Abraham and the city which discouraged the ten unfaithful spies from taking the Promised Land in Moses' day because of the Anakim who lived there (Numbers 13:22-23).

ii. Cundall notes that Judges 1:9 describes the three major geographic divisions of Israel:

- **The mountains**, or more literally *the hill country*, "which describes the mountainous regions between Jerusalem and Hebron."
- **The South**, also known as the *Negev*, which is "the semi-arid area between Hebron and Kadesh-barnea."
- **The lowland**, sometimes called the *Shelphelah* from the Hebrew word used here. This "is the region of foot-hills running north and south between the coastal plain and the central mountain range."

5. (12-15) Othniel's conquest and reward; Achsah's bold request.

Then Caleb said, "Whoever attacks Kirjath Sepher and takes it, to him I will give my daughter Achsah as wife." And Othniel the son of Kenaz, Caleb's younger brother, took it; so he gave him his daughter Achsah as wife. Now it happened, when she came *to him*, that she urged him to ask her father for a field. And she dismounted from *her* donkey, and Caleb said to her, "What do you wish?" So she said to him, "Give me a blessing; since you have given me land in the South, give me also springs of water."

And Caleb gave her the upper springs and the lower springs.

a. **Whoever attacks Kirjath Sepher and takes it**: Caleb was a man of great personal courage and integrity (Numbers 13:30, Joshua 14:6-15). He knew the value of inspiring and motivating bold courage in the next generation. Therefore, he generously offered his daughter **Achsah** in marriage to the man who was bold and courageous enough to attack and conquer the town of **Kirjath Sepher**.

b. **Othniel...took it**: Caleb's nephew **Othniel** was the man who boldly conquered Kirjath Sepher. This same Othniel was later one of the judges of Israel (Judges 3:9-11). He married his cousin Achsah who herself boldly asked for a valuable part of the land: **springs of water**. Boldness seemed to run in Caleb's family.

c. **Give me a blessing**: Charles Spurgeon preached a wonderful sermon on Judges 1:12-15 titled, *Achsah's Asking, A Pattern of Prayer*. Spurgeon showed how the request from a daughter (Achsah) to a father (Caleb) is a parable or illustration of prayer.

> i. Achsah was a good example because *she thought about what she wanted before she went to her father*. Before you pray, know what you need before God. She came to God with a very definite request that had been considered beforehand. "Think what you are going to ask before you begin to pray, and then pray like business men. This woman does not say to her father, 'Father, listen to me,' and then utter some pretty little oration about nothing; but she knows what she is going to ask for, and why she is going to ask it." (Spurgeon)

> ii. Achsah was a good example because *she asked for help with her request*, asking her husband – **she urged him to ask her father for a field**. "A friend, some time ago, said to me, 'My dear pastor, whenever I cannot pray for myself, and there are times when I feel shut up about myself, I always take to praying for you: 'God bless him, at any rate!' and I have not long been praying for you before I begin to feel able to pray for myself.' I should like to come in for many of those odd bits of prayer. Whenever any of you get stuck in the mud, do pray for me. It will do you good, and I shall get a blessing." (Spurgeon)

> iii. Achsah was a good example because *she went humbly, yet eagerly*.

> iv. Achsah's prayer was a good example because she *asked for what she wanted*. It is a pleasure for God to hear His people ask.

> v. Achsah's prayer was a good example of prayer because of the *simplicity* of her prayer. Her prayer was, **give me a blessing**.

> vi. Achsah's prayer was a good example because *she added gratitude to her petition* (**you have given me land in the South**).

> vii. Achsah's prayer was a good example because *she used past blessing as a reason to ask for more*.

> viii. Achsah's prayer was a good example because *she realized that what she had been given before was of no use without continual springs of water*. Spurgeon related this to his dependence on the continual blessing of the Holy Spirit on his preaching. "How can I preach to them if thou

dost not give me springs of water? .... What is the use of the hearers if there be not the power of the Holy Spirit going with the Word to bless them? Give me springs of water." (Spurgeon)

ix. Achsah's prayer was a good example because *her father gave her what she asked.*

x. Achsah's prayer was a good example because her prayer was answered; *her father gave to her in large measure.*

xi. Achsah's prayer was a good example because *her father was not critical of the request in the slightest way.*

6. (16-20) Victory and stalemate for the tribe of Judah in the southern lands of Israel.

Now the children of the Kenite, Moses' father-in-law, went up from the City of Palms with the children of Judah into the Wilderness of Judah, which *lies* in the South *near* Arad; and they went and dwelt among the people. And Judah went with his brother Simeon, and they attacked the Canaanites who inhabited Zephath, and utterly destroyed it. So the name of the city was called Hormah. Also Judah took Gaza with its territory, Ashkelon with its territory, and Ekron with its territory. So the Lord was with Judah. And they drove out the mountaineers, but they could not drive out the inhabitants of the lowland, because they had chariots of iron. And they gave Hebron to Caleb, as Moses had said. Then he expelled from there the three sons of Anak.

a. **The City of Palms**: This was another name for the city of Jericho. The Kenites went from there to **Arad**, a city out in the Judean wilderness, west of Masada and the Dead Sea. **Zephath** isn't too far from there; **Gaza** and **Ashkelon** were out towards the coast and later became Philistine strongholds.

i. Cundall believed that the **City of Palms** was another city further south: "*The city of palm trees* elsewhere indicates Jericho (Judges 3:13), but that identification is ruled out here by the context. Possibly it was located at the southern end of the Dead Sea."

b. **They had chariots of iron**: As impressive as Judah's victory was it was nevertheless incomplete. These Canaanites fought Judah to a stalemate and were not driven out of the land. Judah did not defeat those who had the latest military technology: **chariots of iron**. These were wooden chariots reinforced by iron, making them much stronger and more stable.

i. "Strange! Were the *iron chariots* too strong for Omnipotence?" (Clarke)

ii. This spoke more of Judah's lack of full trust in God than it did of Canaanite military superiority. Chariots were no problem for God's people when they were trusting God (see Exodus 14:7-29, Joshua 11:1-8, and 1 Kings 20:21). Their attitude should have been like that reflected in Psalm 20:7: *Some trust in chariots, and some in horses; but we will remember the name of the LORD our God.*

iii. "If they had believed in God, and gone forth in his name, the horses would soon have fled, as indeed they did when God gave his people faith. When Barak led the way with Deborah, then they smote Jabin, who had nine hundred chariots of iron.... the imperfection of their faith lay in this, as it may do in yours, my brethren, – that they believed one promise of God and did not believe another. There is a kind of faith which is strong in one direction, but utter weakness if tried in other ways." (Spurgeon)

iv. "An unconverted person is here who has been thinking of coming to Christ, but he says: 'I cannot give up all my sins. One of them I must retain: all the rest I can leave, but that one is invincible, for it has chariots of iron. I cannot drive it out.' That sin must die, or you will perish by it. Depend upon it, that sin which you would save from slaughter will slaughter you." (Spurgeon)

c. **Then he expelled from there the three sons of Anak**: Caleb's victory over the **sons of Anak** showed what a trusting Israel could accomplish. The **sons of Anak** were large men and fierce warriors (Numbers 13:33, Deuteronomy 9:2), yet with God's help Caleb defeated them (Joshua 15:13-14).

i. "Yet, as if to rebuke them, they had a singular incident set before them for the vindication of God's power, and of that we read in the twentieth verse. Caleb, that grand old man, who still lived on, the sole survivor of all who came out of Egypt, had obtained Hebron as his portion, and he went up in his old age, when his bones were sore and set, and slew the three sons of Anak, even three mighty giants, and took possession of their city. In this way the Lord's power was trusted and vindicated from the slur which Judah had brought upon it." (Spurgeon)

ii. "I will not speak of Caleb, for you will tell me, 'Ah, he was an old, old man, and belonged to another generation. He was just going off the scene; we do not wonder that he did great things.' Ay, but he had a nephew, one Othniel, a young man.... The young hero stood forward, and went up to the fortress, and took the city, and passed it over to his uncle's hands, and received the promised reward. Oh yes, and we have seen raised up…more young heroes who have been self-denying, self-distrustful, inconsiderate of themselves, who have been willing for Christ's sake to be anything or nothing, and God has been with them, and the power of the Most High has rested upon them." (Spurgeon)

B. Incomplete victory and defeat.

1. (21) The tribe of Benjamin does not take possession of Jerusalem.

But the children of Benjamin did not drive out the Jebusites who inhabited Jerusalem; so the Jebusites dwell with the children of Benjamin in Jerusalem to this day.

    a. **The children of Benjamin did not drive out the Jebusites**: This was a case where the battle had already been won (Judges 1:8); the tribe of Benjamin simply had to take what was already theirs. It would certainly take effort, but the critical battle was over. Jerusalem belonged to them.

    b. **So the Jebusites dwell with the children of Benjamin in Jerusalem to this day**: Up until the time of the writer of the book of Judges, the tribe of Benjamin failed to cast out the Jebusites and therefore lived in constant military and spiritual danger.

2. (22-26) The house of Joseph conquers the city of Bethel.

And the house of Joseph also went up against Bethel, and the LORD *was* with them. So the house of Joseph sent men to spy out Bethel. (The name of the city *was* formerly Luz.) And when the spies saw a man coming out of the city, they said to him, "Please show us the entrance to the city, and we will show you mercy." So he showed them the entrance to the city, and they struck the city with the edge of the sword; but they let the man and all his family go. And the man went to the land of the Hittites, built a city, and called its name Luz, which *is* its name to this day.

    a. **The house of Joseph**: This is an interesting combining of the two tribes that came from Joseph (Ephraim and Manasseh) into one group, **the house of Joseph**.

    b. **The LORD was with them**: The men of Ephraim and Manasseh made effective use of **spies** and the information they gathered. Yet, the real reason for their victory was that the **LORD was with them**.

    c. **But they let the man and all his family go**: They seemed to use the events surrounding Rahab and the conquering of Jericho as a pattern (Joshua 3, 6). This perhaps implies that this **man** and his **family** gave their allegiance to Yahweh, the covenant God of Israel, even as Rahab and her family did.

3. (27-29) Manasseh and Ephraim fail to drive out all the Canaanites.

However, Manasseh did not drive out *the inhabitants of* Beth Shean and its villages, or Taanach and its villages, or the inhabitants of Dor and its villages, or the inhabitants of Ibleam and its villages, or the inhabitants of Megiddo and its villages; for the Canaanites were determined to dwell in that land. And it came to pass, when Israel was strong, that they put the Canaanites under tribute, but did not completely drive them out.

Nor did Ephraim drive out the Canaanites who dwelt in Gezer; so the Canaanites dwelt in Gezer among them.

a. **The Canaanites were determined to dwell in that land**: At first, there were pockets of Canaanites that these tribes were unable to push out of the land. But when the tribes eventually grew strong enough, they compromised with the Canaanites and thought they could use them to their advantage (**they put the Canaanites under tribute**).

i. "The story as here given reveals that whereas the work began in earnest, it gradually weakened. The Lord was with Judah and victories resulted. The Lord was with Joseph and Beth-el was taken. Manasseh and Ephraim and all the rest weakened in the work and Canaanites were left in possession." (Morgan)

b. **Did not completely drive them out**: Their inability – or unwillingness – to drive out the Canaanites can be understood as a pattern for present day believers. In the same way, when someone first begins their Christian life, they may not be strong enough in the LORD to deal with all the things they see that need changing, yet as they grow as a disciple of Jesus Christ, they must not slack in dealing with those areas. Believers are never to make a peace treaty with sins; instead, they must determine to **drive them out**.

i. "The one point that Israel should have borne in mind was that they [the Canaanites] had no right there. The land was not theirs, it had become Israel's. And moreover, God was prepared to drive them out; so that his people would have no fighting to do, but only to chase a flying foe." (Meyer)

ii. **Gezer** didn't belong to Israel until it was given to Solomon by Pharaoh (1 Kings 9:16).

4. (30) The tribe of Zebulun compromises and accommodates the Canaanites, putting them under tribute.

Nor did Zebulun drive out the inhabitants of Kitron or the inhabitants of Nahalol; so the Canaanites dwelt among them, and were put under tribute.

a. **Nor did Zebulun drive out the inhabitants**: Each tribe had its own responsibility and its own battles to fight. In their battle, the tribe of **Zebulun** failed to take all that God had provided for them.

b. **So the Canaanites dwelt among them, and were put under tribute**: The people of Zebulun thought they could make their incomplete obedience work to their advantage, especially economically. They failed to appreciate that the **Canaanites** who **dwelt among them** would eventually bring them into both social and spiritual crisis.

i. Because the crisis was not immediate, it was easy to think that it was not real. Yet it was certain, and only trust and obedience to God could spare them the later cycle of crisis that marks the book of Judges.

5. (31-32) The tribe of Asher fails in taking full possession of their land.

Nor did Asher drive out the inhabitants of Acco or the inhabitants of Sidon, or of Ahlab, Achzib, Helbah, Aphik, or Rehob. So the Asherites dwelt among the Canaanites, the inhabitants of the land; for they did not drive them out.

a. **Nor did Asher drive out**: The tribe of Asher also failed to take what God had apportioned for them. Each tribe that failed made it easier for the other tribes to also fail.

b. **So the Asherites dwelt among the Canaanites**: Of the people of Zebulun we read that *the Canaanites dwelt among them* (Judges 1:30). Yet in Asher it was even worse; it was the **Asherites** who **dwelt among the Canaanites**. They suffered a worse degree of social and spiritual declension.

i. "Whilst most of the tribes were able to occupy at least some part of their allotted territory, the tribe of Asher seems to have failed completely to dislodge the Canaanites." (Cundall)

6. (33) The tribe of Naphtali compromises and accommodates the Canaanites, putting them under tribute.

Nor did Naphtali drive out the inhabitants of Beth Shemesh or the inhabitants of Beth Anath; but they dwelt among the Canaanites, the inhabitants of the land. Nevertheless the inhabitants of Beth Shemesh and Beth Anath were put under tribute to them.

a. **Nor did Naphtali drive out the inhabitants**: The tribe of Naphtali found it difficult to counter the trend of the other tribes. The defeat of one of the tribes affected the condition of the other tribes.

i. God never intended for Israel to conquer the land of Canaan *easily*, and He never intended it to happen quickly. Exodus 23:29-30 and Deuteronomy 7:22-24 both say that God intended to give them the land *little by little*. Though God planned for Israel to take the land through constant trust in Him and frequent battles, they failed to do this and therefore did not **drive out the inhabitants**. It was almost as if Israel said, "If we can't win it easily, then we don't want it at all."

b. **They dwelt among the Canaanites.... Nevertheless the inhabitants of Beth Shemesh and Beth Anath were put under tribute to them**: The people of Naphtali combined both facets of capitulation to the enemy. In some regions of their territory, they lived under the shadow of the dominating Canaanites; in other regions they put the Canaanites **under tribute** to them. Both aspects fell well short of God's command and intent for the people of Israel.

7. (34-36) The tribe of Dan fails in taking full possession of their land.

And the Amorites forced the children of Dan into the mountains, for they would not allow them to come down to the valley; and the Amorites were determined to dwell in Mount Heres, in Aijalon, and in Shaalbim; yet when the strength of the house of Joseph became greater, they were put under tribute.

Now the boundary of the Amorites *was* from the Ascent of Akrabbim, from Sela, and upward.

a. **The Amorites forced the children of Dan into the mountains**: Here, we see the people of God being pushed around by their enemies. This should never be the case when God's people are walking in the strength of their God.

b. **When the strength of the house of Joseph became greater, they were put under tribute**: Again, instead of doing what God said should be done with these enemies (to completely drive them out), they decided to use them as *they* thought best; to put these enemies under tribute.

i. "This they did out of covetousness, that root of all evil, neglecting the command of God to the contrary." (Trapp)

c. **The boundary of the Amorites**: The result was that the **Amorites** had an appointed boundary within the inheritance of God's people. This was an unnecessary and dangerous accommodation to the social and spiritual enemies of the people of God.

i. There is a dangerous and seductive form of pacifism in the Christian life, which ignores the reality of the spiritual battle so clearly described in Ephesians 6:10-20 and referred to by analogy in the book of Judges. This pacifist attitude will happily make a peace with the devil and basically says, "I will not harm your interests if you leave me alone." This attitude of spiritual surrender is unacceptable for the Christian.

ii. Leon Trotsky, the infamous Communist leader said at least one correct thing: "You may not be interested in war, but war is interested in you." To take an attitude of spiritual surrender is to willingly *lose* that war.

iii. At this time, the tribes of Israel at their best experienced incomplete victory; at their worst they simply surrendered to and accommodated the enemy. This makes believers value the complete and glorious victory of Jesus Christ on their behalf even more. There was *nothing* left incomplete in the victory He won for His people on the cross and through the resurrection.

Judges 2 – Israel's Failure, God's Mercy

A. From Gilgal to Bochim.

1. (1-3) The Angel of the LORD preaches to Israel.

Then the Angel of the LORD came up from Gilgal to Bochim, and said: "I led you up from Egypt and brought you to the land of which I swore to your fathers; and I said, 'I will never break My covenant with you. And you shall make no covenant with the inhabitants of this land; you shall tear down their altars.' But you have not obeyed My voice. Why have you done this? Therefore I also said, 'I will not drive them out before you; but they shall be *thorns* in your side, and their gods shall be a snare to you.'"

> a. **The Angel of the LORD came up from Gilgal**: It is likely that this was God Himself, appearing in a human form. There are frequent Old Testament appearances of **the Angel of the LORD** that indicate that it is God Himself.
>
>> i. There is a legitimate question as to if *every* mention of **the Angel of the LORD** is a divine appearance. As G. Campbell Morgan wrote, "This messenger, referred to as 'the angel of the Lord,' may have been a prophet, for the word rendered 'angel' may with equal accuracy be rendered messenger. On the other hand, it may have been a special divine and angelic personality."
>>
>> ii. Assuming this to be a divine appearance (as the author believes it does indicate), we surmise that this was Jesus Christ appearing to the people of Israel before His incarnated appearance in Bethlehem. We know this is Jesus for two reasons.
>>
>>> • Because the **Angel of the LORD** here claimed divinity by saying that He was the one who led Israel up from Egypt, who made

a covenant with Israel (Judges 2:1), and who personally called Israel to obedience (Judges 2:2).

- Because this person, appearing in human form before Israel, cannot be God the Father, because the Father is described as *invisible* (1 Timothy 1:17) and one *whom no man has seen or can see* (1 Timothy 6:16).

iii. The idea of Jesus, the second person of the Trinity, appearing as a man before Bethlehem is provocative, but logical. God the Son *existed* before Bethlehem (Micah 5:2); why should He *not*, on isolated but important occasions, appear in bodily form? This happened on other occasions, such as Genesis 18:1-2, 18:16-33, 32:24-30, and Judges 13:1-23.

iv. "Not in such a body as God had prepared for him when he took upon himself the form of a servant, but in such a form and fashion as seemed most congruous to his divine majesty, and to the circumstances of those he visited, this angel of the divine covenant whom we delight in came and spoke unto this people." (Spurgeon)

b. **I led you up from Egypt and brought you to the land**: The first thing Jesus (as **the Angel of the Lord**) did was to remind Israel of His great love and faithfulness to them. He delivered them from Egypt's bondage; He gave them an abundant land of promise; He gave them a covenant that He would never break.

i. It is God's general pattern to remind believers of His great love and faithfulness *before* calling them to obedience or confronting their sin. God's people love God because He first loved them (1 John 4:19), and they can only really obey Him as they walk in His love and abide in His covenant.

ii. The words, **I will never break My covenant with you** remind believers that even though Israel never fully lived up to their part of the covenant, God promised that He would never break His part of the covenant.

c. **You have not obeyed My voice. Why have you done this?** The **Angel of the Lord** confronted Israel in love. The question was stinging in its simplicity; there is never a *good reason* for our disobedience.

i. Israel's real problem was not one of military power or technology; it was a spiritual problem. "The deplorable spiritual condition of the Israelites, not their lack of chariots, lay behind their failure to dispossess the Canaanites." (Wolf)

d. **I will not drive them out before you; but they shall be thorns in your side**: The **Angel of the LORD** announced that He would allow the work of possessing the land to go unfinished as a way of correcting a disobedient Israel.

> i. **I will not drive them out before you** indicates that God would not do the work of conquering Canaan all by Himself. In the early years of the campaign in Canaan God did fight for Israel in supernatural ways. Yet He never intended it to be that way for the entire campaign of conquering the Canaanites.
>
> ii. Believers often wish that God would do the work of Christian maturity for them; that they would wake up one morning and a certain besetting sin would just be gone. Sometimes God grants such a miraculous deliverance, and He may be praised for that. But more commonly He requires the partnership of the believer with Him in the process of Christian growth. This partnership is important to God because it shows that the believer's heart is where His heart is; that they are truly growing close to God.

e. **They shall be thorns in your side, and their gods shall be a snare to you**: The promise that the Canaanites would remain as problems to the nation was announced beforehand to Israel if they would not faithfully drive out the Canaanites.

> i. *But if you do not drive out the inhabitants of the land from before you, then it shall be that those whom you let remain shall be irritants in your eyes and thorns in your sides, and they shall harass you in the land where you dwell.* (Numbers 33:55)

2. (4-6) The people respond with weeping and sorrow.

So it was, when the Angel of the LORD spoke these words to all the children of Israel, that the people lifted up their voices and wept.

Then they called the name of that place Bochim; and they sacrificed there to the LORD. And when Joshua had dismissed the people, the children of Israel went each to his own inheritance to possess the land.

> a. **The people lifted up their voices and wept**: This emotional response of the people was very hopeful. With all the weeping and wailing, there was reason to believe that God's word had a deep impact upon them, and that they were on their way to a genuine revival of God's work among them.
>
> > i. Sadly, it was not the case. The subsequent record of the book of Judges shows that this initial reaction of sorrow and repentance did not mature into real, lasting repentance. Real repentance shows itself in action, not necessarily in weeping. We can be sorry about the consequences of our sin without being sorry about the sin itself.

ii. One may weep and outwardly show repentance without ever inwardly repenting. This is why the LORD challenged Israel in Joel 2:13: *So rend your heart, and not your garments; return to the LORD your God, for He is gracious and merciful, slow to anger, and of great kindness.*

iii. It is good to see people truly weeping over their sin and it should never be discouraged. However, "The tear is the natural drop of moisture, and soon evaporates; the better thing is the inward torrent of grief within the soul, which leaves the indelible mark within…. One grain of faith is better than a gallon of tears. A drop of genuine repentance is more precious than a torrent of weeping." (Spurgeon)

b. **They sacrificed there to the LORD**: In this, they did the right thing. Any awareness of sin should drive us to God's appointed sacrifice. In their day that meant sin offerings of bulls and rams; for the modern believer it means remembering God's sacrifice on the cross of Jesus Christ.

i. They did this "In testimony of their faith in Christ's merits (for they mourned not desperately) and their thankfulness that God had sent them a preacher, and not an executioner, considering their deserts." (Trapp)

c. **And when Joshua had dismissed the people**: This shows that Judges 2 begins in retrospect, looking back to the days even before the death of Joshua (which was described in Judges 1:1). This hopeful response to the **Angel of the LORD** started when Joshua was still alive.

3. (7-10) The new generation in Israel.

So the people served the LORD all the days of Joshua, and all the days of the elders who outlived Joshua, who had seen all the great works of the LORD which He had done for Israel. Now Joshua the son of Nun, the servant of the LORD, died *when he was* one hundred and ten years old. And they buried him within the border of his inheritance at Timnath Heres, in the mountains of Ephraim, on the north side of Mount Gaash. When all that generation had been gathered to their fathers, another generation arose after them who did not know the LORD nor the work which He had done for Israel.

a. **So the people served the LORD all the days of Joshua**: Joshua's legacy was seen in the godliness of Israel during his leadership. He was truly one of history's great men of God.

b. **The servant of the LORD**: This was a deeply meaningful title for Joshua. It is applied only to great men of God like Moses (Deuteronomy 34:5), and David (Psalm 18:1, title), and the courageous prophets (2 Kings 9:7).

c. **And all the days of the elders who outlived Joshua**: Israel was also faithful to God in the days of Joshua's immediate successors. But afterward, there arose a generation who had *not* **seen all the great works of the LORD which He had done for Israel**.

d. **Another generation arose after them who did not know the LORD nor the work which He had done for Israel**: The new generation had no personal relationship with God, and no personal awareness of His power. God was someone who their parents related to and who did great things for their parents generation.

B. A summary of Israel's history during the time of the judges.

1. (11-13) Israel falls into idolatry.

Then the children of Israel did evil in the sight of the LORD, and served the Baals; and they forsook the LORD God of their fathers, who had brought them out of the land of Egypt; and they followed other gods from *among* **the gods of the people who** *were* **all around them, and they bowed down to them; and they provoked the LORD to anger. They forsook the LORD and served Baal and the Ashtoreths.**

a. **The children of Israel did evil in the sight of the LORD**: Even in the days of Joshua Israel did not fully possess what they could have in the Promised Land. Yet in that time they remained faithful to God, and they did not worship the idols of the Canaanites. After the death of Joshua, they fell into the worship of these grotesque idols.

i. It is strange that anyone would want to trade a personal, real, living God for a false god that is the figment of man's imagination. Yet there is something within man that is afraid of the exact God we need; most people would rather serve a god of their own creation than the real, living God who cannot be controlled. The gods man creates are the gods wanted by man's sinful desires.

b. **And served the Baals**: The Canaanite idol Baal was an attractive rival to Yahweh because he was thought to be the god over the weather and nature for the Canaanites; he was essentially the god of agricultural success. In an agricultural society, people served Baal because they wanted good weather for abundant crops and flocks. One might say that the goal with Baal worship was financial success; he was regarded as a god of personal wealth.

i. "There were also 'Baals' associated with particular places, like the Baal of Peor (Numbers 25:3) or Baal-Berith (Judges 9:4); and this may account for the plural form." (Wolf)

ii. According to Wolf, the word *Baal* also meant "husband" or "owner." Therefore, when Israel worshipped the Canaanite god Baal, they entertained another "husband" or "owner."

c. **They forsook the Lord and served Baal and the Ashtoreths**: The Canaanite idol Ashtoreth was an attractive rival to Yahweh because she was thought to be the goddess of love, sex, and fertility. She was usually honored with the practice of ritual sex with a priestess-prostitute. One might say that the goal with Ashtoreth was sex and love.

i. "The religion of these fertility gods was accompanied by all kinds of lascivious practices, especially in Canaan, where it was found in a degraded form which even incorporated child sacrifice." (Cundall)

d. **They forsook the Lord**: God made it clear that Israel's pursuit of these gods was nothing less than forsaking **the Lord God of their fathers**. Yet in all likelihood Israel did not see their idolatry as *forsaking* God; they probably just thought they were adding a few gods alongside of the **God of their fathers**. Nevertheless, the God of Israel is a jealous God who demands exclusive worship.

i. One biblical illustration of our relationship with God is to describe it as a marriage relationship between husband and wife. It would be wrong for a wife (or a husband) to have many lovers, claiming that she could love them all. A husband or wife has a righteous claim on the exclusive affection of their spouse; God has a righteous claim on our exclusive worship.

e. **In the sight of the Lord**: This implies that the sin was even more offensive to God because it was done right before His eyes. To give an extreme example, it is bad enough for a married person to commit adultery, but to commit adultery before the very eyes of one's spouse would be especially offensive.

f. **They followed other gods from among the gods of the people who were all around them**: This shows another root cause for Israel's tragic idolatry. The influence of the Canaanites that they allowed to remain in their midst led them to idolatry. The result of not fully driving out the Canaanites was far worse than Israel imagined.

i. "We worship other gods – the gods of the nations around the idols of the market-place, the studio, the camp, and the bar." (Meyer)

2. (14-15) God's wrath upon their sin of idolatry.

And the anger of the Lord was hot against Israel. So He delivered them into the hands of plunderers who despoiled them; and He sold them into the hands of their enemies all around, so that they could no longer stand

before their enemies. Wherever they went out, the hand of the LORD was against them for calamity, as the LORD had said, and as the LORD had sworn to them. And they were greatly distressed.

a. **And the anger of the LORD was hot against Israel**: This response of God to the unfaithfulness of Israel was no surprise. He specifically promised that He would do this in the covenant that He made with Israel, which was characterized by blessings for obedience and curses for disobedience (as in Leviticus 26 and Deuteronomy 28).

i. Believers today serve God under the terms of a different covenant, a better covenant (Hebrews 8:6). When they forsake God and do not abide in Jesus Christ, things may (and often do) go badly, but not because God has actively set His hand against the believer as He did against Israel under the old covenant. When God's people do not abide in Jesus and things go badly, it is simply because actions have consequences, and they reap the bitter fruit of not keeping themselves in the love of God (Jude 21).

b. **So He delivered them into the hands of plunderers who despoiled them**: The purpose of all this was so that when Israel was **greatly distressed**, they would turn their hearts back to **LORD**. God's goal wasn't punishment, but repentance.

i. Therefore, this should be seen as a manifestation of God's *love* for Israel instead of His *hate*. The worst judgment God can bring upon a person is to leave them alone, to stop trying to bring them to repentance.

ii. The same principle is seen in the relationship between parents and children. Though children often wish their parents would just leave them alone, it is really their worst fear that no one would love them enough to correct them.

3. (16-19) The cyclical pattern of bondage and deliverance in the days of the judges.

Nevertheless, the LORD raised up judges who delivered them out of the hand of those who plundered them. Yet they would not listen to their judges, but they played the harlot with other gods, and bowed down to them. They turned quickly from the way in which their fathers walked, in obeying the commandments of the LORD; they did not do so. And when the LORD raised up judges for them, the LORD was with the judge and delivered them out of the hand of their enemies all the days of the judge; for the LORD was moved to pity by their groaning because of those who oppressed them and harassed them. And it came

to pass, when the judge was dead, that they reverted and behaved more corruptly than their fathers, by following other gods, to serve them and bow down to them. They did not cease from their own doings nor from their stubborn way.

> a. **Nevertheless, the LORD raised up judges who delivered them**: Because of His great love for His people, God **raised up judges** – heroic leaders – to rescue Israel from their calamity. God did this **nevertheless**; not because Israel ever deserved such a deliverer from God, but in spite of the fact that they were undeserving.
>
> > i. "It was a method made necessary by the repeated failure of the people. That should be clearly understood." (Morgan)
>
> b. **Yet they would not listen to their judges, but played the harlot with other gods**: Though God gave Israel these heroic leaders, they did not **listen to their judges** in matters of spiritual leadership. They wanted the judges as *political* and *military* leaders, but not as spiritual leaders.
>
> > i. Trapp explains the idea behind the phrase, **played the harlot**: "Carried on by a spirit of fornication, a strong inclination, a vehement *impetus* to whoredom; so that they care not how they waste all upon it, and will not be reclaimed: so idolaters."
>
> c. **The LORD was with the judge**: This explains the source of power with the judges God raised up. They were able to lead Israel in dramatic acts of deliverance because **the LORD was with the judge**, not because the judges were necessarily great or powerful in themselves.
>
> d. **The LORD was moved to pity by their groaning**: During the time of the judges, Israel only cried out to God and really depended on Him in times of emergency. When they did cry out to Him with **groaning**, He answered with **pity** and faithfulness.
>
> > i. "This connection of sin, punishment, and deliverance really forms the keynote to the historical movement recorded in the whole of the Book." (Morgan)
> >
> > ii. This principle explains why some people are in a constant state of crisis; God knows that is the only way they can be kept trusting in Him. Instead, God's desire is that we be in a constant relationship of dependence on Him. This is exactly how Jesus lived, as He said in John 5:19: *Most assuredly, I say to you, the Son can do nothing of Himself, but what He sees the Father do; for whatever He does, the Son also does in like manner.*
>
> e. **When the judge was dead, that they reverted and behaved more corruptly than their fathers**: The pattern of bondage, deliverance, and

blessing; followed by sin and bondage again is a discouraging fact in many Christian lives today.

> i. This discouraging cycle was more understandable in ancient Israel than in the life of the modern Christian. This is because the Christian, as part of the new covenant, lives with the indwelling presence of the Holy Spirit and is made a new creature in Jesus. These are privileges that Israel in the days of the judges knew *nothing* of.
>
> ii. "The days of the judges were those in which there was no king over Israel. The fitfulness of our experience is often attributable to our failure to recognize the kingship of Jesus." (Meyer)

f. **They did not cease from their own doings**: Their sin was **their own doings**; they couldn't blame it on anyone or anything else. In the same way, their sin was **their own** – they didn't learn it from God, but it came from their own corrupt natures.

g. **Nor from their stubborn way**: The ancient Hebrew word translated **stubborn** (also translated as *stiff-necked*) is a word that was also applied to Israel many times during the Exodus (Exodus 32:9, 33:3, and 33:5). This shows that a change of location – even coming into the Promised Land – didn't necessarily mean a change of heart for Israel.

> i. Believers should never count on sanctification by relocation; wherever you go, you take *you* with you. A new environment doesn't always mean a new attitude.
>
> ii. The ancient Hebrew word for **stubborn** (*kawsheh*) comes from the idea of being hard or severe. To be stubborn against the LORD is to have a hard and unyielding heart, and it results in a hard life.

4. (20-23) God gives Israel over to their sinful compromise.

Then the anger of the LORD was hot against Israel; and He said, "Because this nation has transgressed My covenant which I commanded their fathers, and has not heeded My voice, I also will no longer drive out before them any of the nations which Joshua left when he died, so that through them I may test Israel, whether they will keep the ways of the LORD, to walk in them as their fathers kept *them*, or not." Therefore the LORD left those nations, without driving them out immediately; nor did He deliver them into the hand of Joshua.

a. **Then the anger of the LORD was hot**: In the covenant God made with Israel, He promised to bless them when they were obedient and faithful to the covenant and curse them when they were not (Leviticus 26, Deuteronomy 27-28). Here, God treated Israel as disobedient and unfaithful to their covenant with Him.

i. "He is not made all of mercy, as some dream, but can be angry: and 'who knoweth the power of his wrath?' (Psalm 90:11). It is such as men can neither avoid nor abide." (Trapp)

b. **Because this nation has transgressed My covenant**: When God said, **this nation** instead of "My nation" it showed that Israel wasn't abiding in their relationship with God.

c. **I also will no longer drive out before them any of the nations which Joshua left**: Israel wanted these Canaanite nations around, so God gave them the worst punishment He could think of: He would allow it.

d. **Therefore the LORD left those nations**: After setting their hearts on sinful things, Israel found that God *gave* what their sinful hearts desired. This illustrates the great danger of setting the heart on sinful things; we may get to the point where God may allow us to have those things – thus bringing sin, bondage, and pain.

Judges 3 – The First Three Judges

A. The pagan nations remaining in the territory of Israel.

1. (1-2) Why God allowed these nations to continue in Israel's territory.

Now these *are* the nations which the Lord left, that He might test Israel by them, *that is,* all who had not known any of the wars in Canaan (*this was* only so that the generations of the children of Israel might be taught to know war, at least those who had not formerly known it),

a. **These are the nations which the Lord left**: God left these Canaanite nations behind because Israel was not faithful in driving them out. One might rightly say that it was a combination of both their choice and God's will.

b. **That He might test Israel by them**: It was within the power of God to eliminate those pagan nations without any help from Israel. God allowed the troublesome peoples to remain for a reason. The word **test** here is used in the sense of "proving." These nations would remain because God wanted to *prove* the faithfulness of Israel to Himself, and to *improve* their reliance on Him.

   i. God doesn't just instantly change *every* area of a Christian's life in order that their relationship with Him can be proved and improved. It is so they may live in true partnership with God.

c. **So that the generations of the children of Israel might be taught to know war**: This was another reason why God allowed the Canaanites to remain where Israel did not drive them out. God wanted His people to be *warriors*, and the presence of these dangerous neighbors would make it necessary for future **generations** to **know war**.

   i. "Israel was to be in a hostile environment for the major part of her history, due either to the pressures of the petty kingdoms which surrounded her or, at a later stage, due to her strategic position between

Judges 3

the successive world-powers of Assyria, Babylonia, Persia and Greece on the one hand and Egypt on the other hand. Military prowess was a necessary accomplishment, humanly speaking, if she was to survive." (Cundall)

ii. No one *likes* the struggle against sin, but the battle is good for us. The symbol of Christianity is a cross, not a feather bed.

2. (3-4) The pagan nations are specifically listed.

Namely, five lords of the Philistines, all the Canaanites, the Sidonians, and the Hivites who dwelt in Mount Lebanon, from Mount Baal Hermon to the entrance of Hamath. And they were *left, that He might* test Israel by them, to know whether they would obey the commandments of the Lord, which He had commanded their fathers by the hand of Moses.

a. **Namely**: God named each of the pagan peoples that stubbornly stayed in the land. After the same pattern, some people could today make a specific list of "pagan territory" in the lives of believers. Such a list may indeed be helpful in the way that it causes us to identify our enemies.

b. **That He might test Israel by them, to know whether they would obey**: The reason that God didn't just eliminate these nations is again stated. It was to *prove* Israel's commitment to God and His word. If they were obedient to the word of God, the other nations would not hinder them and they would grow strong enough to drive them out completely.

B. The first judge: Othniel.

1. (5-7) The apostasy of Israel in the days of Othniel.

Thus the children of Israel dwelt among the Canaanites, the Hittites, the Amorites, the Perizzites, the Hivites, and the Jebusites. And they took their daughters to be their wives, and gave their daughters to their sons; and they served their gods.

So the children of Israel did evil in the sight of the Lord. They forgot the Lord their God, and served the Baals and Asherahs.

a. **They took their daughters to be their wives, and gave their daughters to their sons**: Part of the accommodation of Israel to the pagan peoples surrounding them was their sin of intermarriage with the pagan nations in their midst.

b. **They forgot the Lord their God, and served the Baals and Asherahs**: Their ungodly relationships led them to the worship of the pagan deities Baal and Ashtoreth.

i. Jesus told us that following Him would require that we give up the things we love most (Mark 10:29-30). Often an ungodly romantic relationship falls into this exact category.

2. (8) Israel's servitude to the king of Mesopotamia.

Therefore the anger of the LORD was hot against Israel, and He sold them into the hand of Cushan-Rishathaim king of Mesopotamia; and the children of Israel served Cushan-Rishathaim eight years.

a. **He sold them into the hand of Cushan-Rishathaim king of Mesopotamia**: God gave Israel just what they wanted. They didn't want to serve God, so He allowed them to be in bondage to a pagan king. Israel reaped exactly what they sowed.

i. "The name of *Cushan-Rishathaim* is also suspect, for it reads literally 'Cushan of double wickedness', not likely a personal name, and it would appear that the historian has made a deliberate distortion to cast ridicule upon this oppressor." (Cundall)

ii. "A rather strange designation but perhaps intended to be an intimidating one. It could also be a caricature of the actual name." (Wolf)

iii. "Tyrants delight in terrible names and titles, as Attilas, the Hunne, who would needs be styled *Ira Dei et orbis vastitas*, the wrath of God, and waster of the world." (Trapp)

iv. In those ancient times, the word **Mesopotamia** described the fertile, well-watered area that would be today Eastern Syria and Northern Iraq.

b. **Eight years**: There were many years of bondage before Israel cried out to the LORD.

3. (9-11) God's deliverance through Othniel.

When the children of Israel cried out to the LORD, the LORD raised up a deliverer for the children of Israel, who delivered them: Othniel the son of Kenaz, Caleb's younger brother. The Spirit of the LORD came upon him, and he judged Israel. He went out to war, and the LORD delivered Cushan-Rishathaim king of Mesopotamia into his hand; and his hand prevailed over Cushan-Rishathaim. So the land had rest for forty years. Then Othniel the son of Kenaz died.

a. **When the children of Israel cried out to the LORD**: After the eight years of bondage Israel finally cried out in dependence on God. It often takes many years of bondage and calamity before man looks away from self and looks unto God.

b. **The LORD raised up a deliverer…Othniel**: Othniel was the son-in-law of the great hero Caleb (Judges 1:12-13) and his wife was also a woman of faith (Judges 1:13-15).

i. In his collection of rabbinical fables and traditions titled *The Legends of the Jews*, Louis Ginzberg includes two fanciful additions to the story of Othniel:

- "Among the judges, Othniel represents the class of scholars. His acumen was so great that he was able, by dint of dialectic reasoning, to restore the seventeen hundred traditions which Moses had taught the people, and which had been forgotten in the time of mourning for Moses."

- "Othniel, however, was held so little answerable for the causes that had brought on the punishment of the people, that God granted him eternal life; he is one of the few who reached Paradise alive."

c. **The Spirit of the LORD came upon him**: We don't know very much about Othniel, but this is enough to know. The Holy Spirit empowered him for the job God called him to do.

i. Othniel lived the principle of Zechariah 4:6: *Not by might nor by power, but by My Spirit, says the LORD of hosts.* Empowered by the **Spirit of the LORD**, he delivered Israel.

ii. "Since Pentecost (Acts 2) a more general and permanent endowment of the Holy Spirit has been the privilege of every disciple." (Cundall)

C. The second judge: Ehud.

1. (12-14) The cycle continues: Israel sins and is sold into servitude.

And the children of Israel again did evil in the sight of the LORD. So the LORD strengthened Eglon king of Moab against Israel, because they had done evil in the sight of the LORD. Then he gathered to himself the people of Ammon and Amalek, went and defeated Israel, and took possession of the City of Palms. So the children of Israel served Eglon king of Moab eighteen years.

a. **The children of Israel again did evil in the sight of the LORD**: After God brought deliverance through the work of Othniel, Israel eventually drifted away from their dependence and obedience towards God. Their victory did not automatically last forever; it had to be maintained.

i. Cundall does a good job of describing the three peoples mentioned here as oppressors of Israel:

- "*Moab*, situated to the east of the Dead Sea between the Arnon and the Zered, was settled as a kingdom some fifty years before the Israelite invasion."
- "*Ammon*, to the north-east of Moab, was established about the same time as Israel in the late thirteenth century B.C."
- "The Amalekites, who were akin to the Edomites, were a nomadic race occupying the considerable area south of Judah, and were possibly Israel's bitterest enemy (Exodus 17:8-16; *cf.* 1 Samuel 15:2-3)."

b. **The children of Israel served Eglon**: Israel's sin brought them into bondage. They suffered 8 years of bondage before they cried out to the LORD in the days of Othniel. Then they endured another 18 stubborn years of bondage before they cried out to the LORD.

i. Sin always brings bondage, though it comes deceptively. The fish never contemplates the bondage of the hook when it goes after the bait; Satan snares people by making the bait attractive and hiding the hook.

ii. "Some great men have borne names which, when reduced to their grammatical meaning, appear very ridiculous: the word *Eglon* signifies *a little calf!*" (Clarke) In Eglon's case, it was a fatted calf and was ready for slaughter.

2. (15) God raises up a deliverer for Israel: Ehud.

But when the children of Israel cried out to the LORD, the LORD raised up a deliverer for them: Ehud the son of Gera, the Benjamite, a left-handed man. By him the children of Israel sent tribute to Eglon king of Moab.

a. **When the children of Israel cried out to the LORD, the LORD raised up a deliverer**: This shows the mercy of God. When Israel repeatedly drifted from God, He had every right to cast them off completely. Yet He still responded when they finally did call on Him for deliverance.

b. **Ehud…a left-handed man**: In the ancient world left-handed people were often forced to become right-handed. This made Ehud's standing as **a left-handed man** more unusual.

i. "He is described as a *left-handed* man, literally 'restricted as to his right hand'. In the eyes of an Israelite, this was regarded as a physical defect and it appears often in connection with the Benjaminites, without affecting their prowess in battle (*cf.* 20:16)." (Cundall)

3. (16-26) Ehud's daring assassination of Eglon.

Now Ehud made himself a dagger (it was double-edged and a cubit in length) and fastened it under his clothes on his right thigh. So he brought the tribute to Eglon king of Moab.(Now Eglon *was* a very fat man.) And when he had

finished presenting the tribute, he sent away the people who had carried the tribute. But he himself turned back from the stone images that *were* at Gilgal, and said, "I have a secret message for you, O king."

He said, "Keep silence!" And all who attended him went out from him.

And Ehud came to him (now he was sitting upstairs in his cool private chamber). Then Ehud said, "I have a message from God for you." So he arose from *his* seat. Then Ehud reached with his left hand, took the dagger from his right thigh, and thrust it into his belly. Even the hilt went in after the blade, and the fat closed over the blade, for he did not draw the dagger out of his belly; and his entrails came out. Then Ehud went out through the porch and shut the doors of the upper room behind him and locked them.

When he had gone out, *Eglon's* servants came to look, and *to their* surprise, the doors of the upper room were locked. So they said, "He is probably attending to his needs in the cool chamber." So they waited till they were embarrassed, and still he had not opened the doors of the upper room. Therefore they took the key and opened *them*. And there was their master, fallen dead on the floor.

But Ehud had escaped while they delayed, and passed beyond the stone images and escaped to Seirah.

a. **He brought the tribute to Eglon king of Moab**: Israel had to pay this **tribute** money because they were under the domination of the king of Moab. Ehud came to Eglon as a messenger or courier.

i. "Since the payment was carried by a number of men, it may have been food or wool." (Wolf)

ii. "Presents, tribute, etc., in the eastern countries were offered with very great ceremony; and to make the more parade several persons, ordinarily slaves, sumptuously dressed, and in considerable *number*, were employed to carry what would not be a burden even to *one*. This appears to have been the case in the present instance." (Clarke)

b. **I have a message from God for you**: Ehud certainly told the truth when he said this. The message was, "Those who oppress the people of God touch the apple of His eye and will be judged for it."

i. F.B. Meyer set forth some thoughts from Judges 3:20, and Ehud's statement to Eglon, **I have a message from God for you**.

- God's messages are often secret.
- God's messages must be received with reverence.
- God's messages leap out from unexpected quarters.
- God's messages are sharp as a two-edged sword, and cause death.

ii. "God's Word pierces as a two-edged sword to the dividing of soul and spirit in the recesses of the being, and is a discerner of the thoughts and intents of the heart. When the Eglon of self has received its death-wound, the glad trumpet of freedom is blown on the hills." (Meyer)

iii. God uses many messengers to speak to us, including death. "Ehud said, 'I have a message from God for thee.' It was a dagger which found its way to Eglon's heart, and he fell dead. So shall death deliver his message to you. 'I have a message from God unto thee,' he will say, and ere you shall have time to answer, you shall find that this was the message, 'Because I the Lord will do this, prepare to meet thy God, O Israel; thus saith the Lord, cut it down; why cumbereth it the ground! Set thy house in order, for thou shalt die and not live.' Oh! may you hear the other messengers of God before he sends this last most potent one, from which ye cannot turn away." (Spurgeon)

iv. The preacher should also present the word of God with the sense that he has a message from God. "I am afraid, there are some ministers who hardly think that the gospel is intended to come personally home to the people. They talk, as I read of one the other day, who said that when he preached to sinners he did not like to look the congregation in the face, for fear they should think he meant to be personal; so he looked up at the ventilator, because there was no fear then of any individual catching his eye. Oh! That fear of man has been the ruin of many ministers. They never dared to preach right at the people." (Spurgeon)

c. **Ehud reached with his left hand**: Because most men fought with their right hand, it wasn't expected for a man to use his left hand with a dagger or a sword. This shows how cunning Ehud was and how unexpected the strike was to Eglon.

i. **The fat closed over the blade, for he did not draw the dagger out of his belly; and his entrails came out**: "This is variously understood: either the contents of the bowels issued through the wound, or he had an evacuation in the natural way through the *fright* and *anguish*." (Clarke)

ii. The phrase **and his entrails came out** has caused some problems for translators. One of the words used occurs nowhere else in the Old Testament. "The most plausible, if gruesome, suggestion is that it refers to the opening of the king's body, the downward motion of the dagger being with such force that it passed completely through the abdomen and projected from the vent (*cf.* RV, *it came out behind*). Such sensational details have a habit of impressing themselves indelibly upon the human memory." (Cundall)

iii. "The KJV and RSV translate 'and the dirt came out,' implying an intestinal discharge caused by the sword thrust. Koehler-Baumgartner relates the word to the Akkadian *parasdinum* ('hole'), meaning that Ehud went out through an 'escape hole.' The construction is very similar to 'Ehud went out to the porch' in Judges 3:23." (Wolf)

iv. Some are troubled by this act of assassination; we cannot say that this event is a general approval or commission of those who would assassinate rulers who oppress the people of God. It is significant that this was never suggested or even an issue in the early Christian persecutions. "God did not necessarily approve of the method used by Ehud. It may be significant that the Spirit of the Lord did not come on Ehud and that he was never described as 'judging Israel.'" (Wolf)

v. Nevertheless, the Bible reliably records this incident without giving specific approval of this act of assassination. "Such incidental details as the length of the murder weapon and the fact of Eglon's corpulence (mentioned only because the dagger was completely buried in his body) attest to the historicity of the event." (Cundall)

d. He is probably attending to his needs in the cool chamber: Without being coarse, we can see how real and true-to-life the Bible is. It describes normal, everyday functions but in a dignified way.

i. **Attending to his needs** is literally "covering his feet," a euphemism for elimination also used in 1 Samuel 24:3. Some commentators see this only reluctantly: "He has lain down on his sofa in order to sleep; when this was done they dropped their slippers, lifted up their feet, and covered them with their long loose garments. But the *versions*, in general seem to understand it as implying a certain natural act." (Clarke)

ii. The **stone images** mentioned in Judges 3:19 and 3:26 were probably "the actual stones set up by Joshua to commemorate the miraculous crossing of the Jordan (Joshua 4:19-24) and thus were a well-known landmark." (Cundall)

4. (27-30) Ehud leads the Israelites in battle against the Moabites.

And it happened, when he arrived, that he blew the trumpet in the mountains of Ephraim, and the children of Israel went down with him from the mountains; and he led them. Then he said to them, "Follow me, for the LORD has delivered your enemies the Moabites into your hand." So they went down after him, seized the fords of the Jordan leading to Moab, and did not allow anyone to cross over. And at that time they killed about ten thousand men of Moab, all stout men of valor; not a man escaped. So Moab was subdued that day under the hand of Israel. And the land had rest for eighty years.

a. **And he led them**: As much cunning and courage as Ehud had, he could not do the work by himself. It was essential for brave and faithful men to rally around him. Ehud led, but he had to have followers.

i. In the same way, God lifts leaders up in the church, but they can't do the work by themselves. The whole body needs to work together.

b. **Follow me, for the LORD has delivered**: Ehud asked the Israelites to **follow** him because he was their leader. Yet he also encouraged them to look with faith to the LORD (**for the LORD has delivered your enemies... into your hand**).

i. Like any true leader, Ehud said "**follow me.**" A leader can't expect his followers to go where he or she will not or has not gone. "This was captain-like spoken. Caesar never said to his soldiers, Go ye, but Come along: I will lead you, neither shall ye go farther than ye have me before you. Hannibal was wont to be first in the battle, and last out." (Trapp)

c. **And the land had rest for eighty years**: Ehud's cunning and courage, coupled with Israel's faithful following of a leader, brought Israel's longest period of freedom under the 400-year period of the judges. Ehud is a dramatic example of how in the LORD, one man can make a difference, and how God will call others to work with that one man.

D. The third judge: Shamgar.

1. (31a) The brief story of Shamgar.

After him was Shamgar the son of Anath,

a. **Shamgar the son of Anath**: Shamgar is one of six individuals we call "minor" judges, because not much is written about them. Yet the work they did for God was just as important in their day as anyone else's work.

2. (31b) Shamgar's great accomplishment.

Who killed six hundred men of the Philistines with an ox goad; and he also delivered Israel.

a. **Killed six hundred men of the Philistines**: Shamgar was a man of great accomplishment, yet only one verse describes his work. It is possible that so little is said about Shamgar because his story was so well known.

i. "The significant omissions may indicate that there *was* something unusual about Shamgar; he may not have been a judge after the usual pattern but just a warrior who effected this one local stroke of valour against a nation who afterwards became Israel's principal oppressor." (Cundall)

b. **With an ox goad**: Shamgar is an excellent example of service for God. He simply used what God put in his hand – in his case, an **ox goad**.

i. An ox goad was a stick about 8 feet long (about 2.5 meters), and about 6 inches (15 cm) around at the larger end of the stick. One end of the ox goad was pointed (for poking the ox), and the other end was like a chisel (for scraping the plow clean of dirt).

ii. "In the hands of a strong, skilful man, such an instrument must be more dangerous and more fatal than any sword." (Clarke)

c. **He also delivered Israel**: There was nothing spectacular about an ox goad. But God can use, and wants to use, whatever is in our hands. Shamgar was merely a laborer doing his job, but he took what was in his hand when prompted by God and he rescued the people of God from their enemies.

i. Shamgar was like Moses and his shepherd's staff or David and his shepherd's sling. God uses simple things to accomplish great things.

Judges 4 – Deborah and Barak

A. Deborah, the fourth judge.

1. (1-3) The cycle begins again: apostasy, servitude and supplication.

When Ehud was dead, the children of Israel again did evil in the sight of the LORD. So the LORD sold them into the hand of Jabin king of Canaan, who reigned in Hazor. The commander of his army *was* Sisera, who dwelt in Harosheth Hagoyim. And the children of Israel cried out to the LORD; for Jabin had nine hundred chariots of iron, and for twenty years he had harshly oppressed the children of Israel.

    a. **When Ehud was dead, the children of Israel again did evil in the sight of the LORD**: Seeing the continual drift to disobedience makes one less and less confident of man but more and more impressed with the mercy and grace of God. Though Israel kept forsaking Him, He continued to work with them.

        i. "The sedentary life is most subject to diseases: standing waters soon putrify. It is hard and happy not to grow worse with liberty." (Trapp)

    b. **So the LORD sold them into the hand of Jabin king of Canaan**: God loved Israel too much to let them go their own way. There may be times when we wish God would leave us alone; yet we are ultimately thankful for His continued dealing with us, even when it isn't comfortable.

        i. Even when God deals with people in this way, it still may take a good while until they turn their hearts to Him in repentance. It took Israel twenty years of bondage before they **cried out to the LORD**.

    c. **Jabin king of Canaan**: God used an entirely different oppressor this time. God can, and will, use anything to get the attention of the believer and keep them in line with His will.

2. (4-5) Deborah: a prophetess and a judge for Israel.

Now Deborah, a prophetess, the wife of Lapidoth, was judging Israel at that time. And she would sit under the palm tree of Deborah between Ramah and Bethel in the mountains of Ephraim. And the children of Israel came up to her for judgment.

a. **And Deborah, a prophetess**: Some people consider it unexpected for God to raise up a woman as a prophetess. But the New Testament makes it clear that God may grant the gift of prophecy to women (Acts 21:9), and they are to practice it appropriately (1 Corinthians 11:5).

i. "*Lapidoth*, her husband, appears to have had no hand in the government. But the original may as well be translated *a woman of Lapidoth*, as *the wife of Lapidoth*." (Clarke)

ii. The Bible tells us of several other prophetesses: Miriam (Exodus 15:20), Huldah (2 Kings 22:14), Anna (Luke 2:36), and Philip's four daughters (Acts 21:8-9).

iii. From 1 Corinthians 11:5, we find that the essential element of a woman's ministry as a prophetess in the early church was her clear submission to the male leadership in the church (in that culture, shown by the wearing of a head covering). In the New Testament church, a woman was to use her gifts in the context of order established by the leaders of the church – just like anyone's gift.

iv. This is always possible because the gift of prophecy never "overwhelms" the one who receives it; *the spirits of the prophets are subject to the prophets* (1 Corinthians 14:32).

b. **Deborah…was judging Israel at that time**: Still more people consider it unexpected for God to raise up a woman to be a judge – a *shaphat*, a heroic leader for Israel in a civil, political, and military sense. Deborah was a unique woman in Old Testament history, greatly called and used by God. She was also a woman who respected the other leaders God had appointed for Israel (Judges 4:6, 10).

i. The issue, from a New Testament perspective, is not whether women can be used greatly by God. Of course, they can. The issues are of headship, final accountability, and authority – and God has granted these responsibilities to husbands in the home and to qualified men in the church. Women can be used greatly by God, but it is to be according to this structure of authority and responsibility in the home and the church.

ii. The reasons have nothing to do with any notion of male superiority; they have to do with God's ordained order (1 Corinthians 11:3), considering God's order of creation (1 Corinthians 11:8-9), considering the presence of watching angels (1 Corinthians 11:10), and considering the nature of the fall (1 Timothy 2:14).

iii. The reasons also have nothing to do with any notion or even the suggestion of female inferiority. Jesus was under the headship and authority of His Father (John 5:19) without being inferior in any way (John 1:1, 10:30).

c. **And the children of Israel came up to her for judgment**: Often it is assumed that Deborah was allowed leadership because unspecified men failed to take the position. While later we will see that Barak doesn't seem to be all he should be, we have no indication that he failed to do something God told him to do in taking leadership. Deborah was uniquely called and wonderfully used.

i. Wolf notes, "Her prominence implies a lack of qualified and willing men." Yet this can be regarded as no more than an *implication*, not specifically stated in the text.

3. (6-7) Deborah calls Barak with a message from God.

Then she sent and called for Barak the son of Abinoam from Kedesh in Naphtali, and said to him, "Has not the Lord God of Israel commanded, 'Go and deploy *troops* at Mount Tabor; take with you ten thousand men of the sons of Naphtali and of the sons of Zebulun; and against you I will deploy Sisera, the commander of Jabin's army, with his chariots and his multitude at the River Kishon; and I will deliver him into your hand'?"

a. **And she sent and called for Barak**: Deborah never believed that God called her alone to deliver Israel. She realized that God would do much of the work through Barak.

b. **Has not the Lord God of Israel commanded**: This phrase suggests that Deborah simply *confirmed* something that the Lord had already spoken to Barak. God often brings confirmation when He speaks to us, especially if what we believe He wants us to do will affect other people.

4. (8-10) Barak will only lead if Deborah accompanies.

And Barak said to her, "If you will go with me, then I will go; but if you will not go with me, I will not go!"

So she said, "I will surely go with you; nevertheless there will be no glory for you in the journey you are taking, for the Lord will sell Sisera into the hand of a woman." Then Deborah arose and went with Barak to Kedesh. And Barak called Zebulun and Naphtali to Kedesh; he went up with ten thousand men under his command, and Deborah went up with him.

a. **If you will go with me, then I will go**: It didn't seem unwise of Barak to ask Deborah to come with him. Yet the fact that he *demanded it* suggests that he trusted more in Deborah's relationship with God than in his own relationship with God.

i. "Barak preferred the inspiration of Deborah's presence to the invisible but certain help of Almighty God...He is mentioned in Hebrews 11 as one of the heroes of faith; but his faith lay rather in Deborah's influence with God than in his own. Thus he missed the crown of that great day of victory." (Meyer)

ii. "He is famous for his faith (Hebrews 11:32-33), and yet here he showeth some unbelief. Let us be faithful in weakness, though but weak in faith." (Trapp)

b. **There will be no glory for you**: Because of this, Barak would not be the one to personally defeat Sisera, the commander of Jabin's army – but a **woman** would be the one. The reader would expect this to be fulfilled by Deborah, but this prophecy will be fulfilled unexpectedly.

c. **He went up with ten thousand men under his command**: Nevertheless, Barak and all who went with him showed real courage and trust in God to go out against Sisera and his army. They had essentially no weapons to fight with against a technologically advanced army (having 900 chariots of iron). In addition, God led them to fight on a plain, which gave great advantage to the forces with chariots.

B. Israel's defeat of Sisera.

1. (11-13) The armies gather against one other.

Now Heber the Kenite, of the children of Hobab the father-in-law of Moses, had separated himself from the Kenites and pitched his tent near the terebinth tree at Zaanaim, which *is* beside Kedesh.

And they reported to Sisera that Barak the son of Abinoam had gone up to Mount Tabor. So Sisera gathered together all his chariots, nine hundred chariots of iron, and all the people who *were* with him, from Harosheth Hagoyim to the River Kishon.

a. **Heber the Kenite**: These were distant descendants of Israel, through Jethro, the priest of Midian and the **father-in-law of Moses**, back to Abraham and his second wife Keturah (Genesis 25:1-4).

b. **So Sisera gathered together all his chariots, nine hundred chariots of iron**: The **chariots of iron** were a sophisticated and impressive military technology. The armies of Israel, under the direction of Barak and Deborah, were at a great disadvantage. Israel fought almost only as foot-soldiers.

2. (14-16) Sisera and his army are utterly defeated.

Then Deborah said to Barak, "Up! For this *is* the day in which the LORD has delivered Sisera into your hand. Has not the LORD gone out before you?" So Barak went down from Mount Tabor with ten thousand men following him. And the LORD routed Sisera and all *his* chariots and all *his* army with the edge of the sword before Barak; and Sisera alighted from *his* chariot and fled away on foot. But Barak pursued the chariots and the army as far as Harosheth Hagoyim, and all the army of Sisera fell by the edge of the sword; not a man was left.

> a. **So Barak went down from Mount Tabor with ten thousand men**: This was a wonderful act of faith on the part of Barak, who moved to a flatter battleground where his armies were at a great disadvantage against the enemy's chariots.
>
>> i. "He doth not make use of the advantage of the hill, where he might have been out of the reach of his iron chariots, Joshua 17:16, but boldly marcheth down into the valley, to give Sisera the opportunity of using all his horses and chariots, that so the victory might be more glorious and wonderful." (Poole)
>
> b. **And the LORD routed Sisera and all his chariots**: Because of Barak's great trust in God (as well as the trust his armies had in the LORD) God granted them a great victory against great odds.
>
>> i. **Routed**: "Terrified, as the vulgar Latin hath it, perhaps by thunder and hailstones, as Joshua 10:10; 1 Samuel 7:10, where the same Hebrew word is used; or else by some hurry-noise made in the air by the angels, as 2 Kings 6; but something was certainly done from heaven." (Trapp)
>
> c. **The LORD routed Sisera and all his chariots**: Judges 5:4-5 and 5:21 explain that God helped Israel to victory by bringing a flash flood. The muddy conditions made the chariots of iron a hindrance, not helpful in the battle.
>
> d. **Has not the LORD gone out before you?** This is a phrase that speaks of a king or general leading his troops (1 Samuel 8:20). Therefore, Deborah played a big role in this victory. She was an encourager, building up the faith of Barak and his men. Her encouragement was that God, as a king, would go out before His people into battle.

3. (17-22) The death of Sisera by the hand of a woman.

However, Sisera had fled away on foot to the tent of Jael, the wife of Heber the Kenite; for *there was* peace between Jabin king of Hazor and the house of Heber the Kenite. And Jael went out to meet Sisera, and

said to him, "Turn aside, my lord, turn aside to me; do not fear." And when he had turned aside with her into the tent, she covered him with a blanket.

Then he said to her, "Please give me a little water to drink, for I am thirsty." So she opened a jug of milk, gave him a drink, and covered him. And he said to her, "Stand at the door of the tent, and if any man comes and inquires of you, and says, 'Is there any man here?' you shall say, 'No.'"

Then Jael, Heber's wife, took a tent peg and took a hammer in her hand, and went softly to him and drove the peg into his temple, and it went down into the ground; for he was fast asleep and weary. So he died. And then, as Barak pursued Sisera, Jael came out to meet him, and said to him, "Come, I will show you the man whom you seek." And when he went into her *tent,* there lay Sisera, dead with the peg in his temple.

a. **Sisera had fled away on foot to the tent of Jael, the wife of Heber the Kenite**: Here the story takes an unexpected turn. God promised that a woman would defeat Sisera (Judges 4:9). The reader would naturally assume that this would be Deborah, but God had something else in mind. The LORD instead used the wife of a **Kenite** to accomplish Sisera's end.

i. "Women had their tents apart from their husbands, Genesis 24:67; 31:33. And here he thought to lurk more securely than in her husband's tent." (Poole)

b. **Turn aside, my lord, turn aside to me; do not fear**: Because **there was peace between** the people of Sisera and the people of Jael, he had a reason to trust Jael's invitation. He was desperate, and she seemed to offer safety.

i. In addition, "Any pursuer would hardly think to look in a woman's tent for any man, let alone a weary fugitive, for this would be a breach of etiquette." (Cundall)

ii. "This was a promise of security, and therefore she cannot be excused from dissimulation and treachery in the manner, though the substance of her act was lawful and worthy." (Poole)

c. **Drove the peg into his temple**: The gory detail of this matter supports the idea that this was an eye-witness account. Jael knew how to handle a tent-peg because it was customarily the job of women to set up the tents. She struck the peg so hard that **it went down into the ground**.

i. "Lo, there lay this proud worms' meat sprawling, with his head fastened to the ground, as if it had been now listening to what was become of the soul." (Trapp)

ii. Jael broke a fundamental principle of hospitality and many in the ancient world would think her a treacherous woman. She broke her promise to Sisera and killed a man that her own husband had made peace with.

iii. Yet God used even her treachery to accomplish His purpose. Surely, Sisera deserved to die; he fought against God's people on behalf of a leader who had *harshly oppressed the children of Israel* (Judges 4:3). The lesson for us is important – God can make even the evil of man serve His purpose: *Surely the wrath of man shall praise You* (Psalm 76:10). Yet, that *never* takes away the personal responsibility of the one doing the evil. Judas' betrayal of Jesus served the eternal purpose of God, yet he still answered for that evil deed.

iv. "She was encouraged to do it, partly, by observing that the heavens and all the elements conspired against him, as against one devoted to destruction; partly by the fair opportunity which God's providence put into her hands; and principally, by the secret instinct of God inciting her to it, and assuring her of success in it." (Poole)

v. "But we do not find one word from Jael herself, stating how she was led to do an act repugnant to her feelings as a woman, contrary to good faith, and a breach of the rules of hospitality. Nor does the sacred penman say one word to explain the case; as in the case of Ehud, he states the fact, and leaves his readers to form their own opinion." (Clarke)

vi. Charles Spurgeon preached a wonderful sermon on this passage titled *Sin Slain* on how we may regard Sisera as representing sin, and his master (Jabin) as a type of Satan. Spurgeon insisted that we should not be content to merely *defeat* sin, as Barak defeated Sisera in battle; we should not rest until sin is *dead*. And, just as Jael asked Barak to look at the dead body of Sisera, Spurgeon said we should look at sin slain by the work of Jesus, knowing He has already won the battle. "If you are content merely to conquer your sins and not to kill them, you may depend upon it, it is the mere work of morality – a surface work – and not the work of the Holy Spirit." (Spurgeon)

4. (23-24) After this decisive battle, full victory soon won for Israel.

So on that day God subdued Jabin king of Canaan in the presence of the children of Israel. And the hand of the children of Israel grew stronger and stronger against Jabin king of Canaan, until they had destroyed Jabin king of Canaan.

a. **And the hand of the children of Israel grew stronger and stronger**: The battle against Sisera was important, but it did not end the struggle. It was an important event that Israel had to continue to develop and walk in.

b. **Until they had destroyed Jabin king of Canaan**: The war was not over until **Jabin** was **destroyed**. Israel could not think the war was over when a great battle was won.

Judges 5 – The Song of Deborah

A. Blessing God for the deliverance He brings through His leaders.

1. (1-2) Theme of the song: The joy and blessing in being a willing instrument of God.

Then Deborah and Barak the son of Abinoam sang on that day, saying:
"When leaders lead in Israel,
When the people willingly offer themselves,
Bless the LORD!

    a. **Then Deborah and Barak the son of Abinoam sang that day**: This song is commonly attributed only to Deborah; Barak's role in the composition and perhaps performance of the song is often overlooked.

        i. This song is well within the tradition of other Jewish songs of deliverance and celebration, such as Miriam's song (Exodus 15:20-21) and the songs celebrating David's victory over Goliath (1 Samuel 18:7). "Deborah was a poetess as well as a prophetess." (Trapp)

        ii. "Deborah sang concerning the overthrow of Israel's enemies, and the deliverance vouchsafed to the tribes: we have a far richer theme for music; we have been delivered from worse enemies, and saved by a greater salvation. Let our gratitude be deeper; let our song be more jubilant." (Spurgeon)

        iii. "When he had been most slandered – when the Pope had launched out a new bull [decree], and when the kings of the earth had threatened him fiercely – Luther would gather together his friends, and say, 'Come let us sing a psalm and spite the devil.' He would ever sing the most psalms when the world roared the most." (Spurgeon)

    b. **When leaders lead**: Leadership is important in any endeavor and especially in the work of God. God expects leaders among His people to actually **lead**, showing there is a genuine need for leaders and their leadership.

c. **When the people willingly offer themselves**: Leaders are nothing without followers, and it is the job of **the people** to **willingly offer themselves** to their leaders.

i. We may think of the relation between leader and people as that of the conductor and the orchestra. The conductor *must* lead, and the orchestra *must* be ready and willing to follow the conductor's leadership. When the conductor does his job and the orchestra does their job, then beautiful music is made.

2. (3-5) Remembering God's preservation of Israel in the past.

"Hear, O kings! Give ear, O princes!
I, *even* I, will sing to the Lord;
I will sing praise to the Lord God of Israel.

"Lord, when You went out from Seir,
When You marched from the field of Edom,
The earth trembled and the heavens poured,
The clouds also poured water;
The mountains gushed before the Lord,
This Sinai, before the Lord God of Israel.

a. **Lord, when You went out from Seir**: God won the victory for Israel over Sisera by sending a great rain (**the heavens poured**). In this song Deborah recalled a time when God did the same thing on behalf of Israel in the days of the Exodus (Deuteronomy 33:2).

b. **When You marched from the field of Edom**: It is good to remember that God's goodness to His people didn't just start today. He has been good to His people for a long, long, time.

i. "*Seir* and *Edom* are the same place; and these two expressions note the same thing, even God's marching in the head of his people from Seir or Edom towards the land of Canaan." (Poole)

3. (6-8) Describing life under Canaanite oppression.

"In the days of Shamgar, son of Anath,
In the days of Jael,
The highways were deserted,
And the travelers walked along the byways.
Village life ceased, it ceased in Israel,
Until I, Deborah, arose,
Arose a mother in Israel.
They chose new gods;

Then *there was* war in the gates;
Not a shield or spear was seen among forty thousand in Israel.

    a. **Village life ceased, it ceased in Israel**: Not only was life hard under Israel's oppressors, but they also confiscated all weapons, so the Israelites could not fight (**Not a shield or spear was seen among forty thousand in Israel**).

        i. "The land was full of anarchy and confusion, being everywhere infested with banditti. No public road was safe; and in going from place to place, the people were obliged to use unfrequented paths." (Clarke)

        ii. By spiritual analogy, we can say that Satan doesn't only want to oppress the Christian; he also wants to *disarm* the believer. He wants the believer to lay down the full armor of God that belongs to you in Jesus Christ (Ephesians 6:12-18).

    b. **Until I, Deborah, arose**: This wasn't necessarily pride on Deborah's part. She understood that God works through willing individuals, and she was the willing one in this crisis.

4. (9) Refrain: Bless the LORD for leaders who lead and followers who follow.

My heart *is* with the rulers of Israel
Who offered themselves willingly with the people.
Bless the LORD!

    a. **My heart is with the rulers of Israel**: Deborah didn't only care for *her* job of leadership. She also had a **heart** for other leaders and their work. Her vision was bigger than just getting "her job" done. She wanted to see the Kingdom of God advanced.

    b. **Who offered themselves willingly with the people**: In Judges 5:2 Deborah spoke of the people offering themselves willingly. Here she notes that the sacrifices should also be borne by the leaders. They also must offer **themselves willingly**.

B. The victory remembered.

1. (10-12) A call to recount the great victory.

"Speak, you who ride on white donkeys,
Who sit in judges' attire,
And who walk along the road.
Far from the noise of the archers, among the watering places,
There they shall recount the righteous acts of the LORD,
The righteous acts *for* His villagers in Israel;
Then the people of the LORD shall go down to the gates.

"Awake, awake, Deborah!
Awake, awake, sing a song!
Arise, Barak, and lead your captives away,
O son of Abinoam!

> a. **Speak, you who ride on white donkeys**: The song asked the civic leaders along with Deborah and Barak to tell the **villagers in Israel** the great things God did.
>
>> i. Believers should never hide our light under a bushel (Matthew 5:15-16) but tell others of the great things God has done and is doing. Many need to wake up and sing a song of praise to the LORD.
>
> b. **For His villagers in Israel**: The common people needed to hear of God's great works, and it was the job of leaders to tell them.

2. (13-18) The tribes that helped and the tribes that didn't help.

"Then the survivors came down, the people against the nobles;
The LORD came down for me against the mighty.
From Ephraim *were* those whose roots were in Amalek.
After you, Benjamin, with your peoples,
From Machir rulers came down,
And from Zebulun those who bear the recruiter's staff.
And the princes of Issachar *were* with Deborah;
As Issachar, so *was* Barak
Sent into the valley under his command;
Among the divisions of Reuben
There were great resolves of heart.
Why did you sit among the sheepfolds,
To hear the pipings for the flocks?
The divisions of Reuben have great searchings of heart.
Gilead stayed beyond the Jordan,
And why did Dan remain on ships?
Asher continued at the seashore,
And stayed by his inlets.
Zebulun *is* a people *who* jeopardized their lives to the point of death,
Naphtali also, on the heights of the battlefield.

> a. **The LORD came down for me against the mighty**: As she remembered God's help, Deborah knew that His help came from the tribes of Israel, stirred to join in the battle. Deborah praised the tribes that helped, notably Ephraim, West Manasseh, Benjamin, Zebulun, Issachar, and Naphtali.
>
> b. **Why did you sit among the sheepfolds**: Not every tribe was helpful. Reuben, East Manasseh, Dan, and Asher did not join in the battle.

i. "All these are worthily shamed and shented, though they were not without some sorry pleas and pretences. The labouring Church must be some way helped, if be but by our prayers." (Trapp)

3. (19-23) The battle described and a curse on an unhelpful city.

"**The kings came *and* fought,**
Then the kings of Canaan fought
In Taanach, by the waters of Megiddo;
They took no spoils of silver.
They fought from the heavens;
The stars from their courses fought against Sisera.
The torrent of Kishon swept them away,
That ancient torrent, the torrent of Kishon.
O my soul, march on in strength!
Then the horses' hooves pounded,
The galloping, galloping of his steeds.
'Curse Meroz,' said the angel of the LORD,
'Curse its inhabitants bitterly,
Because they did not come to the help of the LORD,
To the help of the LORD against the mighty.'

a. **They fought from the heavens**: The battle was fought **from the heavens** in the sense that God sent rain that made the Canaanite chariots of no use (**the torrent of Kishon swept them away**).

b. **'Curse Meroz,' said the angel of the LORD**: Apparently the city of Meroz was of no help. God still accomplished His work, but the city of Meroz was cursed because they had no part in it.

4. (24-27) Praise for Jael for her killing of Sisera.

"**Most blessed among women is Jael,**
The wife of Heber the Kenite;
Blessed is she among women in tents.
He asked for water, she gave milk;
She brought out cream in a lordly bowl.
She stretched her hand to the tent peg,
Her right hand to the workmen's hammer;
She pounded Sisera, she pierced his head,
She split and struck through his temple.
At her feet he sank, he fell, he lay still;
At her feet he sank, he fell;
Where he sank, there he fell dead.

a. **Most blessed among women is Jael**: What Jael did would be condemned by many in the days of the Judges. The responsibility to protect and bless a guest was an almost absolute command, and Jael killed a guest. Yet she was **blessed** here because her obedience to the cause of God was greater than her obedience to tradition and custom.

b. **At her feet he sank**: Deborah wanted to increase Sisera's shame by pointing out that it was a woman who ended his life.

i. "Finally the song rejoiced over the death of the tyrant in language that thrills with Eastern imagery and color." (Morgan)

ii. "Here is a lively representation of the thing done. At the first blow or wound he was awakened, and made some attempt to rise; but being astonished and very weak, she also following her first blow with others, he found himself impotent, and fell down dead." (Poole)

5. (28-30) Reflection on the soon disappointment of Sisera's survivors.

**"The mother of Sisera looked through the window,
And cried out through the lattice,
'Why is his chariot *so* long in coming?
Why tarries the clatter of his chariots?'
Her wisest ladies answered her,
Yes, she answered herself,
'Are they not finding and dividing the spoil:
To every man a girl *or* two;
For Sisera, plunder of dyed garments,
Plunder of garments embroidered and dyed,
Two pieces of dyed embroidery for the neck of the looter?'**

a. **The mother of Sisera looked through the window**: Every death has consequences and Deborah thought of and celebrated the consequences of Sisera's death.

b. **To every man a girl or two**: The ancient Hebrew word translated **girl** is a somewhat crude way of referring to a female. It shows the contempt a conqueror would have over their defeated foe, including the women regarded as plunder in battle.

i. Cundall on the ancient Hebrew word translated **girl**: "Elsewhere in the Old Testament it means 'womb', and in the Moabite Stone it has the meaning 'girl-slaves.' The nearest English equivalent is 'wench,' and it is clear that these unfortunate captives would be used to gratify the lusts of their captors."

ii. "The Hebrew word signifieth, *vulvam vel uterum*; so they call the Israelitish damsels by way of contempt." (Trapp)

6. (31) Final praise to God and the long-term effect of the victory.

"Thus let all Your enemies perish, O Lord!
But *let* those who love Him *be* like the sun
When it comes out in full strength."

So the land had rest for forty years.

>a. **Thus let all Your enemies perish**: To love God is to hate His enemies. A man or woman is defined as much by who their enemies are as by who their friends are.
>
>b. **Let those who love Him be like the sun**: How much better it is to be one of **those who love Him** than to be one of God's **enemies**!

Judges 6 – The Call of Gideon

A. Apostasy, servitude, and supplication.

1. (1) Israel's apostasy brings them into servitude.

Then the children of Israel did evil in the sight of the Lord. So the Lord delivered them into the hand of Midian for seven years,

    a. **Then the children of Israel did evil**: The *forty years of rest* (Judges 5:31) following the defeat of Sisera eventually came to an end. In their prosperity and complacency, **Israel did evil in the sight of the Lord.**

    b. **So the Lord delivered them into the hand of Midian**: *God* brought Israel into bondage through the oppression of the Midianites. This was an example of God's *grace* and *mercy* to Israel because the oppression would make them turn back to God. It would have been worse if God had just left them alone.

2. (2-6) The details of Israel's bondage to Midian.

And the hand of Midian prevailed against Israel. Because of the Midianites, the children of Israel made for themselves the dens, the caves, and the strongholds which *are* in the mountains. So it was, whenever Israel had sown, Midianites would come up; also Amalekites and the people of the East would come up against them. Then they would encamp against them and destroy the produce of the earth as far as Gaza, and leave no sustenance for Israel, neither sheep nor ox nor donkey. For they would come up with their livestock and their tents, coming in as numerous as locusts; both they and their camels were without number; and they would enter the land to destroy it. So Israel was greatly impoverished because of the Midianites, and the children of Israel cried out to the Lord.

    a. **The children of Israel made for themselves the dens, the caves, and the strongholds**: The oppression of Midian – coming because of the sin of Israel – brought Israel into humiliation. Before they turned back to God they had to be humbled, living as cave-dwellers instead of properly civilized people.

b. Whenever Israel had sown, Midianites would come up: The Midianites did not continually occupy the land, but only came at the time of harvest to steal what the Israelites grew (**leave no sustenance for Israel**).

> i. Israel's sin made all their hard work profitless. All their produce and livestock were stolen after they worked hard to bring it to fruition. Sin does this; it robs us of what we work hard to gain. There are many accomplished men who lose everything in life because they won't stop their sin. All may be lost to gain what, in retrospect, seems like nothing.
>
> ii. **As far as Gaza**: "That is, the whole *breadth* of the land, from Jordan to the coast of the Mediterranean Sea. Thus the whole land was ravaged and the inhabitants deprived of the necessaries of life." (Clarke)

c. Both they and their camels were without number: The Midianites were a desert-dwelling people, and they dominated Israel because of their effective use of **camels**.

> i. "It is clear that the use of this angular and imposing beast struck terror in the hearts of the Israelites." (Cundall)

d. And the children of Israel cried out to the Lord: After the long season of humiliation, fruitless labor, poverty, and domination by an oppressive power, Israel *finally* **cried out to the Lord**. Unfortunately, prayer was their *last resort* instead of their *first resource*.

3. (7-10) In response to Israel's cry to the Lord, God sends a prophet.

And it came to pass, when the children of Israel cried out to the Lord because of the Midianites, that the Lord sent a prophet to the children of Israel, who said to them, "Thus says the Lord God of Israel: 'I brought you up from Egypt and brought you out of the house of bondage; and I delivered you out of the hand of the Egyptians and out of the hand of all who oppressed you, and drove them out before you and gave you their land. Also I said to you, "I *am* the Lord your God; do not fear the gods of the Amorites, in whose land you dwell." But you have not obeyed My voice.'"

> a. **The Lord sent a prophet**: The delivering judge will appear later. Before Israel could receive and respond to the work of the judge, they first had to be prepared by this un-named prophet.

b. **I brought you up from Egypt**: God spoke through the prophet, reminding Israel of all He did for them in the past. To face their current crisis, Israel needed a reminder of what God did before.

> i. This reminded Israel of the *love* of God. The God loving enough to before deliver from Egypt, still loved them enough to now deliver them from the Midianites.
>
> ii. This reminded Israel of the *power* of God. The God powerful enough to before deliver from Egypt was still powerful enough to now deliver them from the Midianites.

c. **But you have not obeyed My voice**: God sent this messenger to tell them where the real problem was. It wasn't that the Midianites were so strong; it was that Israel was so disobedient.

> i. Israel *thought* the problem was the Midianites, but the real problem was *Israel*. It is human nature to blame *others* for problems that we cause.
>
> ii. The message of the prophet also shows that when Israel **cried out to the Lord**, they didn't understand that *they* were the problem. Their cry to God for help did not mean that they recognized or repented of their sin.

B. The deliverer is called.

1. (11-13) The Angel of the Lord appears to Gideon.

Now the Angel of the Lord came and sat under the terebinth tree which *was* in Ophrah, which *belonged* to Joash the Abiezrite, while his son Gideon threshed wheat in the winepress, in order to hide *it* from the Midianites. And the Angel of the Lord appeared to him, and said to him, "The Lord *is* with you, you mighty man of valor!"

Gideon said to Him, "O my lord, if the Lord is with us, why then has all this happened to us? And where *are* all His miracles which our fathers told us about, saying, 'Did not the Lord bring us up from Egypt?' But now the Lord has forsaken us and delivered us into the hands of the Midianites."

> a. **The Angel of the Lord came and sat under the terebinth tree**: When **the Angel of the Lord** appeared to Gideon, we recognize this is as a *theophany* – an Old Testament appearance of Jesus Christ, in human, bodily form, but before His incarnation in Bethlehem.
>
> > i. The description of the encounter with the **Angel of the Lord** shows that this is not merely an angel speaking on behalf of God. It shows that God himself, appearing in human form, spoke to Gideon:

- *Then the LORD turned to him and said* (Judges 6:14).
- *And the LORD said to him* (Judges 6:16).

ii. Since no man has seen God the Father at any time (John 1:18, John 5:27) and by nature the Holy Spirit is a spirit without bodily form, it is reasonable to see this as an appearance of the *Second Person* of the Trinity, as an appearance of *God the Son*. However, this is not the *incarnation* in the same sense that Jesus was as a baby in Bethlehem. At Bethlehem Jesus was *truly* and *fully* human (while also being truly and fully God). Here, it is more likely that Jesus took the *mere appearance* of humanity, doing so for a specific purpose.

b. **Gideon threshed wheat in the winepress**: This was both difficult and humiliating. Wheat was **threshed** in open spaces, typically on a hill-top so the breeze could blow away the chaff. Wheat was not normally **threshed** in a sunken place like a **winepress**.

i. "This was a place of privacy; he could not make a threshing-floor in open day as the custom was, and bring either the wheel over the grain, or tread it out with the feet of the oxen, for fear of the Midianites, who were accustomed to come and take it away as soon as threshed." (Clarke)

ii. "So God called Moses and David from following the ewes, Elisha from the plough-tail, the apostles from fishing, washing, and mending their nets. He usually appeared to the busy in visions, like as Satan doth to the idle in manifold temptations." (Trapp)

c. **The LORD is with you, you mighty man of valor**: This was a strange greeting to Gideon. It didn't seem like the LORD was **with** him and it didn't seem that he was a **mighty man of valor**. Gideon might have turned to see if there was another person to whom the angel spoke.

i. "Wherein did that valor consist? Apparently, he was a simple man living a very ordinary life. The Angel found him about his daily duty." (Morgan)

d. **Where are all His miracles which our fathers told us about**: Gideon *heard* about the great works of God in the past, yet he wondered why he did not see the same great works in his day. Gideon thought the problem was with God (**now the LORD has forsaken us**) – not with him and with the nation of Israel as a whole. In truth, Israel forsook God – God did not forsake Israel.

i. Yet to his credit, it *bothered* Gideon that Israel was in this condition. He was far from apathetic or fatalistic. "He is revealed as a man continuing his work with the bitterness of the whole situation burning like a fire in his bones." (Morgan)

2. (14-16) Gideon's call to God's service.

Then the LORD turned to him and said, "Go in this might of yours, and you shall save Israel from the hand of the Midianites. Have I not sent you?"

So he said to Him, "O my Lord, how can I save Israel? Indeed my clan *is* the weakest in Manasseh, and I *am* the least in my father's house."

And the LORD said to him, "Surely I will be with you, and you shall defeat the Midianites as one man."

a. **Go in this might of yours**: It is hard to see that Gideon had *any* **might** to go in. Yet the Angel of the LORD didn't mock Gideon when he told him, "**Go in this might of yours**." Gideon indeed had **might**, but not as we might normally think.

- Gideon had the **might** of the *humble*, threshing wheat on the winepress floor.
- Gideon had the **might** of the *caring* because he cared about the low place of Israel.
- Gideon had the **might** of *knowledge* because he knew God did great things in the past.
- Gideon had the **might** of the *spiritually hungry* because he wanted to see God do great works again.
- Gideon had the **might** of the *teachable* because he listened to what the Angel of the LORD said.
- Gideon had the **might** of the *weak*, and God's strength is perfected in weakness (2 Corinthians 12:9).

b. **O my Lord, how can I save Israel**: Gideon had might to go forth in, but he could not see himself as someone who could do great things for God. He thought of himself as insignificant, from the smallest clan in his tribe, and that he was the least in his own family.

i. At the same time, Gideon was correct: *he* could not **save Israel**. But a great God could use a small and weak Gideon to rescue Israel.

c. **Surely I will be with you, and you shall defeat the Midianites as one man**: God's assurance to Gideon was not to build up his self-confidence, but to assure him that God was indeed with him. Gideon did not need more *self*-confidence; he needed more *God*-confidence.

i. It is important to know that God has sent us, but it is even greater to know that He is **with** us. This was the same assurance God gave to Moses (Exodus 3:12) and that Jesus gave all believers (Matthew 28:20).

3. (17-21) A sign from the Angel of the LORD.

Then he said to Him, "If now I have found favor in Your sight, then show me a sign that it is You who talk with me. Do not depart from here, I pray, until I come to You and bring out my offering and set *it* **before You."**

And He said, "I will wait until you come back."

So Gideon went in and prepared a young goat, and unleavened bread from an ephah of flour. The meat he put in a basket, and he put the broth in a pot; and he brought *them* **out to Him under the terebinth tree and presented** *them***. The Angel of God said to him, "Take the meat and the unleavened bread and lay** *them* **on this rock, and pour out the broth." And he did so.**

Then the Angel of the LORD put out the end of the staff that *was* **in His hand, and touched the meat and the unleavened bread; and fire rose out of the rock and consumed the meat and the unleavened bread. And the Angel of the LORD departed out of his sight.**

a. **Then show me a sign that it is You who talk with me**: It was not wrong for Gideon to ask for a confirming sign. It made sense to ask God to confirm some area of direction that was not specifically detailed in His word, and in regard to something as life-or-death as leading Israel into battle against an enemy.

i. For example, we don't need a special sign that God loves us because He forever demonstrated His love at the cross according to Romans 5:8. This is true for many other things specifically detailed in God's word. Yet when it comes to guidance in things not specifically detailed in God's word, it is possible to look for and expect confirmation in various ways.

b. **Fire rose out of the rock and consumed the meat and the unleavened bread**: The miraculous sign alone should not have persuaded Gideon because there are miraculous deceptions. Yet this miracle of fire *together* with the other aspects of this whole experience should have persuaded Gideon that this all was from the LORD.

i. "Here was a sign that the Midianites should be destroyed without man's labour." (Trapp)

4. (22-24) Gideon reacts with awe and worship to the miraculous sign.

Now Gideon perceived that He *was* the Angel of the Lord. So Gideon said, "Alas, O Lord God! For I have seen the Angel of the Lord face to face."

Then the Lord said to him, "Peace *be* with you; do not fear, you shall not die." So Gideon built an altar there to the Lord, and called it The-Lord-*Is*-Peace. To this day it *is* still in Ophrah of the Abiezrites.

- a. **Now Gideon perceived that He was the Angel of the Lord**: This demonstrates that before this, Gideon believed that this person was simply a man. The appearance of **the Angel of the Lord** was completely human in its character.

- b. **Peace be with you; do not fear, you shall not die**: Once Gideon realized the identity of the **Angel of the Lord**, he was terrified. The **Angel of the Lord** brought this comforting word to the terrified Gideon.

    - i. "Why was Gideon afraid? Not because he was a coward-you will scarcely meet with a braver man in all Scripture than this son of Joash-but because even brave men are alarmed at the supernatural. He saw something which he had never seen before, an appearance celestial, mysterious, above what is usually seen of mortal men; therefore, as he feared God, Gideon was afraid." (Spurgeon)

- c. **So Gideon built an altar there to the Lord**: Gideon did this as an act of worship and consecration unto the Lord, whom he had just encountered face-to-face. He was no longer terrified of God, as demonstrated by the title given to the altar: **The-Lord-Is-Peace**.

    - i. "When Gideon is fully at peace, what does he begin to do for God? If God loves you he will use you either for suffering or service; and if he has given you peace you must now prepare for war. Will you think me odd if I say that our Lord came to give us peace that he might send us out to war?" (Spurgeon)

C. The beginning of Gideon's ministry.

1. (25-27) Removing Baal worship from his midst.

Now it came to pass the same night that the Lord said to him, "Take your father's young bull, the second bull of seven years old, and tear down the altar of Baal that your father has, and cut down the wooden image that *is* beside it; and build an altar to the Lord your God on top of this rock in the proper arrangement, and take the second bull and offer a burnt sacrifice with the wood of the image which you shall cut down." So Gideon took ten men from among his servants and did as the

LORD had said to him. But because he feared his father's household and the men of the city too much to do *it* by day, he did *it* by night.

a. **The same night that the LORD said to him**: This happened right away. When Gideon made himself responsive to God, God guided him. Perhaps it happened as soon as Gideon built the altar; with the altar built, now God commanded him to sacrifice something on it.

b. **Tear down the altar of Baal that your father has**: In Gideon's community, Baal was worshipped right alongside of Yahweh. God called Gideon to get his own house in order first.

i. It seems that two bulls were to be offered: one as a sin offering, and the other as a consecration offering. "It appears that the second bullock was offered, because it was just *seven* years old, Judges 6:25, being calved about the time that the Midianitish oppression began; and it was now to be slain to indicate that their slavery should end with its life." (Clarke)

c. **He did it by night**: Gideon probably did this at night and under the cover of secrecy because he **feared** that his **father's household and the men of the city** would *prevent* him from doing what needed to be done.

2. (28-32) The removal of an altar raises a controversy.

And when the men of the city arose early in the morning, there was the altar of Baal, torn down; and the wooden image that *was* beside it was cut down, and the second bull was being offered on the altar *which had been* built. So they said to one another, "Who has done this thing?" And when they had inquired and asked, they said, "Gideon the son of Joash has done this thing." Then the men of the city said to Joash, "Bring out your son, that he may die, because he has torn down the altar of Baal, and because he has cut down the wooden image that *was* beside it."

But Joash said to all who stood against him, "Would you plead for Baal? Would you save him? Let the one who would plead for him be put to death by morning! If he *is* a god, let him plead for himself, because his altar has been torn down!" Therefore on that day he called him Jerubbaal, saying, "Let Baal plead against him, because he has torn down his altar."

a. **Gideon the son of Joash has done this thing**: They didn't have a hard time figuring out who was responsible for the destruction of the altar. Gideon was found out immediately. What he did could not be hidden.

b. **Bring out your son, that he may die, because he has torn down the altar of Baal**: This shows just how powerful Baal worship was in Israel at this time. "The heresy had become the main religion." (Wolf)

i. Ancient Israel worshipped Baal because he was thought to be the god of weather, and they relied on the weather for agricultural prosperity. In the difficult economic times because of the Midianite oppression, people worshipped Baal even more, not understanding that they only made things worse by not turning to God.

ii. "They all felt an interest in the continuance of rites in which they had often many sensual gratifications. Baal and Ashtaroth would have more worshippers than the true God, because their *rites* were more adapted to the fallen nature of man." (Clarke)

c. **If he is a god, let him plead for himself, because his altar has been torn down**: Gideon's father made a very logical argument for preserving his son's life. Since Baal was the offended party, he could defend himself.

i. This is similar to what happened during a great move of God in the South Seas in the 19th Century. One tribal chief was converted to Christianity, and he gathered up all the idols of his people. The chief told the idols he was going to destroy them, and then he gave them the chance to run away. He destroyed all the ones that sat there like dumb statues.

ii. This incident gave Gideon the nickname **Jerubbaal**. The name means, "A man against whom Baal is to strive and contend; a title of honour." (Trapp)

3. (33-35) Gideon gathers an army.

Then all the Midianites and Amalekites, the people of the East, gathered together; and they crossed over and encamped in the Valley of Jezreel. But the Spirit of the LORD came upon Gideon; then he blew the trumpet, and the Abiezrites gathered behind him. And he sent messengers throughout all Manasseh, who also gathered behind him. He also sent messengers to Asher, Zebulun, and Naphtali; and they came up to meet them.

a. **The Spirit of the LORD came upon Gideon**: This follows the familiar pattern of the Spirit's work upon men under the Old Covenant. The Holy Spirit comes upon specific people for specific reasons, usually for divinely empowered leadership. Under the New Covenant, a broad and generous outpouring of the Holy Spirit is promised upon all flesh (Joel 2:28-29, Acts 2:17-18).

b. **Then he blew the trumpet**: Because of this divine empowering, Gideon was able to gather an impressive number of troops on short notice. Judges 7:3 tells us that 32,000 men came to follow him into battle.

64 Judges 6

4. (36-40) God assures Gideon's doubts.

So Gideon said to God, "If You will save Israel by my hand as You have said—look, I shall put a fleece of wool on the threshing floor; if there is dew on the fleece only, and *it is* dry on all the ground, then I shall know that You will save Israel by my hand, as You have said." And it was so. When he rose early the next morning and squeezed the fleece together, he wrung the dew out of the fleece, a bowlful of water. Then Gideon said to God, "Do not be angry with me, but let me speak just once more: Let me test, I pray, just once more with the fleece; let it now be dry only on the fleece, but on all the

ground let there be dew." And God did so that night. It was dry on the fleece only, but there was dew on all the ground.

a. **If You will save Israel by my hand as You have said**: God already gave Gideon a sign (Judges 6:17-21). Here, Gideon asked God to do *a second* miracle to confirm His word – and then *a third* miracle to confirm it again.

i. Sometimes Christians talk about putting out a "fleece" before the Lord. This phrase refers back to what Gideon did here. He used a literal **fleece** in asking God to confirm His Word with a sign.

ii. Adam Clarke described how the early church commentator Origen, who was given to allegorizing, found the "deeper" meaning of this account:

- The fleece represents the Jewish people and the area around it represents the Gentiles.
- The fleece was covered with dew while all around was dry, representing the Jewish nation favored with the law and the prophets.
- The fleece was then dry and all around was wet with dew, representing that the Jewish nation was cast off for rejecting the Gospel and the Gospel was preached to the Gentiles and they converted to God.
- The dew wrung out into the bowl represents the doctrines of Christianity, which are extracted from the Jewish writings. This is also shadowed forth by Christ's pouring water into a basin and washing the disciple's feet.

b. **Then I shall know that You will save Israel by my hand, as You have said**: Gideon showed that he had a weak, imperfect faith. For such a bold, life-endangering mission, one might understand (and encourage) his request for one sign (fulfilled in Judges 6:17-21). But asking for second and third signs showed that his faith was weak.

i. The test was wrong because it was essentially a trick, and it had nothing to do with fighting the Midianites. Gideon probably didn't understand that he was actually dictating his terms to God. Sometimes God shows His displeasure with such requests. In Luke 1:18, when Zechariah, John the Baptist's father, asked for a confirming sign, the Lord made him mute until the birth of his son.

ii. Gideon also did not keep his word. God fulfilled the sign once, and Gideon said that would be enough for him. But he went back on his word after God fulfilled the first sign. Yet the Lord was still merciful and gracious to Gideon. "This is an outstanding example of God's gracious patience with a troubled child." (Wood)

iii. Yet before being too critical of Gideon, we should consider the challenge that was ahead of him. Many of us would immediately refuse such a call, without even considering allowing God to confirm it. Gideon's weak faith was still greater than *no* faith. For this reason, Gideon is rightly included in the register of great men and women of faith (Hebrews 11:32).

Judges 7 – The Battle Against Midian

A. Israel's small army is too big for God to use.

1. (1-3) God tells Gideon to tell all his soldiers who are afraid to go home.

Then Jerubbaal (that *is*, Gideon) and all the people who *were* with him rose early and encamped beside the well of Harod, so that the camp of the Midianites was on the north side of them by the hill of Moreh in the valley.

And the LORD said to Gideon, "The people who *are* with you *are* too many for Me to give the Midianites into their hands, lest Israel claim glory for itself against Me, saying, 'My own hand has saved me.'" Now therefore, proclaim in the hearing of the people, saying, 'Whoever *is* fearful and afraid, let him turn and depart at once from Mount Gilead.'" And twenty-two thousand of the people returned, and ten thousand remained.

> a. **The people who are with you are too many for Me**: This was a great test of Gideon's faith. His army of 32,000 men was already overmatched by 135,000 Midianites. Yet God thought his army was *too big*, and He commanded Gideon to invite all who were afraid to go home. He was left with only 10,000 men.
>
>> i. Gideon was probably surprised at the number of men who were afraid to fight and hoped that only a few hundred would leave. But we are told that they assembled in a place where they could see the 135,000 Midianite troops (Judges 7:8). The sight of a huge opposing army made many Israelite soldiers afraid.
>
> b. **Lest Israel claim glory for itself against Me, saying "My own hand has saved me"**: This explains *why* the army of 32,000 was too large. Israel could still take credit for a victory if they had 32,000 troops. They could believe they were underdogs who triumphed through their own great

Judges 7 67

bravery or strategy. God wanted the odds so bad that the victory would clearly be His alone.

i. If we really believe the principle, *not by might nor by power, but by My Spirit, says the* LORD *of hosts* (Zechariah 4:6), then our smallness does not matter. If we really believe the principle, *some trust in chariots, and some in horses; but we will remember the name of the* LORD *our God* (Psalm 20:7), then smallness does not matter.

2. (4-8) Gideon must separate the men according to a particular test.

But the LORD said to Gideon, "The people *are* still *too* many; bring them down to the water, and I will test them for you there. Then it will be, *that* of whom I say to you, 'This one shall go with you,' the same shall go with you; and of whomever I say to you, 'This one shall not go with you,' the same shall not go." So he brought the people down to the water. And the LORD said to Gideon, "Everyone who laps from the water with his tongue, as a dog laps, you shall set apart by himself; likewise everyone who gets down on his knees to drink." And the number of those who lapped, *putting* their hand to their mouth, was three hundred men; but all the rest of the people got down on their knees to drink water. Then the LORD said to Gideon, "By the three hundred men who lapped I will save you, and deliver the Midianites into your hand. Let all the *other* people go, every man to his place." So the people took provisions and their trumpets in their hands. And he sent away all *the rest of* Israel, every man to his tent, and retained those three hundred men. Now the camp of Midian was below him in the valley.

a. **The people are still too many**: God already reduced Gideon's army from 32,000 to 10,000. Here He reduced it from 10,000 to 300. He did this because 10,000 were **still too many** for God's purpose.

i. We rarely think that bigness can be a hindrance to the work of God. Yet it is harder to truly rely on God when we have many wonderful resources at hand. Though it certainly can be done, it is hard to be big and to rely only on the LORD. When we are big, it is possible to do a lot in human resources and "give the credit" to God.

ii. Paul was in danger of being too strong for his own good. Therefore, God brought a weakness into his life so that Paul would keep relying on the LORD's strength – and be stronger than ever (2 Corinthians 12:7-10).

b. **Bring them down to the water, and I will test them for you there**: This seems a strange test, and there are different ideas as to why God used this to separate the soldiers. Perhaps it was because those who cupped the water in their hands and brought it to their mouth were better soldiers because they kept their eyes on their surroundings even when taking a drink.

> i. **As a dog laps**: The ancient Hebrew word for **laps** is *yalok*, used to imitate the sound a dog makes when lapping water.
>
> ii. "The test was peculiarly military. Men in such a position were not on guard against sudden surprise." (Morgan)
>
> iii. We might say that God eliminated the fearful and those who thought first only of convenience, the easy way. "The thought is disturbing, but it may well be true, that the composition of God's army to fight Satan's hosts in any day is really little different. How many Christians are so fearful of the enemy that they are of no real use in this warfare, and how many of the remainder are so self-centered, rather than God centered, that they find little place for effective ministry." (Wood)

c. **By the three hundred men who lapped I will save you, and deliver the Midianites into your hand**: God assured Gideon that victory was certain, even through only 300 men. Now the Israeli army was less than 1% of its original size and the proportion was 400 Midianite soldiers to each Israeli soldier. Gideon could only trust in God because there was nothing else to trust.

3. (9-11) Gideon must spy on the camp of the Midianites and find encouragement.

It happened on the same night that the LORD said to him, "Arise, go down against the camp, for I have delivered it into your hand. But if you are afraid to go down, go down to the camp with Purah your servant, and you shall hear what they say; and afterward your hands shall be strengthened to go down against the camp." Then he went down with Purah his servant to the outpost of the armed men who *were* in the camp.

a. **Arise, go down against the camp**: God wanted Gideon to find encouragement in this visit to the enemy's camp. This shows that when God asks us to do hard things for Him, He doesn't fold His arms and sit back and expect us to do it on our own. He is there to guide us and to keep us and to encourage us all along the way.

b. **Afterward your hands shall be strengthened to go down against the camp**: This is the tender mercy of God. He dealt with the doubts and fears of Gideon and wanted to assure him.

4. (12-15) God reassures Gideon through the Midianites.

Now the Midianites and Amalekites, all the people of the East, were lying in the valley as numerous as locusts; and their camels *were* without number, as the sand by the seashore in multitude.

And when Gideon had come, there was a man telling a dream to his companion. He said, "I have had a dream: *To my* surprise, a loaf of barley bread tumbled into the camp of Midian; it came to a tent and struck it so that it fell and overturned, and the tent collapsed."

Then his companion answered and said, "This *is* nothing else but the sword of Gideon the son of Joash, a man of Israel! Into his hand God has delivered Midian and the whole camp."

And so it was, when Gideon heard the telling of the dream and its interpretation, that he worshiped. He returned to the camp of Israel, and said, "Arise, for the LORD has delivered the camp of Midian into your hand."

> a. **A loaf of barley bread tumbled into the camp of Midian**: Only the very poor ate **barley bread**. The vision meant that the camp of the Midianites would be knocked over by a humble nobody.
>
>> i. "Barley-meal was rather food for dogs or cattle than for men; and therefore the barley cake would be the emblem of a thing despised." (Spurgeon)
>>
>> ii. "A cake of barley bread might be a worthless thing; but if God were behind it, it would upset a tent!" (Meyer)
>
> b. **This is nothing else but the sword of Gideon**: God allowed Gideon to see a great confirmation of His future work. This was obviously no coincidence and no display of luck. God used this situation to build the faith of Gideon, and it worked so well that all Gideon could do was worship God.
>
>> i. It was no accident that the man dreamed the dream that night; no accident that he told his friend about it at just that moment; no accident that Gideon came to the exact place where he overheard the man telling the dream.
>>
>> ii. "I think if I had been Gideon I should have said to myself, 'I do not so much rejoice in what this dreamer saith as I do in the fact that he has told his dream at the moment when I was lurking near him: I see the hand of the Lord in this, and I am strengthened by the sight. Verily, I perceive that the Lord worketh all things with unfailing wisdom, and faileth not in his designs. He that has ordered this matter can order all things else.'" (Spurgeon)

iii. It must have built the faith of Gideon to know that his enemies were afraid of *him*. When we are weak in faith, we often imagine our enemies to be stronger than they really are. We could say that the devil himself is afraid of the normal Christian – or at least afraid of what they *could* become.

iv. We should take it to heart; our enemies, both human and spiritual, are at their core *afraid of us*. "Behold the host of doubters, and heretics, and revilers, who, at the present time, have come up into the inheritance of Israel, hungry from their deserts of rationalism and atheism! They are eating up all the corn of the land. They cast a doubt upon all the verities of our faith. But we need not fear them; for if we heard their secret counsels, we should perceive that they are afraid of us. Their loud blusterings and their constant sneers, are the index of real fear. Those who preach the cross of our Lord Jesus are the terror of modern thinkers. In their heart of hearts they dread the preaching of the old-fashioned gospel, and they hate what they dread. On their beds they dream of the coming of some evangelist into their neighborhood. What the name of Richard was to the Saracens, that is the name of Moody to these boastful intellects." (Spurgeon)

c. **Arise, for the LORD has delivered the camp of Midian into your hand**: Gideon's encouragement was contagious. Having received encouragement, he could not help but spread that encouragement to others and his encouragement built their faith.

i. "But what a pity it is that we should need such little bits of things to cheer us up, when we have matters of far surer import to make us glad! Gideon had already received, by God's own angel, the word, 'Surely I will be with thee, and thou shalt smite the Midianites as one man.' Was not this enough for him? Whence is it that a boy's dream comforts him more than God's own word." (Spurgeon)

B. The army is small enough to be used by God to win the battle.

1. (16-18) Gideon announces a strange battle plan.

Then he divided the three hundred men *into* three companies, and he put a trumpet into every man's hand, with empty pitchers, and torches inside the pitchers. And he said to them, "Look at me and do likewise; watch, and when I come to the edge of the camp you shall do as I do: When I blow the trumpet, I and all who *are* with me, then you also blow the trumpets on every side of the whole camp, and say, '*The sword of* the LORD and of Gideon!'"

a. **He divided the three hundred men into three companies**: There is no specific mention that God gave Gideon this plan through supernatural revelation. Yet, because Gideon was a Spirit-filled man (Judges 6:34), the supernatural can operate very naturally in his life.

b. **Look at me and do likewise**: This plan probably came very naturally to Gideon, but upon reflection one can clearly see how the Holy Spirit prompted him.

2. (19-23) God strikes the army of Midian with a surprise attack.

So Gideon and the hundred men who *were* with him came to the outpost of the camp at the beginning of the middle watch, just as they had posted the watch; and they blew the trumpets and broke the pitchers that *were* in their hands. Then the three companies blew the trumpets and broke the pitchers—they held the torches in their left hands and the trumpets in their right hands for blowing—and they cried, "The sword of the Lord and of Gideon!" And every man stood in his place all around the camp; and the whole army ran and cried out and fled. When the three hundred blew the trumpets, the Lord set every man's sword against his companion throughout the whole camp; and the army fled to Beth Acacia, toward Zererah, as far as the border of Abel Meholah, by Tabbath.

And the men of Israel gathered together from Naphtali, Asher, and all Manasseh, and pursued the Midianites.

a. **Then the three companies blew the trumpets and broke the pitchers**: The Midianite soldiers awoke to an explosion of noise, light, and movement coming down on them from all directions. No wonder they thought they were being attacked by an army even bigger than they were.

b. **And they cried, "The sword of the Lord and of Gideon"**: This cry was not the result of pride on Gideon's part. Instead, it showed wisdom in the attack because clearly the Midianites were already afraid of **the sword of Gideon** (Judges 7:14), and shouting helped to send them into panic.

i. Perhaps the Midianites did not know who the Lord was, but they knew there was a man from the Lord named Gideon. It was appropriate for Gideon to take this leadership role.

c. **The Lord set every man's sword against his companion throughout the whole camp**: The first phase of the battle wasn't between Israel and Midian, but as the Midianites fought themselves. This is a good example of how we can be *more than conquerors through Him who loved us* (Romans 8:37). We get the spoils of victory though Jesus won the battle for us.

i. The early Christian writer Origen often emphasized elaborate spiritual meanings to Biblical accounts. In this story he made the 300 men types of preachers of the gospel. Their trumpets were a picture of preaching Christ crucified. Their torchlights represented the holy conduct of the preachers.

ii. **And the men of Israel gathered together from Naphtali, Asher, and all Manasseh, and pursued the Midianites**: "If some have the courage to strike the enemy, there are others who will come out of their hiding-places to hunt the beaten foe. When you really want help, often you cannot get it; but when you can afford to do without assistance, you will sometimes be embarrassed by it." (Spurgeon)

3. (24-25) Working towards total defeat of Midian.

Then Gideon sent messengers throughout all the mountains of Ephraim, saying, "Come down against the Midianites, and seize from them the watering places as far as Beth Barah and the Jordan." Then all the men of Ephraim gathered together and seized the watering places as far as Beth Barah and the Jordan. And they captured two princes of the Midianites, Oreb and Zeeb. They killed Oreb at the rock of Oreb, and Zeeb they killed at the winepress of Zeeb. They pursued Midian and brought the heads of Oreb and Zeeb to Gideon on the other side of the Jordan.

a. **Come down against the Midianites**: This was *not* unbelief on Gideon's part. Though God started the work with a small number of soldiers, once the work began, Gideon wanted many to get involved in the work.

b. **They pursued Midian**: God blessed the effort of people of Ephraim, and they made good success against the enemy and their leaders.

Judges 8 – Pursuing After Midian

A. Gideon battles Midianite kings and contentious Israelites.

1. (1-3) Ephraim's complaint and Gideon's answer.

Now the men of Ephraim said to him, "Why have you done this to us by not calling us when you went to fight with the Midianites?" And they reprimanded him sharply.

So he said to them, "What have I done now in comparison with you? *Is* not the gleaning *of the grapes* of Ephraim better than the vintage of Abiezer? God has delivered into your hands the princes of Midian, Oreb and Zeeb. And what was I able to do in comparison with you?" Then their anger toward him subsided when he said that.

> a. **And they reprimanded him sharply**: The **men of Ephraim** joined in the fight against Midian when Gideon called out to them (Judges 7:24-25). Yet they were upset that Gideon did not call them *before* the battle started. Gideon's initial call for help went out to the tribes of Manasseh (his own tribe), Asher, Zebulun, and Naphtali (Judges 6:35).
>
>> i. The **men of Ephraim** seem to have cared more about recognition than the overall good of Israel. Instead of being jealous about the recognition that others received, they should have been happy that God's people were rescued and that they had some part in the victory. Jealousy often hinders the work of God.
>
> b. **What have I done now in comparison with you?** Gideon did not challenge their pride; instead, he soothed their pride by complimenting them and giving them the recognition they seemed to crave. Most importantly, he challenged them to get involved in the work of God that was at hand. His reply is a wise way to deal with contention when there is work for the Lord to be done.

i. Yet, Gideon seems to have had a continuing controversy with the men of Ephraim. His later making of an ephod (Judges 8:27) was a disservice to Israel and may have been prompted by a competitive attitude towards Ephraim.

2. (4-9) The sins of Succoth and Penuel.

When Gideon came to the Jordan, he and the three hundred men who *were* with him crossed over, exhausted but still in pursuit. Then he said to the men of Succoth, "Please give loaves of bread to the people who follow me, for they are exhausted, and I am pursuing Zebah and Zalmunna, kings of Midian."

And the leaders of Succoth said, "*Are* the hands of Zebah and Zalmunna now in your hand, that we should give bread to your army?"

So Gideon said, "For this cause, when the LORD has delivered Zebah and Zalmunna into my hand, then I will tear your flesh with the thorns of the wilderness and with briers!" Then he went up from there to Penuel and spoke to them in the same way. And the men of Penuel answered him as the men of Succoth had answered. So he also spoke to the men of Penuel, saying, "When I come back in peace, I will tear down this tower!"

a. **He and the three hundred men who were with him crossed over, exhausted but still in pursuit**: We can imagine how tired they were. They fought hard and pursued the enemy over a long distance.

i. "If you, dear brethren and sisters, will give yourselves wholly to God's work, although you will never get tired of it, you will often get tired in it. If a man has never tired himself with working for God, I should think he never has done any work that was worth doing." (Spurgeon)

ii. "Let us also serve the Lord when every movement is painful, when even to think is wearisome. These men were faint. You know what it is for a soldier to be faint; it is no nonsense, no pretense, it is real fainting. Yet to go running on when you are ready to faint, to keep right on when you are ready to drop, this is very trying work; yet let us do it, brethren, by God's grace. Some people only pray when they feel like praying; but we need most to pray when we feel that we cannot pray. If we were only to preach, – some of us, – when we felt like preaching, we should not often preach." (Spurgeon)

b. **Please give loaves of bread to the people who follow me**: Through Gideon, the call came to the people of the city of Succoth to support those who fought the battle. They were not asked to engage in the actual battle, but simply to support those on the front lines.

c. **Are the hands of Zebah and Zalmunna now in your hand, that we should give bread to your army?** Instead of offering help, the people of Succoth and Penuel made an excuse. They didn't want to support Israel in the fight against Midian until the battle was already won.

> i. We can suppose that this was discouraging for Gideon and those fighting the battle. They didn't ask the people of Succoth and Penuel to fight on the front lines, only to support those who did. Yet they were unwilling and made excuses. When we set out to do the LORD's work, often the resistance we face is from our friends. We can't allow this to hinder or discourage our work.

d. **When the LORD has delivered…. When I come back in peace, I will tear down this tower**: With or without the help of the people of Succoth and Penuel, Gideon knew he would win the battle (saying **when**, not *if*). Yet he vowed to take revenge on these cities that refused to help the army of Israel at this strategic time.

> i. "Some have said that this showed resentment and harshness, but when a man is at war, he is not in the habit of sprinkling his adversaries with rosewater. War is in itself so great an evil that there are many other evils necessarily connected with it. It seems to me that if, when Gideon was trying to deliver his own countrymen, they scoffed at him, and refused him bread for his soldiers in the day of their hunger, they deserved to be punished with great severity." (Spurgeon)

3. (10-12) Two Midianite kings and their armies are routed.

Now Zebah and Zalmunna *were* at Karkor, and their armies with them, about fifteen thousand, all who were left of all the army of the people of the East; for one hundred and twenty thousand men who drew the sword had fallen. Then Gideon went up by the road of those who dwell in tents on the east of Nobah and Jogbehah; and he attacked the army while the camp felt secure. When Zebah and Zalmunna fled, he pursued them; and he took the two kings of Midian, Zebah and Zalmunna, and routed the whole army.

> a. **He attacked the army while the camp felt secure**: Gideon, continuing in the boldness of the LORD, led a courageous surprise attack. This wasn't the same as 300 attacking the vast army described in Judges 7:12, but it was still a small army against a much larger army.
>
> > i. We may suppose that Gideon was bold enough to do this because he saw God do great things in similar circumstances before. The previous work of God encouraged him to trust God for great things in the present.

b. **He pursued them…and routed the whole army**: This shows the *persistence* of Gideon. He fought until the battle was won, and he went after the leaders of the opposition.

4. (13-17) Gideon repays Succoth and Penuel.

Then Gideon the son of Joash returned from battle, from the Ascent of Heres. And he caught a young man of the men of Succoth and interrogated him; and he wrote down for him the leaders of Succoth and its elders, seventy-seven men. Then he came to the men of Succoth and said, "Here are Zebah and Zalmunna, about whom you ridiculed me, saying, 'Are the hands of Zebah and Zalmunna now in your hand, that we should give bread to your weary men?'" And he took the elders of the city, and thorns of the wilderness and briers, and with them he taught the men of Succoth. Then he tore down the tower of Penuel and killed the men of the city.

a. **He came to the men of Succoth and said**: The men of this city didn't want to help Gideon or his army before victory was assured. They refused to help Gideon by *faith*, and so Gideon would punish them as he had promised.

b. **He took the elders of the city, and thorns of the wilderness and briers, and with them he taught the men of Succoth**: Gideon publicly whipped the leaders of the city of Succoth with **thorns** and **briers** as a method of public rebuke.

c. **He tore down the tower of Penuel and killed the men of the city**: The text does not make it clear, but we suppose there was a justification for this severe penalty. Perhaps the people of Penuel were significant supporters of the Midianites and traitors against Israel.

5. (18-21) Gideon repays the two Midianite kings.

And he said to Zebah and Zalmunna, "What kind of men *were they* whom you killed at Tabor?"

So they answered, "As you *are*, so *were* they; each one resembled the son of a king."

Then he said, "They *were* my brothers, the sons of my mother. *As* the LORD lives, if you had let them live, I would not kill you." And he said to Jether his firstborn, "Rise, kill them!" But the youth would not draw his sword; for he was afraid, because he *was* still a youth.

So Zebah and Zalmunna said, "Rise yourself, and kill us; for as a man *is, so is* his strength." So Gideon arose and killed Zebah and Zalmunna, and took the crescent ornaments that *were* on their camels' necks.

a. **They were my brothers, the sons of my mother**: These two Midianite kings were responsible for the death of Gideon's **brothers**. Gideon wanted this known and confessed before he executed these kings.

b. **Rise yourself, and kill us**: Zebah and Zalmunna knew they deserved death and even encouraged their executioner.

B. Israel under Gideon as a judge.

1. (22-23) Gideon refuses to be made king.

Then the men of Israel said to Gideon, "Rule over us, both you and your son, and your grandson also; for you have delivered us from the hand of Midian."

But Gideon said to them, "I will not rule over you, nor shall my son rule over you; the LORD shall rule over you."

a. **Rule over us**: The desire for a human king over Israel started early in the nation's history. Hundreds of years later (in the days of Samuel the prophet and judge), God gave Israel the king they asked for.

i. "They found relief in the judges who were raised up of God, and began to hanker after some ruler, visible, and of their own number. They thought that, by securing this, they would preserve themselves from the recurrence of these troubles." (Morgan)

b. **I will not rule over you**: This was a good response from Gideon. He understood that it was not his place to take the throne over Israel, and that the LORD God was King over Israel.

i. "That is the true attitude of all those whom God raised up to lead and deliver His people. Their leadership must ever stop short of sovereignty. Their business is never that of superseding the Divine rule; but of interpreting it, and of leading the people to recognition of it, and submission to it. This is true, not only of kings, but also of priests, prophets, and preachers." (Morgan)

ii. Gideon gave the right answer when he *said* he didn't want to be a king, yet in the rest of the chapter, he acted like one. His words were humble, but his actions were not. It is easier to talk about humility and service to God than it is to live it.

2. (24-26) Gideon gathers a fortune.

Then Gideon said to them, "I would like to make a request of you, that each of you would give me the earrings from his plunder." For they had golden earrings, because they *were* Ishmaelites.

So they answered, "We will gladly give *them*." And they spread out a garment, and each man threw into it the earrings from his plunder. Now the weight of the gold earrings that he requested was one thousand seven hundred *shekels* of gold, besides the crescent ornaments, pendants, and purple robes which *were* on the kings of Midian, and besides the chains that *were* around their camels' necks.

a. **That each of you would give me the earrings from his plunder**: This didn't seem like much to ask for, yet when it was added up, it came to more than 50 pounds (22 kilograms) of gold. That was quite a fortune.

b. **We will gladly give them**: The people were happy to give this, and it is hard to say that Gideon did not *deserve* this huge fortune. At the same time, it was inappropriate, because it lifted him far above the level of the people he would lead, and it was at their expense.

i. A general rule of thumb is that Christian leaders who make their living from the gifts of God's people should live at the level of their own people – not below or above.

3. (27) Gideon, using the riches he received, assumes an inappropriate role of religious leadership and leads Israel into idolatry.

Then Gideon made it into an ephod and set it up in his city, Ophrah. And all Israel played the harlot with it there. It became a snare to Gideon and to his house.

a. **Gideon made it into an ephod and set it up in his city**: An ephod is a shirt-like garment worn by the priests of Israel (Exodus 28). This was obviously wrong, and it is not immediately apparent why Gideon did this. It is possible he did this to work against the prestige and influence of the tribe of Ephraim. At this time the tabernacle – the center of worship for Israel – was at Shiloh, in the territory of Ephraim. Gideon perhaps set up this rival place of worship to compete against the tribe that troubled him in the battle against Midian.

i. "While this was probably done out of a sense of the religious failure of the people, the effect produced was evil and resulted in deterioration of the character of Gideon himself." (Morgan)

ii. "He did not set up an idol, but he made an ephod, an imitation of that wonderful vestment worn by the high priest. Perhaps he made it of solid gold, not to be worn, but to be looked at, simply to remind the people of the worship of God, and not to be itself worshipped. But ah, dear friends, you see here that, if we go half an inch beyond what God's Word warrants we always get into mischief!" (Spurgeon)

b. **And all Israel played the harlot with it there**: The people of Israel *enjoyed* this idolatrous worship. The beautiful and expensive ephod **became a snare** to Gideon, his family, and all Israel.

> i. Artistic beauty has a way of impressing us and giving a sense of awe, but it is not necessarily a godly impression or awe. Many times, it can distract our focus from the Lord. In contrast to this ephod, God commanded that His altars be made of unfinished stone (Exodus 20:25), so that no one's attention was focused on the beauty of the stone carver's work.
>
> ii. Gideon was remarkably obedient and filled with faith in the extreme moment of battle. The routine of daily living seems to have been a greater test of his character. This is true for many, and the challenges of daily living are more difficult than those of the extreme moment.
>
> iii. "Perhaps it is easier to honour God in some courageous action in the limelight of a time of national emergency than it is to honour Him consistently in the ordinary, everyday life, which requires a different kind of courage." (Cundall)

4. (28-30) Gideon assumes a kingly harem.

Thus Midian was subdued before the children of Israel, so that they lifted their heads no more. And the country was quiet for forty years in the days of Gideon.

Then Jerubbaal the son of Joash went and dwelt in his own house. Gideon had seventy sons who were his own offspring, for he had many wives.

a. **Thus Midian was subdued**: Regarding the security of the nation, Gideon's rule as a judge over Israel was a success. Yet in many ways he was a spiritual failure.

b. **For he had many wives**: A harem was not only a reflection of a man's inability to control his sexual lust, but it was also a way for him to proudly express his wealth, by saying "Look at all the wives and children I can support."

> i. The Old Testament never directly condemns polygamy (though the New Testament does in Matthew 19:4-6 and 1 Timothy 3:2). Yet the Old Testament shows the bitter fruit of polygamy. The stories of polygamous families in the Old Testament (such as those of Jacob or David) are the stories of conflict and crisis.

5. (31-32) Gideon assumes – or hopes for – a hereditary rule.

And his concubine who *was* in Shechem also bore him a son, whose name he called Abimelech. Now Gideon the son of Joash died at a good old age, and was buried in the tomb of Joash his father, in Ophrah of the Abiezrites.

> a. **Whose name he called Abimelech**: The name **Abimelech** means, "my father, a king." It is the kind of name that a king himself would bear. It seems that Gideon intended that his son would become the leader of Israel after Gideon himself was gone.
>
> b. **Gideon the son of Joash died at a good old age**: Throughout his career, we see Gideon as a man who slipped from great heights of faith to a place of outright apostasy and rebellion against God. We could say that Gideon handled adversity better than success. Success, riches, and prominence brought him down.
>
>> i. It isn't enough for us to begin well with God. We must continue on throughout our whole Christian life. Gideon, in his later years, had to *look back* to see anything done for God. All those works were in the past.

6. (33-35) After Gideon, Israel rebels and makes a covenant with Baal.

So it was, as soon as Gideon was dead, that the children of Israel again played the harlot with the Baals, and made Baal-Berith their god. Thus the children of Israel did not remember the LORD **their God, who had delivered them from the hands of all their enemies on every side; nor did they show kindness to the house of Jerubbaal (Gideon) in accordance with the good he had done for Israel.**

> a. **As soon as Gideon was dead…the children of Israel again played the harlot with the Baals**: In a sense, Israel served the memory of Gideon well, especially the Gideon of his later years. By serving Baal, Israel said, "What really matters is money and success," and in this they followed the example of Gideon in his later years.
>
> b. **And made Baal-Berith their god**: The name **Baal-Berith** means "Baal of the covenant." The Israelites sadly regarded Baal as their covenant god.

Judges 9 – The Rise and Fall of Abimelech

A. Abimelech's rise to power.

1. (1-3) Abimelech forces his uncles to submit to him.

Then Abimelech the son of Jerubbaal went to Shechem, to his mother's brothers, and spoke with them and with all the family of the house of his mother's father, saying, "Please speak in the hearing of all the men of Shechem: 'Which is better for you, that all seventy of the sons of Jerubbaal reign over you, or that one reign over you?' Remember that I *am* your own flesh and bone."

And his mother's brothers spoke all these words concerning him in the hearing of all the men of Shechem; and their heart was inclined to follow Abimelech, for they said, "He is our brother."

    a. **Then Abimelech the Son of Jerubbaal went to Shechem**: Abimelech was the son of **Jerubbaal** (another name for Gideon given in Judges 8:35), but he was not the clear successor to his father's place of leadership. This was for two reasons: God had not established a hereditary monarchy in Israel, and there were sixty-nine other sons of Gideon (Judges 8:30) who might also want to succeed their father.

    b. **Their heart was inclined to follow Abimelech**: At the city of Shechem, Abimelech convinced his uncles on his mother's side to support him as king over his brothers on his father's (Gideon's) side. So, the **men of Shechem** agreed to accept Abimelech as the new leader – perhaps even the king – of Israel.

        i. "The reference to the *men of Shechem* (Judges 9:2) is literally 'the baals of Shechem', the word having here its original meaning of 'lord' or 'owner'." (Cundall)

2. (4-5) Abimelech murders his brothers.

So they gave him seventy *shekels* of silver from the temple of Baal-Berith, with which Abimelech hired worthless and reckless men; and they followed him. Then he went to his father's house at Ophrah and killed his brothers, the seventy sons of Jerubbaal, on one stone. But Jotham the youngest son of Jerubbaal was left, because he hid himself.

> a. **So they gave him seventy shekels of silver from the temple of Baal-Berith**: The relatives of Abimelech on his mother's side gave him some "start-up money" to establish his leadership. He did this, but in a way that they never imagined – he hired **worthless and reckless men** to kill all his brothers, making certain there would never be a challenger to his leadership.
>
>> i. **From the temple of Baal-Berith**: Abimelech received his pay from the temple dedicated to Baal. "A work begun under the name and influence of the devil is not likely to end to the glory of God, or to the welfare of man." (Clarke)
>
> b. **Killed his brothers, the seventy sons of Jerubbaal**: Therefore, Abimelech killed his brothers with the support of his relatives on his mother's side. The *men of Shechem* (Judges 9:2-3) supported the plan because it was good *for them*, not because it was morally good or right.

3. (6) The men of Shechem make Abimelech their king.

And all the men of Shechem gathered together, all of Beth Millo, and they went and made Abimelech king beside the terebinth tree at the pillar that *was* in Shechem.

> a. **They went and made Abimelech king**: It is almost hard to tell who was worse; Abimelech who did the murdering, or the **men of Shechem** who approved of it. This was an ungodly leader given to an ungodly people, who first rejected God's leadership over the nation and then embraced a cruel and brutal man.
>
>> i. **Beth Millo**: "The word *millo* derives from a verb meaning 'to be filled', and originally referred to a rampart or earthwork; but its association with fortifications may have developed into a reference to fortresses generally. Thus *Beth-millo* may be identical with *the tower of Shechem*." (Cundall)
>
> b. **Beside the terebinth tree at the pillar that was in Shechem**: Ironically, Abimelech's coronation took place at the same tree where Joshua had solemnly placed a copy of the Law of God (Joshua 24:26). The Law was present among them, but Israel refused to read or heed it.

i. "Nevertheless, Abimelech became the first person ever to be crowned king in Israel. His abortive rule, however, ran roughshod over the divine requirements for that office." (Wolf)

ii. "The associations of such sites were very tenacious and it is of interest to note that Rehoboam went to Shechem, following the death of Solomon, to secure the acclamation of the Israelites although the city itself was in ruins at the time (1 Kings 12:1, 25)." (Cundall)

B. Jotham's warning.

1. (7-15) The parable of the trees.

Now when they told Jotham, he went and stood on top of Mount Gerizim, and lifted his voice and cried out. And he said to them:

**"Listen to me, you men of Shechem,
That God may listen to you!**

**"The trees once went forth to anoint a king over them.
And they said to the olive tree,
'Reign over us!'
But the olive tree said to them,
'Should I cease giving my oil,
With which they honor God and men,
And go to sway over trees?'**

**"Then the trees said to the fig tree,
'You come *and* reign over us!'
But the fig tree said to them,
'Should I cease my sweetness and my good fruit,
And go to sway over trees?'**

**"Then the trees said to the vine,
'You come *and* reign over us!'
But the vine said to them,
'Should I cease my new wine,
Which cheers *both* God and men,
And go to sway over trees?'**

**"Then all the trees said to the bramble,
'You come *and* reign over us!'
And the bramble said to the trees,
'If in truth you anoint me as king over you,
Then come *and* take shelter in my shade;
But if not, let fire come out of the bramble
And devour the cedars of Lebanon!'**

a. **Now when they told Jotham**: Jotham was the only son of Gideon to escape the massacre at the stone (Judges 9:5). Here he told a parable to rebuke the men of Shechem for their choice of Abimelech as a king.

> i. He made this speech from the **top of Mount Gerizim**, the mountain from which Israel heard the blessings of God pronounced upon the obedient (Deuteronomy 11:29 and 27:12; Joshua 8:33) about 150 years before.

b. **The trees once went forth to anoint a king over them**: In the parable told by Jotham, the worthy trees (such as the **olive**, the **fig**, and the **vine**) didn't want to be king; but the unworthy **bramble** agreed to be king.

> i. The promise of the bramble, **take shelter in my shade**, was intended as ironic and ridiculous. The bramble was a low, thorny bush and offered shade to no one, especially to trees.

c. **Let fire come out of the bramble and devour the cedars of Lebanon**: The bramble warned that he would be an oppressive ruler and destroy anyone who disagreed with him.

> i. One test of the character of a man is to see how he treats those who disagree with him. If his only desire is to destroy those who disagree, then he is much like the **bramble** – plenty of good points, but no real substance for good.

> ii. "Finally, the position was offered to the *bramble*, which not only produced nothing of value and was quite worthless as timber, but was a positive menace to the farmer who had to wage continual war against its encroachments." (Cundall)

> iii. "The condensed moral of the whole fable is this: Weak, worthless, and wicked men, will ever be foremost to thrust themselves into power; and, in the end, to bring ruin upon themselves, and on the unhappy people over whom they preside." (Clarke)

2. (16-21) Jotham applies the parable: the city of Shechem will be repaid for choosing such a worthless man.

"Now therefore, if you have acted in truth and sincerity in making Abimelech king, and if you have dealt well with Jerubbaal and his house, and have done to him as he deserves—for my father fought for you, risked his life, and delivered you out of the hand of Midian; but you have risen up against my father's house this day, and killed his seventy sons on one stone, and made Abimelech, the son of his female servant, king over the men of Shechem, because he is your brother—if then you have acted in truth and sincerity with Jerubbaal and with his house this day, *then* rejoice in Abimelech, and let him also rejoice in you.

But if not, let fire come from Abimelech and devour the men of Shechem and Beth Millo; and let fire come from the men

of Shechem and from Beth Millo and devour Abimelech!" And Jotham ran away and fled; and he went to Beer and dwelt there, for fear of Abimelech his brother.

    a. **If you have acted in truth and sincerity**: Jotham raised this just for the sake of argument. He didn't believe that 69 of his brothers were murdered for the sake of **truth and sincerity**.

    b. **Because he is your brother**: The real reason the men of Shechem supported Abimelech was because he was their **brother**. Abimelech's mother, though only a **female servant** to Gideon, was from Shechem. Abimelech probably grew up in Shechem (Judges 8:31).

        i. **Abimelech, the son of his female servant**: "Abimelech's mother is called a 'slave girl', a term usually referring to a wife's servant who is also a concubine, such as Hagar or Bilhah." (Wolf)

    c. **Let fire come from Abimelech and devour the men of Shechem**: Jotham's warning to the men of Shechem was that their unwise choice would come back to hurt them. He predicted that "**fire**" would come from Abimelech and devour them. After this bold warning he **ran away and fled** for fear of his life.

        i. "The prophecy of Jotham was not to be immediately fulfilled. The fire smoldered for three years but at last manifested itself." (Morgan)

C. Jotham's warning fulfilled.

1. (22-25) A spirit of ill will between Abimelech and Shechem.

After Abimelech had reigned over Israel three years, God sent a spirit of ill will between Abimelech and the men of Shechem; and the men of Shechem dealt treacherously with Abimelech, that the crime *done* to the seventy sons of Jerubbaal might be settled and their blood be laid on Abimelech their brother, who killed them, and on the men of Shechem, who aided him in the killing of his brothers. And the men of Shechem set men in ambush against him on the tops of the mountains, and they robbed all who passed by them along that way; and it was told Abimelech.

    a. **God sent a spirit of ill will between Abimelech and the men of Shechem**: Everything seemed fine between the men of Shechem and Abimelech for three years. Then, in judgment, God removed the peace that was between them and sent this **spirit of ill will**.

i. The writer of Judges used an interesting word to say that Abimelech had **reigned** over Israel. This word "is unique to the book and is perhaps chosen to distinguish Abimelech's ill-fated rule from that of the true judges. Abimelech was more like a tyrant than a king." (Wolf)

ii. "The extent of Abimelech's kingdom was very limited; only Shechem, Beth-millo, Arumah (Judges 9:41) and Thebez (Judges 9:50) are mentioned as under his jurisdiction and it is unlikely that it extended beyond a portion of western Manasseh." (Cundall)

iii. "God gave the devil commission to enter into or work upon their minds and hearts; knowing that he of himself, and by his own inclinations, would fill them with mistakes, and jealousies, and dissensions, and heart-burnings, which would end in civil wars and mutual ruin." (Poole)

b. **Set men in ambush…they robbed all who passed by**: Prompted by the **spirit of ill will**, the men of Shechem set ambushes on the mountain roads, hoping to disrupt the trade routes that profited Abimelech.

i. "This would have the effect of reducing the number of travellers and caravans in such a troubled area, thus emptying the pockets of Abimelech as well as hitting at his pride, for he could not guarantee the safety of travel in his domain." (Cundall)

2. (26-29) The men of Shechem choose a new leader.

Now Gaal the son of Ebed came with his brothers and went over to Shechem; and the men of Shechem put their confidence in him. So they went out into the fields, and gathered *grapes* from their vineyards and trod *them*, and made merry. And they went into the house of their god, and ate and drank, and cursed Abimelech. Then Gaal the son of Ebed said, "Who *is* Abimelech, and who *is* Shechem, that we should serve him? *Is he* not the son of Jerubbaal, and *is not* Zebul his officer? Serve the men of Hamor the father of Shechem; but why should we serve him? If only this people were under my authority! Then I would remove Abimelech." So he said to Abimelech, "Increase your army and come out!"

a. **The men of Shechem put their confidence in him**: The men of Shechem lost their confidence in Abimelech, so they chose a new leader named Gaal, the son of Ebed.

b. **They went into the house of their god, and ate and drank, and cursed Abimelech**: The men of Shechem were so confident that their new leader Gaal could protect them against Abimelech that they started throwing drunken parties and openly cursing Abimelech and challenging him to a fight (**Increase your army and come out!**).

3. (30-33) The role of Zebul, the **ruler of the city**.

When Zebul, the ruler of the city, heard the words of Gaal the son of Ebed, his anger was aroused. And he sent messengers to Abimelech secretly, saying

, "Take note! Gaal the son of Ebed and his brothers have come to Shechem; and here they are, fortifying the city against you. Now therefore, get up by night, you and the people who *are* **with you, and lie in wait in the field. And it shall be, as soon as the sun is up in the morning,** *that* **you shall rise early and rush upon the city; and** *when* **he and the people who are with him come out against you, you may then do to them as you find opportunity."**

> a. **When Zebul, the ruler of the city, heard the words of Gaal the son of Ebed, his anger was aroused**: Zebul, the "city manager" on behalf of Abimelech, told Abimelech all about Gaal and this rebellion. Zebul advised Abimelech to come and attack the city.
>
> b. **You shall rise early and rush upon the city**: Zebul advised Abimelech to organize a surprise attack against the rebels of Shechem.

4. (34-41) Abimelech defeats the rebellion of the men of Shechem, organized by Gaal.

So Abimelech and all the people who *were* **with him rose by night, and lay in wait against Shechem in four companies. When Gaal the son of Ebed went out and stood in the entrance to the city gate, Abimelech and the people who** *were* **with him rose from lying in wait. And when Gaal saw the people, he said to Zebul, "Look, people are coming down from the tops of the mountains!"**

But Zebul said to him, "You see the shadows of the mountains as *if they were* **men."**

So Gaal spoke again and said, "See, people are coming down from the center of the land, and another company is coming from the Diviners' Terebinth Tree."

Then Zebul said to him, "Where indeed *is* **your mouth now, with which you said, 'Who is Abimelech, that we should serve him?'** *Are* **not these the people whom you despised? Go out, if you will, and fight with them now."**

So Gaal went out, leading the men of Shechem, and fought with Abimelech. And Abimelech chased him, and he fled from him; and

many fell wounded, to the *very* entrance of the gate. Then Abimelech dwelt at Arumah, and Zebul drove out Gaal and his brothers, so that they would not dwell in Shechem.

a. **So Abimelech and all the people who were with him rose by night, and lay in wait**: Abimelech agreed with and followed the plan suggested by Zebul.

b. **Zebul said to him, "You see the shadows of the mountains as if they were men"**: Zebul deceived Gaal, allowing Abimelech's troops to take position. With the advantage of their superior position, Abimelech and his soldiers drove out Gaal and his men.

c. **Where indeed is your mouth now**: When Zebul knew that Gaal was at a disadvantage, he could not resist rebuking him for his proud, arrogant words against Abimelech, an enemy he could not defeat.

> i. "Gaal probably was not prepared for a siege; so he had little choice but to leave the city walls behind and confront Abimelech out in the open." (Wolf)

5. (42-45) Abimelech attacks the citizens of Shechem and conquers the city.

And it came about on the next day that the people went out into the field, and they told Abimelech. So he took his people, divided them into three companies, and lay in wait in the field. And he looked, and there were the people, coming out of the city; and he rose against them and attacked them. Then Abimelech and the company that *was* with him rushed forward and stood at the entrance of the gate of the city; and the *other* two companies rushed upon all who *were* in the fields and killed them. So Abimelech fought against the city all that day; he took the city and killed the people who *were* in it; and he demolished the city and sowed it with salt.

a. **It came about on the next day**: With the resistance of Gaal overcome, Abimelech would find it easy to again establish his control over the city of Shechem. Both outside and inside the city, they effectively attacked and killed the people of Shechem (even those not directly involved in the rebellion).

> i. "The people, apparently confident that the matter was concluded, *went out into the fields* as usual to engage in their daily occupations." (Cundall)

b. **He took the city and killed the people who *were* in it; and he demolished the city and sowed it with salt**: Abimelech then turned his fury against the people of Shechem, and killed as many of them as he could, and he demolished their city.

i. "Indeed, Shechem was not rebuilt until the reign of Jeroboam I, almost two centuries later (1 Kings 12:25)." (Wolf)

ii. This shows the problem of following a man who comes to power through violence. Commonly, it is only a matter of time until the same violence is turned against those who helped him come to power.

6. (46-49) The massacre at the tower of Shechem.

Now when all the men of the tower of Shechem had heard *that*, they entered the stronghold of the temple of the god Berith. And it was told Abimelech that all the men of the tower of Shechem were gathered together. Then Abimelech went up to Mount Zalmon, he and all the people who *were* with

him. And Abimelech took an ax in his hand and cut down a bough from the trees, and took it and laid *it* on his shoulder; then he said to the people who were with him, "What you have seen me do, make haste *and* do as I *have done.*" So each of the people likewise cut down his own bough and followed Abimelech, put *them* against the stronghold, and set the stronghold on fire above them, so that all the people of the tower of Shechem died, about a thousand men and women.

a. **Abimelech took an ax in his hand and cut down a bough…. "What you have seen me do, make haste and do as I have done"**: Though Abimelech was an ungodly and violent man, he did understand some basic principles of leadership. He understood the importance of leading through the example of one's own actions. He could tell his troops to **do as I have done**, and they did.

b. **All the people of the tower of Shechem died, about a thousand men and women**: With this, Abimelech massacred the last survivors of the city of Shechem, killing about a thousand men and women. This graphically fulfilled the warning of Jotham earlier in the chapter (Judges 9:19-20).

i. "This was as if a man should run into a stack of straw or barrel of gunpowder, to secure himself from a raging fire. Their covenant with Baal, that image of jealousy (Ezekiel 8:3), was the cause of their ruin. They looked upon this hold as both a fort and a sanctuary; but it saved them not." (Trapp)

ii. For the people of Shechem, even a secure tower could not protect them. Yet there is a more secure tower than the tower of Shechem. *The name of the* LORD *is a strong tower; the righteous run to it and are safe* (Proverbs 18:10). *For You have been a shelter for me, a strong tower from the enemy* (Psalm 61:3).

7. (50-55) God's judgment on Abimelech.

Then Abimelech went to Thebez, and he encamped against Thebez and took it. But there was a strong tower in the city, and all the men and women—all the people of the city—fled there and shut themselves in; then they went up to the top of the tower. So Abimelech came as far as the tower and fought against it; and he drew near the door of the tower to burn it with fire. But a certain woman dropped an upper millstone on Abimelech's head and crushed his skull. Then he called quickly to the young man, his armorbearer, and said to him, "Draw your sword and kill me, lest men say of me, 'A woman killed him.'" So his young man thrust him through, and he died. And when the men of Israel saw that Abimelech was dead, they departed, every man to his place.

> a. **Abimelech came as far as the tower and fought against it**: After his brutal victory at the tower of Shechem, Abimelech probably thought he was an expert at attacking towers. He went to **Thebez** and attacked the city and the tower there.
>
> b. **A certain woman dropped an upper millstone on Abimelech's head and crushed his skull**: At Thebez, a woman dropped a millstone on Abimelech's head and mortally wounded him.
>
>> i. This was probably a stone used to grind grain by hand. "Such handstones averaged ten to fourteen inches long and weighed five pounds or more." (Wood)
>
> c. **Draw your sword and kill me, lest men say of me, "A woman killed him."**: Abimelech considered it more manly to be killed by his armorbearer; but he was still dead afterward. Proud even in death, he then had to answer to God for his wicked actions.
>
>> i. "Yet long after his death, the credit continued to be given to the woman (cf. 2 Samuel 11:21)." (Wolf)
>>
>> ii. "But commentators observe it for a just hand of God upon Abimelech, that upon one stone he had slain his seventy brethren, and now a stone slayeth him: his head had stolen the crown of Israel, and now his head is smitten." (Trapp)

8. (56-57) Summation: The certainty of God's judgments.

Thus God repaid the wickedness of Abimelech, which he had done to his father by killing his seventy brothers. And all the evil of the men of Shechem God returned on their own heads, and on them came the curse of Jotham the son of Jerubbaal.

a. **Thus God repaid the wickedness of Abimelech**: We can be certain that God will repay wickedness, either in this life or the life to come. Often God finds a way to do it *both* in this life and the life to come.

b. **On them came the curse of Jotham the son of Jerubbaal**: God had warned the men of Shechem through Jotham. Yet they rejected the warning of God and therefore came to ruin.

> i. We should each consider if God is warning us about something in the present time. The story of Abimelech, the men of Shechem, and Jotham shows us that there is a real and terrible price to pay for rejecting God's warnings.

Judges 10 – Two Minor Judges and More Oppression

A. Two "minor" judges.

1. (1-2) Tola.

After Abimelech there arose to save Israel Tola the son of Puah, the son of Dodo, a man of Issachar; and he dwelt in Shamir in the mountains of Ephraim. He judged Israel twenty-three years; and he died and was buried in Shamir.

> a. **There arose to save Israel Tola**: We are not told much about the career of the judge, Tola; only that his service as a judge lasted a relatively long time (**twenty-three years**).

2. (3-5) Jair.

After him arose Jair, a Gileadite; and he judged Israel twenty-two years. Now he had thirty sons who rode on thirty donkeys; they also had thirty towns, which are called "Havoth Jair" to this day, which *are* in the land of Gilead. And Jair died and was buried in Camon.

> a. **After him arose Jair**: We also know little about Jair's service as a leader of Israel. We do know that he served for about the same number of years as Tola before him (**twenty-two years**).
>
> b. **Now he had thirty sons who rode on thirty donkeys; they also had thirty towns**: This shows that Jair was a polygamous man, and a man of wealth and prestige. His many sons had prestigious transportation and their own territory to rule. Jair never took the title of king, but it seems that he acted like one.

B. Apostasy, servitude, and supplication.

1. (6) Israel's seven-fold apostasy.

Then the children of Israel again did evil in the sight of the LORD, and served the Baals and the Ashtoreths, the gods of Syria, the gods of Sidon, the gods of Moab, the gods of the people of Ammon, and the gods of the Philistines; and they forsook the LORD and did not serve Him.

a. **Then the children of Israel again did evil in the sight of the LORD**: This phrase is repeated seven times in the book of Judges. It shows that the evil of Israel was even worse because they did it before the eyes of God. We could say that it is bad to commit adultery, but it is far more offensive to commit adultery before the eyes of your spouse.

b. **And served the Baals and the Ashtoreths**: The essence of Israel's sin was that they **served** other gods. Here, seven different ethnic and national gods are mentioned that Israel worshipped in their idolatry.

i. Israel was attracted to these other gods not because of the beauty of an idol image, but because of what was associated with the pagan deity. Baal, the weather god, was associated with financial success. Ashtoreth, the goddess of fertility, was associated with love, sex, and romance. As for the other gods of the neighboring nations around them, it was a matter of conforming to the popular culture and doing what everyone else did.

ii. Israel's worship of neighboring gods reminds us that the people of God are often in danger of worshipping what the world worships.

c. **They forsook the LORD and did not serve Him**: Perhaps Israel did not *consciously* forsake God. Yet adding the worship of pagan gods to the worship of the true God was to forsake the LORD. It seems that Israel was willing to worship just about anything *except* the true God. When a man stops believing in God, he does not believe in nothing; he believes in anything.

i. "Accordingly Peter Martyr giveth these two reasons here why the Israelites went so a whoring after these false gods of the several neighbour nations: (1.) Because they so flourished in wealth and honour, when themselves were so poor and contemptible; (2.) Because the worship of the true God was so severe, but the heathenish superstition licentious and pleasing to flesh and blood." (Trapp)

2. (7-9) Israel's servitude.

So the anger of the LORD was hot against Israel; and He sold them into the hands of the Philistines and into the hands of the people of Ammon. From that year they harassed and oppressed the children of Israel for eighteen years—all the children of Israel who *were* on the other side of the Jordan in the land of the Amorites, in Gilead. Moreover the people

of Ammon crossed over the Jordan to fight against Judah also, against Benjamin, and against the house of Ephraim, so that Israel was severely distressed.

a. **He sold them into the hands of the Philistines and into the hands of the people of Ammon**: If Israel wanted to serve the gods of the Philistines and the Ammonites, God would allow them to do so. He allowed them in the fullest sense, by *selling* them into servitude to the Philistines and Ammonites.

b. **They harassed and oppressed the children of Israel**: Of course, Israel was never *blessed* when they served these other gods. Instead, they were **harassed and oppressed**; they were **severely distressed** – but God gave them what they wanted.

3. (10-14) Israel calls to the LORD; God's response to Israel.

And the children of Israel cried out to the LORD, saying, "We have sinned against You, because we have both forsaken our God and served the Baals!"

So the LORD said to the children of Israel, "*Did I* not *deliver you* from the Egyptians and from the Amorites and from the people of Ammon and from the Philistines? Also the Sidonians and Amalekites and Maonites oppressed you; and you cried out to Me, and I delivered you from their hand. Yet you have forsaken Me and served other gods. Therefore I will deliver you no more. Go and cry out to the gods which you have chosen; let them deliver you in your time of distress."

a. **We have sinned against You**: The *words* of this cry seem fine, but God's response seems to indicate that He saw something lacking in Israel's repentance. One may cry out to the LORD, yet really just *wish* things were different. Crying out to God with the voice is not necessarily the same as crying out to Him with the heart.

i. God wanted from Israel the same thing He wants from us – a heart to put one's hand to the plow and not look back (Luke 9:62). He wants us to come to the place where we know that there is nothing worth following except God.

b. **Therefore I will deliver you no more**: God was harsh with Israel because they had to be genuinely sick of their sin before they would genuinely turn to God. God allowed Israel to experience the sickness of their sin.

i. "For the first time it is recorded that He refused to save them, reminding them of how repeatedly He had delivered them, and yet they had turned back to their evil courses. In the message of His anger there was clearly evident a purpose of love." (Morgan)

ii. "This apparent rejection, and the apparent indifference to the pleas of His people, was designed to test the sincerity of their response." (Cundall)

iii. One technique used to help people stop smoking is to put them in a small, unventilated room and make them smoke for hours on end, until they can hardly bear it. It makes them sick of smoking and makes them truly want to stop. In the same way, sometimes God will allow the natural consequences of our sin to crash upon us in concentrated form, so we can become sick of our sin.

iv. **Which you have chosen**: "You have not been forced to worship these gods by your oppressors and tyrants; but you have freely chosen these gods before me." (Poole)

4. (15-16) Repentance from Israel, mercy from God.

And the children of Israel said to the LORD, "We have sinned! Do to us whatever seems best to You; only deliver us this day, we pray." So they put away the foreign gods from among them and served the LORD. And His soul could no longer endure the misery of Israel.

a. **Do to us whatever seems best to You**: This indicates that Israel came to a place of total surrender to God. The prayer that comes most naturally to us is, "Do to me whatever seems best to me." The change in heart meant that the season of affliction eventually did affect Israel in a good way.

b. **So they put away the foreign gods from among them and served the LORD**: Israel finally discovered that the *worst* of serving God is better than the *best* of serving idols.

c. **His soul could no longer endure the misery of Israel**: God looked upon disobedient Israel with compassion, not hatred. It was "difficult" for God to allow Israel to stay in their misery, though it was best for them. Like the perfect loving parent, God hated to see Israel suffer, even when suffering was good for them. He longed to rescue them but would not do so until that was *good* for them.

i. "God *grieves* for the miseries to which his creatures are reduced by their own sins. Be astonished ye heavens, at this; and shout for joy, all ye inhabitants of the earth! For, through the love whence this compassion flowed, God has visited and redeemed a lost world!" (Clarke)

ii. "*His soul was grieved*; not properly, or as to inward affection, for God being infinitely happy, is not capable of grieving; but figuratively, and as to outward expression. He acted towards them like one that felt their sufferings." (Poole)

iii. "And now He grieves over you. If only you would forsake your sins and turn to Him, He would assuredly raise up a Jephthah for your help." (Meyer)

5. (17-18) Israel gathers, but without a leader.

Then the people of Ammon gathered together and encamped in Gilead. And the children of Israel assembled together and encamped in Mizpah. And the people, the leaders of Gilead, said to one another, "Who *is* the man who will begin the fight against the people of Ammon? He shall be head over all the inhabitants of Gilead."

a. **The children of Israel assembled together and encamped in Mizpah**: In response to the Ammonite threat, Israel gathered together for defense.

b. **Who is the man who will begin the fight against the people of Ammon?** Israel gathered but had no leader. God's pattern for doing great works among His people is to raise up a man. He could do the work all by Himself; He could send angels to do the work for Him; He could use a leaderless mob or a committee. Yet God's normal means of operating is to raise up a man, and through that man to do a great work. God uses leaders.

Judges 11 – Jephthah and the Ammonites

A. Jephthah negotiates with the Ammonites.

1. (1-3) Jephthah's background before his rise to leadership.

Now Jephthah the Gileadite was a mighty man of valor, but he *was* the son of a harlot; and Gilead begot Jephthah. Gilead's wife bore sons; and when his wife's sons grew up, they drove Jephthah out, and said to him, "You shall have no inheritance in our father's house, for you *are* the son of another woman." Then Jephthah fled from his brothers and dwelt in the land of Tob; and worthless men banded together with Jephthah and went out *raiding* with him.

> a. **Now Jephthah the Gileadite was a mighty man of valor**: This brave and notable man in Israel had a clouded pedigree. His mother was a **harlot**, a common heathen prostitute.
>
>> i. The *area* of Gilead was the part of Israel that lay *east* of the Jordan River, comprising the territory of Reuben, Gad, and half the tribe of Manasseh. Coincidentally, Jephthah's father was also named **Gilead**.
>
> b. **Jephthah fled from his brothers and dwelt in the land of Tob**: Rejected by his family because of he was not a legitimate heir, Jephthah grew up in this area in what would be modern-day Syria.
>
>> i. Though rejected by his family, God blessed and used Jephthah. "Howbeit God made choice of such a one here to be a deliverer of his people; and hath registered him among other of his worthies, famous for their faith (Hebrews 11). This is for the comfort of bastards, if believers, and born of God (John 1:12-13)." (Trapp)
>>
>> ii. "The one thing which we emphasize is that God did not count the wrong for which he was not responsible, a disqualification. He raised him up; He gave him His Spirit; He employed him to deliver His people in the hour of their need." (Morgan)

iii. "*Tob* has been tentatively identified with the modern el-Taiyibeh, about 15 miles east-north-east of Ramoth-gilead, in the desolate area which lay just outside the eastern boundary of Israel and the northern frontier of Ammon." (Cundall)

c. **Worthless men banded together with Jephthah and went out raiding with him**: Jephthah wasn't necessarily the leader of a band of criminals. Adam Clarke explains that the term **worthless men** doesn't necessarily mean a bandit: "The word may, however, mean in this place *poor persons*, without property, and without employment."

i. Wood states, "He and his band probably operated more in the manner of David and his group years later, protecting cities and settlements from marauders." David did the same in the period described in 1 Samuel 25:4-8, receiving pay from those whom they helped. It is also possible that they only plundered the villages of enemy peoples, such as the Ammonites.

2. (4-8) The elders of Gilead call upon the leadership of Jephthah.

It came to pass after a time that the people of Ammon made war against Israel. And so it was, when the people of Ammon made war against Israel, that the elders of Gilead went to get Jephthah from the land of Tob. Then they said to Jephthah, "Come and be our commander, that we may fight against the people of Ammon."

So Jephthah said to the elders of Gilead, "Did you not hate me, and expel me from my father's house? Why have you come to me now when you are in distress?"

And the elders of Gilead said to Jephthah, "That is why we have turned again to you now, that you may go with us and fight against the people of Ammon, and be our head over all the inhabitants of Gilead."

a. **The people of Ammon made war against Israel**: The nation of Ammon, the Ammonites, lived to the south of Israel. They were a semi-nomadic group of people who descended from Abraham's nephew Lot.

i. **Why have you come to me now when you are in distress?** "May not God justly say as much to most of us? We seldom seek to him till needs must." (Trapp)

b. **Come and be our commander, that we may fight against the people of Ammon**: Because of the crisis of the Ammonites, the leaders of Gilead were desperate for an able leader, and they turned to Jephthah. They were willing to give him the authority as **head** over Gilead.

3. (9-11) Jephthah's response to the leaders of Gilead.

So Jephthah said to the elders of Gilead, "If you take me back home to fight against the people of Ammon, and the LORD delivers them to me, shall I be your head?"

And the elders of Gilead said to Jephthah, "The LORD will be a witness between us, if we do not do according to your words." Then Jephthah went with the elders of Gilead, and the people made him head and commander over them; and Jephthah spoke all his words before the LORD in Mizpah.

> a. **If you take me back home to fight against the people of Ammon, and the LORD delivers them to me, shall I be your head?** Jephthah was only willing to assume leadership in the crisis if he could also remain a leader after the crisis. He didn't want to be rejected again as a worthless man.
>
> b. **Before the LORD in Mizpah**: This was the same place where the famous agreement between Laban and Jacob was made (Genesis 31:43-50). The idea of **Mizpah** ("watch") is "If you do wrong according to this promise, God will see it and may He punish."

4. (12-13) Jephthah negotiates with the king of the Ammonites.

Now Jephthah sent messengers to the king of the people of Ammon, saying, "What do you have against me, that you have come to fight against me in my land?"

And the king of the people of Ammon answered the messengers of Jephthah, "Because Israel took away my land when they came up out of Egypt, from the Arnon as far as the Jabbok, and to the Jordan. Now therefore, restore those *lands* peaceably."

> a. **What do you have against me, that you have come to fight against me in my land?** Jephthah asked a simple question: why are you in the land of Israel? Perhaps the whole dispute could be solved by negotiations and diplomacy instead of warfare.
>
> b. **Because Israel took away my land when they came up out of Egypt**: The king of Ammon gave a simple reply, saying that they were in Israel because it was really their own land, and Israel took it from them unjustly.

5. (14-28) Jephthah's response to the king of the Ammonites.

So Jephthah again sent messengers to the king of the people of Ammon, and said to him, "Thus says Jephthah: 'Israel did not take away the land of Moab, nor the land of the people of Ammon; for when Israel came up from Egypt, they walked through the wilderness as far as the Red Sea and came to Kadesh. Then Israel sent messengers to the king of Edom, saying, "Please let me pass through your land." But the king of Edom would not heed. And in like manner they sent to the king of Moab, but he would not *consent.* So

Israel remained in Kadesh. And they went along through the wilderness and bypassed the land of Edom and the land of Moab, came to the east side of the land of Moab, and encamped on the other side of the Arnon. But they did not enter the border of Moab, for the Arnon *was* the border of Moab. Then Israel sent messengers to Sihon king of the Amorites, king of Heshbon; and Israel said to him, "Please let us pass through your land into our place." But Sihon did not trust Israel to pass through his territory. So Sihon gathered all his people together, encamped in Jahaz, and fought against Israel. And the LORD God of Israel delivered Sihon and all his people into the hand of Israel, and they defeated them. Thus Israel gained possession of all the land of the Amorites, who inhabited that country. They took possession of all the territory of the Amorites, from the Arnon to the Jabbok and from the wilderness to the Jordan.

'And now the LORD God of Israel has dispossessed the Amorites from before His people Israel; should you then possess it? Will you not possess whatever Chemosh your god gives you to possess? So whatever the LORD our God takes possession of before us, we will possess. And now, *are* you any better than Balak the son of Zippor, king of Moab? Did he ever strive against Israel? Did he ever fight against them? While Israel dwelt in Heshbon and its villages, in Aroer and its villages, and in all the cities along the banks of the Arnon, for three hundred years, why did you not recover *them* within that time? Therefore I have not sinned against you, but you wronged me by fighting against me. May the LORD, the Judge, render judgment this day between the children of Israel and the people of Ammon.'" However, the king of the people of Ammon did not heed the words which Jephthah sent him.

> a. **Israel did not take away the land of Moab, nor the land of the people of Ammon**: Jephthah's written response to the king of the Ammonites carefully explained why Israel had a right to the land that the Ammonites claimed was theirs.
>
> b. **Thus Israel gained possession of all the land of the Amorites, who inhabited that country**: Jephthah reminded the king of the Ammonites that the Amorites conquered the Ammonites and took control of their land. When Israel defeated the Amorites in battle, they justly took the land of the Amorites – which also happened to be the previous land of the Ammonites. The war against the Amorites was prompted by the vicious Amorite war against Israelite civilians.

c. **And now the L**ORD **God of Israel has dispossessed the Amorites from before His people Israel; should you then possess it?** Jephthah argued that since God gave this land to Israel, the Ammonites had no claim over it.

d. **Will you not possess whatever Chemosh your god gives you to possess?** Jephthah argued that the Ammonite god Chemosh must show himself worthy to conquer the land of Israel. Since Israel held this land **for three hundred years**, it demonstrated that Chemosh was not greater than the God of Israel.

i. "The *three hundred years* is remarkably close to the total of the various figures for the judges and the periods of oppression given up to this point. The exact figure is 319 years." (Cundall)

ii. This was an inherent challenge: "If your god is mighty enough to give you the land, then let him do it. Let us see who is stronger – Yahweh or Chemosh."

iii. Jephthah did not see this battle as primarily between two armies, but between the God of Israel and the false god of Ammon. Jephthah showed true wisdom in seeing this as a spiritual battle *first*.

iv. **Chemosh your god**: Chemosh was traditionally the god of the Moabites, not the Ammonites. But they may have worshipped each other's gods, and they may also have considered Chemosh and Milcom to be the same god with different names.

e. **However, the king of the people of Ammon did not heed the words which Jephthah sent him**: Jephthah's logical, reasoned response had no effect on the king of Ammon. War was therefore inevitable.

B. Victory and a vow.

1. (29) Jephthah gathers troops and advances courageously on Ammon.

Then the Spirit of the LORD **came upon Jephthah, and he passed through Gilead and Manasseh, and passed through Mizpah of Gilead; and from Mizpah of Gilead he advanced *toward* the people of Ammon.**

a. **Then the Spirit of the L**ORD **came upon Jephthah**: This was the source of Jephthah's courage and can be the source of courage for believers today as well. When believers are beset by fears and anxieties, they need to fill their lives with Jesus and be filled with the Holy Spirit.

b. **He advanced toward the people of Ammon**: The filling of the Spirit makes God's people *advance*. They go forward in the sense of spiritual progress, and they go forward in the sense of confronting the enemies of God.

2. (30-31) Jephthah makes a rash vow, thinking it will help his cause before God.

And Jephthah made a vow to the LORD, and said, "If You will indeed deliver the people of Ammon into my hands, then it will be that whatever comes out of the doors of my house to meet me, when I return in peace from the people of Ammon, shall surely be the LORD's, and I will offer it up as a burnt offering."

    a. **Jephthah made a vow to the LORD**: Though well-intentioned, this was a foolish vow. Such vows can be attempts to manipulate God or put Him under obligation to ourselves. It is far more important to be on God's side than to try to persuade Him to be on your side.

        i. Even a Spirit-filled man can do foolish things. The Holy Spirit does not overwhelm and control us, He guides us – and that guidance can be resisted or ignored.

        ii. "There is no need to bribe God's help, as Jephthah did, by his rash promise. He will give gladly and freely out of His own heart of love the help and deliverance we need, if only our course is rightly ordered before Him." (Meyer)

    b. **Whatever comes out of the doors of my house to meet me…I will offer it up as a burnt offering**: Jephthah did not have a human sacrifice in mind. This is indicated by the ancient Hebrew grammar: "The masculine gender could be translated 'whatever comes out' or 'whoever comes out' and 'I will sacrifice it.'" (Wolf)

        i. Commentator Adam Clarke agreed that according to the most accurate Hebrew scholars, the best translation is *I will consecrate it to the LORD, or I will offer it for a burnt-offering*. As he wrote, "If it be a thing fit for a *burnt-offering*, it shall be made one; if fit for the *service of God*, it shall be consecrated to him."

        ii. Human sacrifice was strictly forbidden by the Mosaic Law in passages such as Leviticus 18:21 and Deuteronomy 12:31. It is almost certain that Jephthah was familiar with such passages because when he negotiated with the Ammonites he demonstrated that he knew God's word.

3. (32-33) God grants Israel victory over the Ammonites.

So Jephthah advanced toward the people of Ammon to fight against them, and the LORD delivered them into his hands. And he defeated them from Aroer as far as Minnith—twenty cities—and to Abel Keramim, with a very great slaughter. Thus the people of Ammon were subdued before the children of Israel.

Judges 11

- a. **And the LORD delivered them into his hands**: God won a great and important victory for Israel through Jephthah. He overcame bitterness and family rejection to meet a great need. Despite his difficult past, God still wonderfully used him.

- b. **Thus the people of Ammon were subdued before the children of Israel**: This was another victory for Israel won under the leadership of a Spirit-filled judge.

4. (34-35) A difficult vow to fulfill.

When Jephthah came to his house at Mizpah, there was his daughter, coming out to meet him with timbrels and dancing; and she *was his* only child. Besides her he had neither son nor daughter. And it came to pass, when he saw her, that he tore his clothes, and said, "Alas, my daughter! You have brought me very low! You are among those who trouble me! For I have given my word to the LORD, and I cannot go back on it."

- a. **When he saw her, he tore his clothes**: Jephthah made his foolish vow sincerely, fully intending to keep it. Yet he had not seriously considered the consequences of the vow. Therefore, he was grieved when his daughter was first to greet him out of his house.

- b. **I have given my word to the LORD, and I cannot go back on it**: Jephthah's oath was foolish, and he should not have kept it. He had no right to punish or afflict his daughter in *any way* because of the vow he made to God.

    i. It was one thing to make and keep the vow when Jephthah believed that a cow or a sheep would come out of the house at his arrival; yet when his daughter came he should have immediately said, "I have made a foolish vow, and it would be more sinful for me to keep it than to break it. I will repent before God for my foolish vow."

    ii. "He had made a rash vow, and such things are much better broken than kept. If a man makes a vow to commit a crime his vow to do so is in itself a sin, and the carrying out of his vow will be doubly sinful. If a man's vowing to do a thing made it necessary and right for him to do it, then the whole moral law might be suspended by the mere act of vowing, for a man might vow to steal, to commit adultery, or to murder, and then say, 'I was right in all those acts, because I vowed to do them.' This is self-evidently absurd, and to admit such a principle would be to destroy all morality." (Spurgeon)

    iii. Ecclesiastes 5:1-2 and 5:4-6 speak of the danger of making foolish vows. This passage makes it clear that it is better to not make vows at all than to make foolish vows. This does not mean that vows are bad

– they can be good. It means we must take them seriously. Christians need to take seriously the sin of broken vows and must either repent and keep them or repent of the foolishness in ever making the vow, and seek God's release from the vow.

c. **I have given my word to the LORD, and I cannot go back on it**: At the same time, for the sake of principle only, there was something wonderful about the spirit of Jephthah's willingness to keep his vows, even when it cost him something. In the specific vow he was foolish and should not have kept it, but the tenacity of character that says, "**I have given my word to the LORD, and I cannot go back on it**" is glorious and should be the word of every follower of Jesus Christ.

i. As followers of Jesus Christ, Jephthah's statement reminds us of *what we have done*: **I have given my word to the LORD**.

- We have confessed our faith in Jesus Christ.
- We have declared ourselves as followers and disciples of Jesus Christ.
- We have praised God with our songs and words.
- We have proclaimed our part together with God's people.

ii. As followers of Jesus Christ, Jephthah's statement reminds us of *what we cannot do*: **I cannot go back on it**.

- We cannot go back because we are being persecuted.
- We cannot go back because we are being mocked.
- We cannot go back, even a little way.
- To go back might show that our faith was always false.
- To go back would disgrace the work of Jesus on the cross.
- To go back would forsake heavenly reward.
- To go back would make no sense.

5. (36-40) Jephthah fulfills his vow to God.

So she said to him, "My father, *if* you have given your word to the LORD, do to me according to what has gone out of your mouth, because the LORD has avenged you of your enemies, the people of Ammon." Then she said to her father, "Let this thing be done for me: let me alone for two months, that I may go and wander on the mountains and bewail my virginity, my friends and I."

So he said, "Go." And he sent her away *for* two months; and she went with her friends, and bewailed her virginity on the mountains. And it

was so at the end of two months that she returned to her father, and he carried out his vow with her which he had vowed. She knew no man.

And it became a custom in Israel *that* the daughters of Israel went four days each year to lament the daughter of Jephthah the Gileadite.

a. **He carried out his vow with her which he had vowed**: Some people think that Jephthah did really offer his daughter as a burnt offering. If he did, this was clearly an example of misguided zeal for God because God never *asked* him to make such a foolish vow or to fulfill it so foolishly.

i. Later in their history, Israel began to serve a terrible pagan god named Molech, who was thought to be appeased by child sacrifice in the most terrible way imaginable. God never asked to be served in this terrible way, and therefore it can't be blamed on God.

b. **She went with her friends, and bewailed her virginity.... She knew no man**: These words indicate that it is more likely that Jephthah set his daughter aside according to the principle of Leviticus 27:2-4, where persons set apart to God in a vow were not required to be sacrificed (as animals were) but were "given" to the tabernacle in monetary value.

i. We know that there were women who were set apart for the tabernacle service; they were called *the women who assembled at the door of the tabernacle of meeting* (Exodus 38:8; 1 Samuel 2:22). It is likely that Jephthah's daughter became one of these women who served at the tabernacle.

ii. His daughter and her friends were rightly grieved that she was given to the tabernacle service before she was ever married. Probably most of the women who *assembled at the door of the tabernacle* were older widows.

iii. By sending his unmarried, only daughter to the service of the tabernacle for the rest of her life, it shows how seriously both Jephthah and his daughter took his promise to God.

iv. Many commentators object and see no other option than to say that Jephthah fulfilled his vow in a horrible way, by the human sacrifice of his own daughter. "The attempt to commute the sentence of death to one of perpetual virginity cannot be sustained." (Cundall)

v. Yet her committal to be one of the *women who assembled at the tabernacle* still seems like the best explanation because Jephthah is listed as a hero of the faith (Hebrews 11:32). It is hard to think of him as doing something so contrary to God's ways as offering his daughter as a human sacrifice and still being mentioned as a man of faith in Hebrews 11.

Judges 12 – Jephthah and the Ephraimites; Three Minor Judges

A. Jephthah and the Ephraimites conflict.

1. (1) The men of the tribe of Ephraim are angry with Jephthah.

Then the men of Ephraim gathered together, crossed over toward Zaphon, and said to Jephthah, "Why did you cross over to fight against the people of Ammon, and did not call us to go with you? We will burn your house down on you with fire!"

> a. **Why did you cross over to fight against the people of Ammon, and did not call us to go with you?** The tribe of Ephraim felt slighted by Jephthah and were angry that they did not have a central and prestigious role in the victorious battle over the Ammonites.
>
> > i. There is a tendency within all of us to not want to do a job unless we receive credit. It is evident that the people of the tribe of Ephraim were more concerned with getting the credit than with seeing a job done.
> >
> > ii. "Why should the Ephraimites complain about a victory accomplished through God's intervention for the benefit of all the tribes? It was a strange jealousy that spurred on Ephraim." (Wolf)
> >
> > iii. This seems to be a consistent problem with the people of the tribe of Ephraim; they gave a similar response to Gideon in Judges 8:1-3. Then Gideon answered the complaining men of Ephraim with tact and diplomacy. Jephthah was a very different sort of man.
>
> b. **We will burn your house down on you with fire**: The people of Ephraim also backed up their anger with a threat. They threatened to burn down Jephthah's house with him in it.

i. "This clearly again reveals the sad disintegration of the nation. The consciousness of the unity of the people seems largely to have been lost." (Morgan)

2. (2-3) Jephthah responds to the people of the tribe of Ephraim.

And Jephthah said to them, "My people and I were in a great struggle with the people of Ammon; and when I called you, you did not deliver me out of their hands. So when I saw that you would not deliver *me*, I took my life in my hands and crossed over against the people of Ammon; and the LORD delivered them into my hand. Why then have you come up to me this day to fight against me?"

a. **The LORD delivered them into my hand**: Jephthah's idea was clear. God won a great victory through him when the Ephraimites stood by, though they had the opportunity to help. In this, he pointed out the essentially unjust character of their complaint.

b. **When I called you, you did not deliver me**: The people of Ephraim here seem to be simply chronic complainers. When they had a chance to step out boldly for God they did not do it. Yet when the work was done and God was glorified, they complained that they didn't get to participate.

i. "The fact that a victory had been gained over their common enemy appears to have been overlooked. Accusation and counter-accusation followed in bewildering succession; the claim that they had been passed over was met by the charge that an appeal *had* been made to them to which they had not responded." (Cundall)

3. (4-6) The Gileadites (led by Jephthah) overwhelm the people of the tribe of Ephraim.

Now Jephthah gathered together all the men of Gilead and fought against Ephraim. And the men of Gilead defeated Ephraim, because they said, "You Gileadites *are* fugitives of Ephraim among the Ephraimites *and* among the Manassites." The Gileadites seized the fords of the Jordan before the Ephraimites *arrived*. And when *any* Ephraimite who escaped said, "Let me cross over," the men of Gilead would say to him, "*Are* you an Ephraimite?" If he said, "No," then they would say to him, "Then say, 'Shibboleth'!" And he would say, "Sibboleth," for he could not pronounce *it* right. Then they would take him and kill him at the fords of the Jordan. There fell at that time forty-two thousand Ephraimites.

a. **The men of Gilead defeated Ephraim**: Apparently, the men of Ephraim were better at talking than fighting, because the men of Gilead seemed to conquer them easily.

b. **Then they would say to him, "Then say, 'Shibboleth'"**: The word **shibboleth** means either "ear of grain" or "flowing stream." With this word the people from the tribe of Ephraim were easily identified by their dialect. They had a hard time pronouncing the "h" in **Shibboleth** and said *Sibboleth* instead, therefore giving themselves away.

i. According to Herbert Wolf, it is said that during the Second World War, the German soldiers sometimes identified Russian Jews by the way they pronounced the word for corn: "*kookoorooza*." Their distinctive pronunciation revealed their ethnic background. So it was for these men of Ephraim. "The Ephraimites were betrayed by their speech; so was Peter many years afterward (Matthew 26:73)." (Cundall)

ii. The term **shibboleth** therefore came into the English language as something which determines which side you are on. In modern English usage a shibboleth is the same as an "acid test."

iii. Today, there are certain true shibboleths in a person's vocabulary. In Jephthah's time, you could know something about a person by how they said "**Shibboleth**" (Judges 12:6). Today when someone talks about Jesus, you can listen to what they say and learn something about them. You can listen as they speak about the Bible, and you know something about them. It is also true that as much as our dialect gives us away, so does our everyday speech. Others should be able to tell that we are Christians by the way we talk.

iv. At the same time, "How thankful we should be, that our admission to the privilege of the Kingdom of God does not depend upon our pronunciation; that the reality of the new-birth is not tested by the accuracy with which we utter the creed; that we shall not be excluded from the gates of the New Jerusalem because we fail in the utterance of an 'h'!" (Meyer)

4. (7) The remainder of Jephthah's time as a judge.

And Jephthah judged Israel six years. Then Jephthah the Gileadite died and was buried in among the cities of Gilead.

B. Three minor judges.

1. (8-10) The judge Ibzan.

After him, Ibzan of Bethlehem judged Israel. He had thirty sons. And he gave away thirty daughters in marriage, and brought in thirty daughters from elsewhere for his sons. He judged Israel seven years. Then Ibzan died and was buried at Bethlehem.

a. **Ibzan of Bethlehem**: This does not seem to be the same city called "House of Bread" that David, son of Jesse, would later make famous.

> i. "*Beth-lehem* is not to be identified with Bethlehem in Judah, which is usually written as Bethlehem-judah…. The likelihood is that this Beth-lehem was the town in western Zebulun, about 10 miles north of Megiddo (Joshua 19:15)." (Cundall)

b. **He had thirty sons. And he gave away thirty daughters in marriage**: Ibzan practiced the traditional custom of making alliances through marriage and was wealthy and prestigious enough to have so many children and so many alliances through marriage.

2. (11-12) The judge Elon.

After him, Elon the Zebulunite judged Israel. He judged Israel ten years. And Elon the Zebulunite died and was buried at Aijalon in the country of Zebulun.

a. **Elon the Zebulunite**: He was next in a succession of briefly reigning judges. He was also from a different tribe than the past few judges before him. God called leaders from various tribes, instead of from one tribe only.

3. (13-15) The judge Abdon.

After him, Abdon the son of Hillel the Pirathonite judged Israel. He had forty sons and thirty grandsons, who rode on seventy young donkeys. He judged Israel eight years. Then Abdon the son of Hillel the Pirathonite died and was buried in Pirathon in the land of Ephraim, in the mountains of the Amalekites.

a. **He had forty sons and thirty grandsons, who rode on seventy young donkeys**: This was a demonstration of the wealth, prestige, and influence of this briefly reigning judge.

> i. "Pirathon was the birth-place of David's captain, Benaiah (2 Samuel 23:30; 1 Chronicles 11:31, 27:14)." (Cundall)

b. **In the mountains of the Amalekites**: These were the same Amalekites that God had put a curse upon for their treatment of the weakest and most vulnerable in Israel's wilderness wanderings (Exodus 17:8-13; Deuteronomy 25:17-19; 1 Samuel 15:2-3).

Judges 13 – The Birth of Samson

A. The Angel of the LORD announces the birth of Samson to Manoah's wife.

1. (1) Life in Israel at the time of Samson's birth.

Again the children of Israel did evil in the sight of the LORD, and the LORD delivered them into the hand of the Philistines for forty years.

> a. **Again the children of Israel did evil in the sight of the LORD**: The cycle of sin, bondage, repentance, deliverance, blessing, and sin again continued in the history of Israel. Into these times was born the next judge of Israel, Samson. In this sense, Samson was truly a man of his times. He is a study in contrasts, a man of great strengths and great weaknesses. In this, he is a picture of Israel's history both during this period and generally, a picture of great heights and deep lows.
>
>> i. Samson is also an important example of unfulfilled potential. Though he did great things for God, it is staggering to consider what he *might* have done and been for God.
>>
>> ii. "We have one of the strangest stories of the Old Testament, the story of Samson. It is the story of a great opportunity and a disastrous failure in the case of a man who might have wrought a great deliverance but failed." (Morgan)
>
> b. **And the LORD delivered them into the hand of the Philistines**: Because of Israel's sin and rebellion, God gained their attention again by bringing them into subjugation to the Philistines.

2. (2-3) The Angel of the LORD appears to Manoah's wife.

Now there was a certain man from Zorah, of the family of the Danites, whose name *was* Manoah; and his wife *was* barren and had no children. And the Angel of the LORD appeared to the woman and said to her, "Indeed now, you are barren and have borne no children, but you shall conceive and bear a son.

a. **A certain man from Zorah**: The town of **Zorah** is about 14 miles (22.5 kilometers) west of Jerusalem. It was in the land of the tribe of Dan.

b. **And the Angel of the LORD appeared**: From the rest of the chapter, we see that we should regard this **Angel** as no mere angel. As seen before in the book of Judges (Judges 2:1-5 and 6:11-24), this was Jesus on a special mission, appearing as a man before His incarnation in Bethlehem.

c. **You are barren and have borne no children, but you shall conceive and bear a son**: This promise came as a great blessing to this woman burdened by childlessness.

3. (4-5) Special instructions regarding the child to come.

Now therefore, please be careful not to drink wine or *similar* drink, and not to eat anything unclean. For behold, you shall conceive and bear a son. And no razor shall come upon his head, for the child shall be a Nazirite to God from the womb; and he shall begin to deliver Israel out of the hand of the Philistines."

a. **The child shall be a Nazirite to God**: Numbers 6:1-21 describes the vow of a Nazirite. When under the vow, people regarded themselves as specially devoted to God, leaving their hair uncut, drinking no wine and eating no grape products, and avoiding any contact with anything dead.

b. **From the womb**: There was nothing particularly unusual about someone taking the vow of a Nazirite for a specific period of time. What was unusual in Samson's case was that he was to live under the vow from his birth, and that his vow was intended to be a lifetime vow.

c. **Please be careful not to drink wine or similar drink, and not to eat anything unclean**: Manoah's wife also had to share in the Nazirite vow during the time she carried Samson.

d. **He shall begin to deliver Israel out of the hand of the Philistines**: "There is almost a weird suggestiveness in the phrase used by the angel concerning him, 'He shall begin to save Israel.' His ultimate failure was as certainly foreknown as was his opportunity." (Morgan)

4. (6-7) Manoah's wife reports the appearance of the Angel of the LORD to her husband.

So the woman came and told her husband, saying, "A Man of God came to me, and His countenance *was* like the countenance of the Angel of God, very awesome; but I did not ask Him where He *was* from, and He did not tell me His name. And He said to me, 'Behold, you shall conceive and bear a son. Now drink no wine or *similar* drink, nor eat anything unclean, for the child shall be a Nazirite to God from the womb to the day of his death.'"

a. **A Man of God came to me**: This indicates that the *Angel of the* LORD appearing to Manoah's wife generally appeared to be a **Man**, yet **His countenance was like the countenance of the Angel of God**.

b. **I did not ask Him where He was from, and He did not tell me His name**: This shows the profound impact the appearance of the **Man of God** had upon Manoah's wife. He was **very awesome**; so much so that she did not ask questions about where **He was from** or what His **name** was.

B. The Angel of the LORD **announces the birth of Samson to Manoah.**

1. (8-14) The Angel of the LORD confirms the words spoken before.

Then Manoah prayed to the LORD**, and said, "O my Lord, please let the Man of God whom You sent come to us again and teach us what we shall do for the child who will be born."**

And God listened to the voice of Manoah, and the Angel of God came to the woman again as she was sitting in the field; but Manoah her husband *was* **not with her. Then the woman ran in haste and told her husband, and said to him, "Look, the Man who came to me the** *other* **day has just now appeared to me!"**

So Manoah arose and followed his wife. When he came to the Man, he said to Him, "Are You the Man who spoke to this woman?"

And He said, "I *am*.**"**

Manoah said, "Now let Your words come *to pass!* **What will be the boy's rule of life, and his work?"**

So the Angel of the LORD **said to Manoah, "Of all that I said to the woman let her be careful. She may not eat anything that comes from the vine, nor may she drink wine or** *similar* **drink, nor eat anything unclean. All that I commanded her let her observe."**

a. **Please let the Man of God whom You sent come to us again and teach us what we shall do for the child who will be born**: Manoah already knew what God wanted him to do because the Angel of the LORD told his wife earlier. Here he asked for confirmation of the word previously spoken.

b. **What will be the boy's rule of life, and his work?** God honored Manoah's request for confirmation, but He did not answer this request to know the future. He simply called Manoah and his wife to obey what God already told them to do.

2. (15-18) Manoah offers the Angel of the LORD a meal; the Angel of the LORD will only accept an offering.

Then Manoah said to the Angel of the Lord, "Please let us detain You, and we will prepare a young goat for You."

And the Angel of the Lord said to Manoah, "Though you detain Me, I will not eat your food. But if you offer a burnt offering, you must offer it to the Lord." (For Manoah did not know He *was* the Angel of the Lord.)

Then Manoah said to the Angel of the Lord, "What *is* Your name, that when Your words come *to pass* we may honor You?"

And the Angel of the Lord said to him, "Why do you ask My name, seeing it *is* wonderful?"

> a. **I will not eat your food. But if you offer a burnt offering, you must offer it to the Lord**: Here, the Angel of the Lord showed Himself to be God, in the sense that He did not need a meal but would accept a sacrificial offering intended to honor the Lord.
>
> b. **Why do you ask My name, seeing it is wonderful?** Here the Angel of the Lord shows Himself to be Jesus, in taking the name **wonderful** (Isaiah 9:6).

3. (19-21) The Angel of the Lord displays His authority to Manoah and his wife.

So Manoah took the young goat with the grain offering, and offered it upon the rock to the Lord. And He did a wondrous thing while Manoah and his wife looked on—it happened as the flame went up toward heaven from the altar—the Angel of the Lord ascended in the flame of the altar! When Manoah and his wife saw *this,* they fell on their faces to the ground. When the Angel of the Lord appeared no more to Manoah and his wife, then Manoah knew that He *was* the Angel of the Lord.

> a. **He did a wondrous thing while Manoah and his wife looked on**: The Angel of the Lord proved He was *wonderful* by doing a **wondrous** thing – ascending in the flame of sacrifice to heaven.
>
>> i. "The first remark arising out the story of Manoah and his wife is this – that oftentimes we pray for blessings which will make us tremble when we receive them.... A second remark is this – Very frequently deep prostration of spirit is the forerunner of some remarkable blessing." (Spurgeon)
>
> b. **Then Manoah knew that He was the Angel of the Lord**: For the first time, Manoah and his wife understood that this person was no mere man or messenger from God. They realized they spoke with God Himself.

4. (22-23) The reaction of Manoah and his wife.

And Manoah said to his wife, "We shall surely die, because we have seen God!"

But his wife said to him, "If the LORD had desired to kill us, He would not have accepted a burnt offering and a grain offering from our hands, nor would He have shown us all these *things*, nor would He have told us *such things* as these at this time."

> a. **We shall surely die, because we have seen God**: Manoah perhaps knew what God said to Moses in Exodus 33:20: *You cannot see My face; for no man shall see Me, and live.* Manoah feared that because they had just seen the LORD, they would shortly die.
>
> b. **If the LORD had desired to kill us, He would not have accepted a burnt offering**: This was a perceptive response from Manoah's wife. She understood that God had not done so much for them to abandon them now. God's past work in our lives is a promise of His future care and blessing for us.
>
>> i. Manoah's wife was an invaluable source of encouragement for his faith. She didn't criticize Manoah. She didn't say, "What a silly man you are. What a stupid man you must be to be so frightened." We can never strengthen someone's faith by criticizing. We must do as Manoah's wife did – encourage them and build faith up.
>
> c. **He would not have accepted a burnt offering**: The basis of the faith of Manoah's wife was that she knew that the LORD had accepted their offering to Him. The same principle works for the Christian believer today: If the LORD wanted to do you evil, He would have never accepted an offering on your behalf – the offering of Jesus on the cross.
>
>> i. "Brother, if the Lord had meant to destroy us, he would not have shown us our sin, because we were happy enough previously, were we not? In our own poor way we were content enough, and if he did not mean to pardon us, it was not like the Lord to show us our sin, and so to torment us before our time, unless he meant to take it away." (Spurgeon)

5. (24-25) Samson is born, and the Holy Spirit comes upon him.

So the woman bore a son and called his name Samson; and the child grew, and the LORD blessed him. And the Spirit of the LORD began to move upon him at Mahaneh Dan between Zorah and Eshtaol.

> a. **So the woman bore a son and called his name Samson**: The promise from the Angel of LORD was fulfilled. It was proven to be true.

b. **And the Lord blessed him…. And the Spirit of the Lord began to move upon Him**: This is the source of the great strength we see in Samson later. Samson is often imagined as a man with huge, rippling muscles; but others couldn't understand why he was so strong. It is reasonable to think that he did not *look* very strong. Whether he looked strong or not, it was the Spirit of God who made him strong.

Judges 14 – Samson's First Failed Marriage

A. Samson seeks a Philistine wife.

1. (1-3) Samson demands a Philistine wife.

Now Samson went down to Timnah, and saw a woman in Timnah of the daughters of the Philistines. So he went up and told his father and mother, saying, "I have seen a woman in Timnah of the daughters of the Philistines; now therefore, get her for me as a wife."

Then his father and mother said to him, *"Is there* **no woman among the daughters of your brethren, or among all my people, that you must go and get a wife from the uncircumcised Philistines?"**

And Samson said to his father, "Get her for me, for she pleases me well."

> a. **Saw a woman in Timnah of the daughters of the Philistines**: This seemed to be a case of "love at first sight" for Samson. He saw this woman and he instantly wanted to marry her.
>
>> i. **She pleases me well** is literally, "she is right in my eyes." What Samson really cared about was how things *looked* to himself, not how they looked to the Lord.
>>
>> ii. Love at first sight is a powerful, but dangerous thing. It is entirely possible for us to fall in love with someone that we have no business falling in love with – which was exactly the case with Samson here. As well, love at first sight feels wonderful, but doesn't last in its initial form forever. We can be attracted more to the *feeling of love* itself than the person we focus upon – whom we don't really know at first sight.
>
> b. **Samson said to his father, "Get her for me, for she pleases me well"**: In demanding a Philistine wife, Samson showed a sinful disregard for his parents and for God's will (Deuteronomy 7:3-4). Bound by romantic feelings, many people still demand from God a mate not of God's will.

i. "His parents attempted to dissuade him, but he allowed himself to be swept by his passion and determined to realize his own desires." (Morgan)

ii. The command to the Israelites to not intermarry with the pagan nations around them applies to the Christian today, in that a believer must not marry someone who is not a Christian, joining themselves together with an unbeliever (2 Corinthians 6:14).

iii. It isn't because those who are not Christians are not lovable – they sometimes may be more lovable than believers. It is not because they aren't good enough, or worthy of our love, or that they are somehow inherently incapable of being a good marriage partner. It is simply because to be a Christian means Jesus Christ is the most important thing in your life; and when a Christian and a non-Christian get together, there are two people who disagree on the most important things in life.

iv. By extension, a Christian should never *date* a non-Christian. Those who do run a serious risk of falling in love with someone they have no business falling in love with.

v. Additionally, a Christian is advised to carefully discern the Christian commitment of the one they are interested in. There have been many pretended conversions, calculated to merely entice a Christian to marriage.

vi. If someone goes against God's plan and marries an unbeliever or if someone becomes a Christian before their spouse, there are specific commands applying to their situation. The apostle Paul clearly wrote that someone must do all that is possible to stay in the marriage and be the best spouse that they can be (1 Corinthians 7:10-16).

vii. God did use Samson mightily; but God used Samson *despite* his sin, not because of it. It is fair to suppose that God may have used Samson in a far greater way if he made himself a clean vessel according to the principle of 2 Timothy 2:20-21.

2. (4) God's will behind the scenes of Samson's desire to marry a Philistine woman.

But his father and mother did not know that it was of the LORD—that He was seeking an occasion to move against the Philistines. For at that time the Philistines had dominion over Israel.

a. **His father and mother did not know that it was of the LORD**: As the rest of the chapter shows, some good ultimately came out of this ungodly marriage. Many Philistines were killed, and they were kept off-balance in their attempts to dominate the Israelites.

> i. However, *none* of that justified Samson's actions. Though God can make even the evil of man serve His purposes, it never justifies the evil that man does.

> b. **He was seeking an occasion to move against the Philistines**: In accomplishing this purpose, God did not *make* a reluctant Samson pursue the Philistine woman for marriage. God allowed Samson to do what he wanted to do, though the act itself was sinful. God allowed it for reasons in both Samson's life and for reasons on a larger scale.

>> i. Someone today might justify their desire to marry a non-Christian because they trust some good will come out of it – such as their non-Christian partner eventually coming to Jesus. Things may work out that way, but even though God used Samson's marriage to a Philistine woman, it all came at a great personal cost to Samson.

>> ii. No matter how much good God can bring out of even the bad things we do, He can always bring far more good out of our obedience – and we ourselves experience much less pain.

3. (5-9) Samson slays a lion and eats some wild honey.

So Samson went down to Timnah with his father and mother, and came to the vineyards of Timnah.

Now *to his* surprise, a young lion *came* roaring against him. And the Spirit of the LORD came mightily upon him, and he tore the lion apart as one would have torn apart a young goat, though *he had* nothing in his hand. But he did not tell his father or his mother what he had done.

Then he went down and talked with the woman; and she pleased Samson well. After some time, when he returned to get her, he turned aside to see the carcass of the lion. And behold, a swarm of bees and honey *were* in the carcass of the lion. He took some of it in his hands and went along, eating. When he came to his father and mother, he gave *some* to them, and they also ate. But he did not tell them that he had taken the honey out of the carcass of the lion.

> a. **Came to the vineyards of Timnah**: Samson was dedicated to God with a lifelong vow of a Nazirite (Judges 13:4-5). Nazirites were to have nothing to do with grape products in any form (Numbers 6:3-4). Samson was dangerously close to a significant compromise.

> b. **He tore the lion apart as one would have torn apart a young goat**: Though Samson flirted with compromise – both with his impending

marriage and the **vineyards of Timnah** – he still had miraculous strength because **the Spirit of the Lord came mightily upon him**.

> i. "If that roaring lion, that goes about continually seeking whom he may devour, find us alone among the vineyards of the Philistines, where is our hope? Not in our heels, he is swifter than we: not in our weapons, we are naturally unarmed: not in our hands, which are weak and languishing; but in the Spirit of God, by whom we can do all things. If God fight in us, who can resist us? There is a stronger lion in us than that against us." (Spurgeon, quoting Bishop Hall)
>
> ii. The Holy Spirit of God wants to come upon us and give us power but power for something far more important than ripping apart lions. The Holy Spirit comes upon us to empower us to live for God as we should and for the power to tell others about Jesus effectively.

c. She pleased Samson well: This does not mean that she was a good woman for Samson to be attracted to or to marry. It is possible to fall in love with someone who is the wrong person to have a committed relationship with. This is why Proverbs 4:23 says: *Keep* (literally, *guard* or *protect*) *your heart with all diligence, for out of it spring the issues of life.* The unguarded heart often ends up in trouble.

> i. If we find that we are already in love with the wrong person, the only thing to do is to give them up, because it is right thing to do before God. Jesus told us that following Him would require giving up the things we love most (Mark 10:29-30).

d. He took some of it in his hands and went along: When Samson gathered honey from the dead carcass of a lion, he expressly violated his Nazirite vow, which stipulated that a Nazirite should never touch a dead body or carcass (Numbers 6:6-7).

> i. Significantly, Samson did this *after* he was remarkably filled with the Holy Spirit. This shows that an outpouring of the Holy Spirit does not automatically make a person godlier. An outpouring of the Holy Spirit gives one the *resources* to be godlier, but it doesn't "do it to" them. A person can be wonderfully gifted by the Holy Spirit and yet very spiritually immature.

e. He did not tell them that he had taken the honey out of the carcass of the lion: Samson did not tell his parents where he got the honey from because he knew it was a compromise of his Nazirite vow.

> i. Samson had *consecration* (at least the appearance of it) without *communion*. This was only good for the sake of image. The empty nature of his consecration would eventually be evident.

ii. Scripture is full of pictures of Christ but none of them are perfect. In the killing of the lion and the sharing of the honey, Spurgeon saw a spiritual picture of the work of Jesus Christ for us: "And what a type we have here of our Divine Lord and Master. Jesus, the conqueror of death and hell. He has destroyed the lion that roared upon us and upon him.... I see our triumphant Lord laden with sweetness, holding it forth to all his brethren, and inviting them to share in his joy." (Spurgeon)

iii. In the same way, Samson *shared* the sweetness of his victory over the lion with others. Spurgeon pointed out that this is, by analogy, a pattern for the way we should share the gospel.

- Samson brought the honey first to those nearest to him.
- Samson brought the honey in his hands, in the simplest way available to him.
- Samson gave them some of the honey to taste.
- Samson brought the honey modestly, not boasting about killing the lion.

B. The feast and the riddle.

1. (10-11) Samson hosts a "bachelor party" for his Philistine friends.

So his father went down to the woman. And Samson gave a feast there, for young men used to do so. And it happened, when they saw him, that they brought thirty companions to be with him.

a. **Samson gave a feast there**: Literally, this was a *drinking feast*. If Samson didn't break his Nazirite vow by partaking in the wine, he certainly put himself in a situation where it would be easy to do so.

b. **They brought thirty companions to be with him**: It was not – and is not – difficult to get many people to be part of a *drinking feast*.

2. (12-14) Samson poses a riddle concerning the lion and the honey.

Then Samson said to them, "Let me pose a riddle to you. If you can correctly solve and explain it to me within the seven days of the feast, then I will give you thirty linen garments and thirty changes of clothing. But if you cannot explain *it* to me, then you shall give me thirty linen garments and thirty changes of clothing."
And they said to him, "Pose your riddle, that we may hear it."
So he said to them:
"Out of the eater came something to eat,

And out of the strong came something sweet."
Now for three days they could not explain the riddle.

> a. **Changes of clothing**: This literally describes a fine suit of clothes one would wear to an important occasion; therefore 30 fine suits were wagered. Like most betting, this "friendly wager" would turn into something not quite so friendly.
>
> b. **Out of the eater came something to eat**: This was a clever riddle, and Samson showed that even if he was weak morally, he was not weak intellectually.

3. (15-18) Samson's Philistine wife extracts the answer to the riddle from Samson and tells it to the Philistines.

But it came to pass on the seventh day that they said to Samson's wife, "Entice your husband, that he may explain the riddle to us, or else we will burn you and your father's house with fire. Have you invited us in order to take what is ours? *Is that* not *so*?"

Then Samson's wife wept on him, and said, "You only hate me! You do not love me! You have posed a riddle to the sons of my people, but you have not explained *it* to me."

And he said to her, "Look, I have not explained *it* to my father or my mother; so should I explain *it* to you?" Now she had wept on him the seven days while their feast lasted. And it happened on the seventh day that he told her, because she pressed him so much. Then she explained the riddle to the sons of her people. So the men of the city said to him on the seventh day before the sun went down:

**"What *is* sweeter than honey?
And what *is* stronger than a lion?"**

And he said to them:

**"If you had not plowed with my heifer,
You would not have solved my riddle!"**

> a. **Then Samson's wife wept on him, and said, "You only hate me! You do not love me"**: Samson's Philistine wife knew how to manipulate the situation and how to make herself a burden to her husband until she got what she wanted from him.
>
> > i. Some wives will make themselves a burden to their husbands until they get what they want. This tactic is used because it often works in the short term but it can poison the relationship and ends up costing more than it gains.

b. **He told her, because she pressed him so much**: A woman easily manipulated the world's strongest man. This weakness of Samson will later be the cause of his downfall.

> i. The willingness of Samson's Philistine wife to side with her people against Samson shows a fundamental weakness in their marriage. She did not fulfill the idea essential to marriage of leaving one's father and mother to be joined in a one-flesh relationship with their spouse (Genesis 2:24; Matthew 19:5). Yet this also shows why it was wrong for Samson to marry a Philistine. We cannot expect someone who does not love the God of Israel to build a marriage on God's principles.

> ii. However, we see that the reason Samson's wife conspired against her husband was also complicated. She acted out of fear because of their threat (**else we will burn you and your father's house with fire**). If she had told Samson about the threats, he could have more than handled the situation. She apparently did not feel safe with Samson, but he was her best safety.

c. **If you had not plowed with my heifer, you would not have solved my riddle**: Samson's use of this proverb showed the anger and bitterness he felt at being manipulated. Samson's wife "won" what she wanted through manipulation, but she lost her husband's heart.

> i. When a man gives in to his wife's manipulations to keep the peace, it often builds anger and resentment in the man – and guilt in the woman for what she did. The way of manipulation is tempting (because it works) but always brings real destruction.

4. (19-20) Samson's anger and revenge.

Then the Spirit of the LORD came upon him mightily, and he went down to Ashkelon and killed thirty of their men, took their apparel, and gave the changes *of clothing* to those who had explained the riddle. So his anger was aroused, and he went back up to his father's house. And Samson's wife was *given* to his companion, who had been his best man.

> a. **Then the Spirit of the LORD came upon him mightily**: The Spirit of the LORD did not come upon Samson to avenge the hurt feelings of a husband. God's strategy was larger: *He was seeking an occasion to move against the Philistines* (Judges 14:4). Therefore, He used this occasion to pour out His Spirit on Samson to fight against the Philistines.

> b. **Killed thirty of their men, took their apparel, and gave the changes of clothing to those who had explained the riddle**: Samson paid off the bet, but he did it at the expense of the Philistines. He killed thirty of these enemies of Israel and gave their garments to satisfy the debt.

c. **Samson's wife was given to his companion, who had been his best man**: Samson won the battle but lost the war. His wife left him and went to his best man. It is interesting to think what Samson and his wife might say if they went in for marriage counseling.

> i. What Samson might say to a marriage counselor: *I love my wife, but it seems that we are not moving in the same direction. All I hear is nag, nag, nag; I finally do what she nags me to do, but by then I'm angry and the situation is worse than ever. I need to feel that she supports me and that she's on my side. I think she wants to give up on the marriage if she hasn't already.*
>
> ii. What Samson's wife might say to a marriage counselor: *My husband is a good guy, but he does not meet my needs. It was love at first sight for us, but now things have gone downhill. There are things I need him to do and to be that he just can't or won't. He doesn't respond to my needs and then we just get into a big fight, and no one is happy. I wonder if he loves me anymore.*
>
> iii. Samson was at fault for not guarding his heart against falling in love with a woman he had no business falling in love with. He was at fault for not founding the marriage on God's principles. He was also at fault for not responding to his wife's manipulations with love, free from anger.
>
> iv. At the same time, Samson's wife was at fault for siding with others against her husband. She was at fault for not telling her husband what the real problem was. And she was at fault for manipulating her husband by being such a bother until she got her way. Most of all, she was at fault for *giving up on the marriage*. Samson didn't leave her; she left him. No matter what the problems in a relationship, what God commands us most of all is to not give up on the marriage.
>
> v. We might rightly say with Charles Spurgeon: "Samson himself is a riddle. He was not only a riddle-maker; but he was himself an enigma very difficult to explain." (Spurgeon)

Judges 15 – Samson Against the Philistines

A. Retaliation back and forth.

1. (1-3) Samson's rage at discovering that his wife is given to another.

After a while, in the time of wheat harvest, it happened that Samson visited his wife with a young goat. And he said, "Let me go in to my wife, into *her* room." But her father would not permit him to go in.

Her father said, "I really thought that you thoroughly hated her; therefore I gave her to your companion. *Is* not her younger sister better than she? Please, take her instead."

And Samson said to them, "This time I shall be blameless regarding the Philistines if I harm them!"

> a. **I really thought that you thoroughly hated her**: It's hard to know why Samson's father-in-law thought that Samson hated his wife. Perhaps this was just an excuse to explain why he did what he did or perhaps Samson's Philistine wife poisoned her father's opinion of Samson (Judges 14:16).
>
> b. **Samson said to them**: Even though Samson was angry with his wife's father, the real root of the problem was the bad choices Samson made in love. He had no business allowing himself to fall in love with an ungodly, pagan woman.
>
>> i. No wonder Proverbs 4:23 tells us: *Keep* (literally, *guard* or *protect*) *your heart with all diligence, for out of it spring the issues of life*. Failure to guard the heart can result in great trouble.
>
> c. **This time I shall be blameless regarding the Philistines if I harm them**: God used Samson's ungodly anger for His purposes. As Psalm 76:10 says, *Surely the wrath of man shall praise You*. This doesn't justify Samson's anger, but it shows the glory and power of God to use all things for His purposes.

2. (4-5) Samson strikes out against the Philistines by burning their crops.

Then Samson went and caught three hundred foxes; and he took torches, turned *the foxes* tail to tail, and put a torch between each pair of tails. When he had set the torches on fire, he let *the foxes* go into the standing grain of the Philistines, and burned up both the shocks and the standing grain, as well as the vineyards *and* olive groves.

> a. **Samson went and caught three hundred foxes**: Samson seemed to act like a juvenile delinquent. Yet God used it all for His purpose of fighting against the Philistines.
>
> b. **Put a torch between each pair of tails**: Some people object that Samson could not have captured 300 foxes. Yet the word translated **foxes** probably refers to a jackal, not a fox, and jackals are known to run in large packs, sometimes up to 200. Second, there is nothing that says Samson did this all by himself. Third, there is nothing that says he did it all in one day.

3. (6-7) The Philistines retaliate by killing Samson's wife and family.

Then the Philistines said, "Who has done this?"

And they answered, "Samson, the son-in-law of the Timnite, because he has taken his wife and given her to his companion." So the Philistines came up and burned her and her father with fire.

Samson said to them, "Since you would do a thing like this, I will surely take revenge on you, and after that I will cease."

> a. **So the Philistines came up and burned her and her father with fire**: God used all this to advance His plan for Israel and redemption. Yet because of Samson's disobedience, it all happened at great personal cost to Samson. It is fair to suppose that if Samson were obedient, God would have furthered His plan in a way that *blessed* Samson.
>
> b. **I will surely take revenge on you, and after that I will cease**: We have here the bitter story of retaliation – of trying to avenge wrongs done to us. Retaliation is a never-ending story, and one that never ends well. Those who trust in God must be able to say, "Retaliation belongs to God. I'll let Him settle the score."
>
>> i. Much of the war, disaster, deep-seated hatred, and pain in our world come from this instinct to retaliate. But Jesus told us to not retaliate an eye for an eye but to take control of the situation by being even more generous (Matthew 5:38-42). When we do this, we act like God, who did not retaliate against man for his sin and rebellion, but instead gave His only Son to die for man.

4. (8) Samson repays the Philistines for the murder of his wife.

So he attacked them hip and thigh with a great slaughter; then he went down and dwelt in the cleft of the rock of Etam.

> a. **He attacked them hip and thigh**: This was an expression for a cruel, unsparing slaughter. Samson was a one-man army against the Philistines.
>
> b. **Dwelt in the cleft of the rock of Etam**: Samson had no more family and could trust virtually no one. He lived like a fugitive, alone in a cave.

B. Samson slays one thousand Philistines.

1. (9-13) Judah surrenders Samson to the Philistines.

Now the Philistines went up, encamped in Judah, and deployed themselves against Lehi. And the men of Judah said, "Why have you come up against us?"

So they answered, "We have come up to arrest Samson, to do to him as he has done to us."

Then three thousand men of Judah went down to the cleft of the rock of Etam, and said to Samson, "Do you not know that the Philistines rule over us? What *is* this you have done to us?"

And he said to them, "As they did to me, so I have done to them."

But they said to him, "We have come down to arrest you, that we may deliver you into the hand of the Philistines."

Then Samson said to them, "Swear to me that you will not kill me yourselves."

So they spoke to him, saying, "No, but we will tie you securely and deliver you into their hand; but we will surely not kill you." And they bound him with two new ropes and brought him up from the rock.

> a. **We have come up to arrest Samson, to do to him as he has done to us**: The fact that soldiers from the tribe of Judah gave up Samson to the Philistines shows just how much they were under the oppression of the Philistines. They would rather *please their oppressors* than *support their deliverer*.
>
> > i. This is a strangely common phenomenon. Often, when someone stands up to evil, people are angrier at the one who stood up to the evil than they are angry at the evil itself.
>
> b. **Do you not know that the Philistines rule over us?** Samson didn't want to hear this or recognize it. As far as he was concerned, the Philistines *should not* rule over the people of God.

Judges 15

c. **They bound him with two new ropes and brought him up from the rock**: It seems that Samson submitted to this. Assuming this was true; it showed great faith on Samson's part. He was willing to put himself in a difficult position and to trust God to take care of him.

2. (14-17) Samson uses the jawbone of a donkey to kill a thousand Philistines.

When he came to Lehi, the Philistines came shouting against him. Then the Spirit of the LORD came mightily upon him; and the ropes that *were* on his arms became like flax that is burned with fire, and his bonds broke loose from his hands. He found a fresh jawbone of a donkey, reached out his hand and took it, and killed a thousand men with it. Then Samson said:

**"With the jawbone of a donkey,
Heaps upon heaps,
With the jawbone of a donkey
I have slain a thousand men!"**

And so it was, when he had finished speaking, that he threw the jawbone from his hand, and called that place Ramath Lehi.

a. **He found a fresh jawbone of a donkey, reached out his hand and took it, and killed a thousand men with it**: Samson was unique among the judges because he was a "one-man army" against the Philistines. Other judges of Israel led *armies* against their enemies, but Samson fought alone.

i. With this remarkable victory, "We are conscious of what he might have done had he been wholly yielded to that 'Spirit of Jehovah' who came mightily upon him, instead of being so largely governed by the fires of his own passion." (Morgan)

b. **With the jawbone of a donkey, heaps upon heaps**: Samson's bold declaration of victory has a poetic touch that is difficult to render in translation. One effort goes like this: "With the jawbone of an ass I have piled them in a mass!"

c. **And called that place Ramath Lehi**: This name essentially means "Jawbone Hill." It was an obviously appropriate name for this place of Samson's great victory.

i. One preacher came up with a five-point sermon on the jawbone of an ass, likening it to the weapon of the gospel:

- It was a novel weapon.
- It was a most convenient weapon.
- It was a simple weapon.

- It was a ridiculous weapon.
- It was a successful weapon.

3. (18-20) God provides for Samson miraculously.

Then he became very thirsty; so he cried out to the LORD and said, "You have given this great deliverance by the hand of Your servant; and now shall I die of thirst and fall into the hand of the uncircumcised?" So God split the hollow place that *is* in Lehi, and water came out, and he drank; and his spirit returned, and he revived. Therefore he called its name En Hakkore, which is in Lehi to this day. And he judged Israel twenty years in the days of the Philistines.

a. **Then he became very thirsty**: Samson needed this thirst to remind himself of his own weakness and need right after such a great victory. After a great victory we need to remember our mortality.

i. "*It is very usual for God's people, when they have had some great deliverance, to have some little trouble that is too much for them.* Samson slays a thousand Philistines, and piles them up in heaps, and then he must needs die for want of a little water!" (Spurgeon)

ii. Matthew Poole comments on Samson's great thirst: it was "partly sent by God, that by the experience of his own impotency he might be forced to ascribe the victory to God only, and not to himself."

b. **God split the hollow place that is in Lehi, and water came out, and he drank; and his spirit returned, and he revived**: This is an example of the principle that God's work, done God's way, will always be provided for by God. Here the LORD showed His faithfulness to Samson by supplying the needs of His servant.

i. In his sermon *The Fainting Hero*, Charles Spurgeon pointed out that the believer can look at *heaps upon heaps* of defeated enemies: Heaps of your sins, heaps of your doubts and fears, heaps of your temptations, heaps of many of your sorrows. Yet, despite all these victories, fresh challenges will come, even as a deadly thirst and fatigue overcame Samson. Through this all, Samson could count on the fact that the *past victory* was a promise of *future deliverance*.

ii. "With that simple minded faith which was so characteristic of Samson, who was nothing but a big child, he turned his eye to his heavenly Father, and cried, 'O Jehovah, thou hast given me this great deliverance, and now shall I die for thirst? After all that thou hast done for me, shall the uncircumcised rejoice over me because I die for want of a drink of water?' Such confidence had he, that God would interpose on his behalf." (Spurgeon)

iii. "Be of good courage, fainting warrior! The God who made thee, and has used thee, knows thy frame, and what thou needest before thou askest." (Meyer)

Judges 16 – Samson's Disgrace and Death

A. Samson and Delilah.

1. (1-3) Samson and the harlot at Gaza.

Now Samson went to Gaza and saw a harlot there, and went in to her. When the Gazites *were told*, "Samson has come here!" they surrounded *the place* and lay in wait for him all night at the gate of the city. They were quiet all night, saying, "In the morning, when it is daylight, we will kill him." And Samson lay *low* till midnight; then he arose at midnight, took hold of the doors of the gate of the city and the two gateposts, pulled them up, bar and all, put *them* on his shoulders, and carried them to the top of the hill that faces Hebron.

> a. **Saw a harlot there, and went in to her**: Samson was in obvious sin here. This is a clear example of how a man so used of God can also sin, and sin blatantly.
>
>> i. Samson wanted to be used by God, but he also yielded to the deceitfulness of sin. He kept the external features of his Nazirite vow zealously, while at the same time sinning blatantly with a prostitute.
>>
>> ii. Samson did what we nearly all do when deceived by sin. He put his life into categories, and believed that some categories God cared about, and some categories God did not care about. Understanding that Jesus has claim over our entire life is a radical change of perspective.
>
> b. **Put them on his shoulders, and carried them to the top of the hill**: Despite his sin, God still gave Samson supernatural strength to escape from the Philistines. God did this because God's purpose was bigger than Samson himself, and because God used Samson *despite* Samson's sin, not because of it.

2. (4-5) Delilah agrees to betray Samson.

Afterward it happened that he loved a woman in the Valley of Sorek, whose name *was* Delilah. And the lords of the Philistines came up to her and said to her, "Entice him, and find out where his great strength *lies*, and by what *means* we may overpower him, that we may bind him to afflict him; and every one of us will give you eleven hundred *pieces* of silver."

    a. **He loved a woman…whose name was Delilah**: Samson fell in love again and fell for a woman completely wrong for him. This is another example of the pain and ruin that came into Samson's life because he did not guard his heart.

    b. **Every one of us will give you eleven hundred pieces of silver**: Delilah was also deeply in love; but she was in love with money, not Samson. 1,100 shekels made up more than 140 pounds (63 kilograms) of silver.

3. (6-9) Samson lies to Delilah about the source of his strength.

So Delilah said to Samson, "Please tell me where your great strength *lies*, and with what you may be bound to afflict you."

And Samson said to her, "If they bind me with seven fresh bowstrings, not yet dried, then I shall become weak, and be like any *other* man."

So the lords of the Philistines brought up to her seven fresh bowstrings, not yet dried, and she bound him with them. Now *men were* lying in wait, staying with her in the room. And she said to him, "The Philistines *are* upon you, Samson!" But he broke the bowstrings as a strand of yarn breaks when it touches fire. So the secret of his strength was not known.

    a. **Please tell me where your great strength lies**: The source of Samson's strength was not obvious. This means that he probably was not a large, heavily muscled man like a modern-day bodybuilder. He may have looked small and skinny, and unlikely to have such strength.

    b. **And with what you may be bound to afflict you**: Delilah knew that Samson was strong yet she also knew that *he could be bound with something*, and this was indeed true of Samson. One might say that the honest answer to her question would be, "I may be bound with the attention and affection of an ungodly yet attractive woman."

    c. **And she bound him**: Samson could have easily seen Delilah's heart by the way she immediately tried to bind him with what he deceptively said he could be bound with. The fact that he did not tell her the truth *proved* that he knew she had a dangerous intention.

4. (10-12) Samson lies to Delilah about the source of his strength a second time.

Then Delilah said to Samson, "Look, you have mocked me and told me lies. Now, please tell me what you may be bound with."

So he said to her, "If they bind me securely with new ropes that have never been used, then I shall become weak, and be like any *other* man."

Therefore Delilah took new ropes and bound him with them, and said to him, "The Philistines *are* upon you, Samson!" And *men were* lying in wait, staying in the room. But he broke them off his arms like a thread.

> a. **Now, please tell me what you may be bound with**: Seemingly, romantic attraction made Samson lose all sense. There was no good or rational reason Samson continued this relationship with Delilah or entertained her prying into the secret of his strength. Samson is a good example of how an ungodly relationship can warp our thinking.
>
> b. **Delilah took new ropes and bound him**: Samson allowed this bondage because he refused to escape the situation. Many people today are in similar places of sin, compromise, and bondage – and refuse to escape the situation.

5. (13-15) Samson lies to Delilah about the source of his strength for the third time.

Delilah said to Samson, "Until now you have mocked me and told me lies. Tell me what you may be bound with."

And he said to her, "If you weave the seven locks of my head into the web of the loom"—

so she wove *it* tightly with the batten of the loom, and said to him, "The Philistines *are* upon you, Samson!"

But he awoke from his sleep, and pulled out the batten and the web from the loom. Then she said to him, "How can you say, 'I love you,' when your heart *is* not with me? You have mocked me these three times, and have not told me where your great strength *lies*."

> a. **Tell me what you may be bound with**: Delilah obviously cared nothing for Samson. His continued commitment to her is a remarkable testimony to the power of blind, irresponsible love.
>
> b. **How can you say, "I love you," when your heart is not with me?** Tragically, Samson's heart *was* **with** Delilah. Her accusation was a manipulative projection of her own heart, which was not **with** Samson.

6. (16-19) Samson finally betrays the source of his strength.

And it came to pass, when she pestered him daily with her words and pressed him, *so* that his soul was vexed to death, that he told her all his heart,

Judges 16

and said to her, "No razor has ever come upon my head, for I *have been* a Nazirite to God from my mother's womb. If I am shaven, then my strength will leave me, and I shall become weak, and be like any *other* man."

When Delilah saw that he had told her all his heart, she sent and called for the lords of the Philistines, saying, "Come up once more, for he has told me all his heart." So the lords of the Philistines came up to her and brought the money in their hand. Then she lulled him to sleep on her knees, and called for a man and had him shave off the seven locks of his head. Then she began to torment him, and his strength left him.

> a. **When she pestered him daily with her words and pressed him, so that his soul was vexed to death…he told her all his heart**: Earlier Samson gave in to the nagging of his Philistine wife (Judges 14:15-18). Now he yielded to the nagging of Delilah. She certainly sinned by using such terrible manipulation, but Samson also sinned by yielding to that manipulation.
>
>> i. Her previous complaint was that Samson's love for her was empty was a hollow protest. Delilah had no love for him, and she expected Samson to destroy himself and his service for God to "prove" his love for her.
>
> b. **He told her all his heart**: When Samson did this, it was a very sad scene. He had to know what was to come. He faced the choice between faithfulness to his God and continuing an ungodly relationship.
>
>> i. In this we see the strongest man in the world weak under the power of an ungodly relationship. Perhaps Samson thought that because he was strong in one area of his life, he was strong in all areas. In this he was desperately wrong.
>
> c. **Then she lulled him to sleep on her knees**: No doubt, Delilah used sweet words to lull Samson to sleep. Her pretended love for Samson for the sake of money is deeply troubling.
>
>> i. "As long as he is consecrated he is strong; break that, he is weak as water. Now there are a thousand razors with which the devil can shave off the locks of a consecrated man without his knowing it. Samson is sound asleep; so clever is the barber that he even lulls him to sleep as his fingers move across the pate, the fool's pate, which he is making bare. The devil is cleverer far than even the skillful barber; he can shave the believer's locks while he scarcely knows it." (Spurgeon)
>
> d. **Then she began to torment him**: This was fitting. We might say that Delilah **began to torment** Samson long before this.

e. **And his strength left him**: There was nothing magical in Samson's hair. We might also say that Samson began breaking his Nazirite vow before this. Yet there came a time when Samson finally had to reckon with his rejection of God's mercy.

> i. "Not that his hair made him strong, but that his hair was the symbol of his consecration, and was the pledge of God's favour to him. While his hair was untouched he was a consecrated man; as soon as that was cut away, he was no longer perfectly consecrated, and then his strength departed from him." (Spurgeon)
>
> ii. "In the opinion of some persons Samson looked much improved when his matted hair was gone. He was more presentable; more fit for good society. And so in the case of churches, the notion is that they are all the better for getting rid of their peculiarities." (Spurgeon)

B. Samson's arrest and death.

1. (20) Samson is seized by the Philistines.

And she said, "The Philistines *are* upon you, Samson!" So he awoke from his sleep, and said, "I will go out as before, at other times, and shake myself free!" But he did not know that the LORD had departed from him.

> a. **I will go out as before**: Samson didn't know things were different. He lived in compromise for so long that he thought it would never make a difference.
>
> > i. "The story is one to fill the soul with holy fear. The possibility of going on in an attempt to do the work of God after God has withdrawn Himself, is an appalling one." (Morgan)
> >
> > ii. This is a tragic example of wasted potential and rejection of God's warnings. Samson thought he could "get away" with sin and escape its consequences. He misinterpreted the merciful delay of God's judgment or correction as a sign that He really didn't care. He therefore presumed upon God's mercy and continued in his sin, making things far worse.
>
> b. **He did not know that the LORD had departed from him**: Samson's strength was not in his hair, it was in his relationship with God. He worked against that relationship to the point where God finally **departed from him**, in the sense that He no longer blessed Samson with supernatural strength.

2. (21-22) Samson's Philistine imprisonment.

Then the Philistines took him and put out his eyes, and brought him down to Gaza. They bound him with bronze fetters, and he became a grinder in

the prison. However, the hair of his head began to grow again after it had been shaven.

a. **Then the Philistines took him and put out his eyes**: It was fitting that Samson was first blinded in his imprisonment. He was attracted to ungodly relationships through his eyes. His failure to restrain this attraction to women brought him into bondage.

b. **They bound him with bronze fetters**: Samson didn't humble himself in obedience before God – he insisted on the "freedom" of doing what he wanted to do. This left him with no freedom at all.

i. "There is nothing perhaps in the sacred writings at once more pathetic and tragic than the vision of Samson with his eyes put out, grinding in the prison house of the Philistines. It is a picture and a parable needing no enforcement of exposition to make it powerful." (Morgan)

ii. Sin has its wages, and this was Samson's payday. His sin left him blind, in bondage, and a slave. Before Samson's blindness, bondage, and slavery were only inward, but they eventually became evident outwardly.

c. **The hair of his head began to grow again**: God gave Samson hope in the middle of a dungeon. His hair began to return, and we can suppose that his heart also began to return.

i. "I wonder why these Philistines did not take care to keep his hair from growing to any length. If cutting his hair once had proved so effectual, I wonder that they did not send in the barber every morning, to make sure that not a hair grew upon his scalp or chin. But wicked men are not in all matters wise men: indeed, they so conspicuously fail in one point or another that Scripture calls them fools." (Spurgeon)

ii. "When Samson's hair began to grow, what did it prophesy? Well, first, it prophesied *hope for Samson*. I will be bound to say that he put his hand to his head, and felt that it was getting bristly, and then he put his hand to his beard, and found it rough. Yes, yes, yes, it was coming, and he thought within himself, 'It will be all right soon. I shall not get my eyes back. *They* will not grow again. I am an awful loser by my sin, but I shall get my strength back again, for my hair is growing. I shall be able to strike a blow for my people and for my God yet." (Spurgeon)

3. (23-25) Samson is mocked by his enemies.

Now the lords of the Philistines gathered together to offer a great sacrifice to Dagon their god, and to rejoice. And they said:

"Our god has delivered into our hands
Samson our enemy!"

When the people saw him, they praised their god; for they said:

"Our god has delivered into our hands our enemy,
The destroyer of our land,
And the one who multiplied our dead."

So it happened, when their hearts were merry, that they said, "Call for Samson, that he may perform for us." So they called for Samson from the prison, and he performed for them. And they stationed him between the pillars.

> a. **Our god has delivered into our hands Samson our enemy**: When Samson pursued his ungodly relationships, he might have justified it to himself by thinking that the only harm was done to himself. Yet here we see that his disobedience led to giving glory to false gods. Samson became a trophy for worshippers of false gods.
>
> b. **When the people saw him, they praised their god**: The message preached by the followers of Dagon was clear. They said, "Our god is stronger than the God of Israel because we have conquered Samson." Often the disobedience of God's leaders causes others to deny God.

4. (26-31) Samson's bittersweet death.

Then Samson said to the lad who held him by the hand, "Let me feel the pillars which support the temple, so that I can lean on them." Now the temple was full of men and women. All the lords of the Philistines *were* there—about three thousand men and women on the roof watching while Samson performed.

Then Samson called to the LORD, saying, "O Lord GOD, remember me, I pray! Strengthen me, I pray, just this once, O God, that I may with one *blow* take vengeance on the Philistines for my two eyes!" And Samson took hold of the two middle pillars which supported the temple, and he braced himself against them, one on his right and the other on his left. Then Samson said, "Let me die with the Philistines!" And he pushed with *all his* might, and the temple fell on the lords and all the people who *were* in it. So the dead that he killed at his death were more than he had killed in his life.

And his brothers and all his father's household came down and took him, and brought *him* up and buried him between Zorah and Eshtaol in the tomb of his father Manoah. He had judged Israel twenty years.

a. **Samson said to the lad who held him by the hand**: The Philistines continued to mock Samson. At this large demonstration, they used a boy to guard him.

> i. This makes us think even more that Samson was not a muscle-bound man who was naturally strong. His strength was truly supernatural, not natural.

b. **That I may with one blow take vengeance on the Philistines**: Samson's end was both bitter and sweet. God answered his last prayer, and he achieved his greatest victory against the Philistines at the cost of his own life.

> i. In this Samson is a picture of the believer in disobedience. God used him, but he did not benefit from it. His life ended in personal tragedy, shadowed by the waste of great potential.

c. **Let me die with the Philistines**: This was suicide, but different from suicide in the strict sense in that his purpose really wasn't to kill himself but to kill as many Philistines as he could. There is a sense in which Samson was like modern suicide bombers.

> i. Samson was a hero, even mentioned among the heroes of faith in Hebrews 11 (Hebrews 11:32). Yet there is no glorification of Samson and his end; he was not a *glorious* hero to be emulated, as modern suicide bombers are glorified by some. Instead, Samson was a *tragic* hero, whose life *should have ended* much differently.
>
> ii. We can also say that Samson's suicide and killing of others was not sought out; the opportunity *came to him* tragically.
>
> iii. Suicide is clearly sin, the sin of self-murder. Yet we are wrong if we regard it as the unforgivable sin. Most people who commit suicide have given in to the lies and deceptions of Satan, whose purpose is to kill and destroy (John 10:10).

d. **And he pushed with all his might, and the temple fell on the lords and all the people who were in it**: This could only happen with God supernaturally empowering Samson. This shows that God never forsook Samson, even when he was disobedient. God's mercies were there for Samson even in a Philistine prison. All Samson had to do was to turn his heart back towards God and receive them.

> i. We could say that Samson was restored with self-renunciation. This last great victory came only after he was broken, humiliated, and blind. He could no longer look to himself. Prior to this we don't see Samson as a man of prayer, but here he prayed. He was humbled enough to allow a little boy to help him.

ii. In summary, Samson shows the danger of underestimating our own sinfulness. He probably believed he had things under control with his own fleshly lusts, but his desire for love, romance, and sex led directly to his destruction. Samson was the great conqueror who never allowed God to properly conquer him.

iii. Samson *had* to be deceived to keep going back to tempting and dangerous places. It seemed that just about every time he went to the land of the Philistines, he fell into moral compromise. He should have learned from this. Instead of putting himself in tempting situations, he should have fled from youthful lusts (2 Timothy 2:22) like Joseph did (Genesis 39:12). "Rather than break his relationship with Delilah, he allowed it to break him." (Wolf)

iv. Samson also shows the danger of being a loner as a leader. Everything Samson did he did alone. He judged for 20 years and never sought or used help from others.

v. Most of all, Samson is a powerful picture of wasted potential. He could have been, and should have been, one of the greatest men of God in the Old Testament but he wasted his potential.

vi. "The Old Testament biographies were never written for our imitation, but they were written for our instruction. Upon this one matter, what a volume of force there is in such lessons! 'See,' says God, 'what faith can do. Here is a man, full of infirmities, a sorry fool; yet, through his childlike faith, he lives. 'The just shall live by faith.' He has many sad flaws and failings, but his heart is right towards his God; he does trust in the Lord, and he does give himself up as a man consecrated to his Lord's service, and, therefore, he is saved.' I look upon Samson's case as a great wonder, put in Scripture for the encouragement of great sinners." (Spurgeon)

Judges 17 – Micah's Idolatry

G. Campbell Morgan on Judges 17-21: *"The events here recorded must have taken place closely following the death of Joshua. They give us a picture of the internal condition of the people, and it is probable that they were added with that intention by the historian."*

A. Micah makes a shrine for idols.

1. (1-2) He returns a large amount of stolen silver to his mother.

Now there was a man from the mountains of Ephraim, whose name *was* Micah. And he said to his mother, "The eleven hundred *shekels* of silver that were taken from you, and on which you put a curse, even saying it in my ears—here *is* the silver with me; I took it."

And his mother said, *"May you be* blessed by the LORD**, my son!"**

> a. **Now there was a man**: Judges 17 and 18 present a detailed example of the spiritual confusion and sin in Israel during the days of the judges. These two chapters show us just how bad things were.
>
> b. **Whose name was Micah**: Micah, from the tribe of Ephraim, stole 1,100 shekels of silver from his mother and then returned them. His mother **blessed** her son for returning the money, even though he had originally taken it.
>
>> i. This account reveals a lot about the character of Micah, his mother, and the general spiritual state of Israel during this period.
>>
>> ii. Judges 17:10 indicates that ten shekels a year was an adequate wage. Therefore, 1,100 shekels was a great fortune.

2. (3-4) Micah's mother directs that some of the money be used to make an image to be used in worship.

So when he had returned the eleven hundred *shekels* of silver to his mother, his mother said, "I had wholly dedicated the silver from my hand to the LORD

for my son, to make a carved image and a molded image; now therefore, I will return it to you." Thus he returned the silver to his mother. Then his mother took two hundred *shekels* of silver and gave them to the silversmith, and he made it into a carved image and a molded image; and they were in the house of Micah.

a. **To make a carved image and a molded image**: Some people believe this was an image of a false god (such as Baal or Ashtoreth). Others believe that it was an image representing Yahweh. Either way, God strictly forbade such an image, whether it was meant to represent the true God or not.

i. The gold calf that Aaron made was actually meant to represent Yahweh (Exodus 32:4-5). But this violated the second commandment: *You shall not make for yourself a carved image, or any likeness of anything that is in heaven above, or that is in the earth beneath, or that is in the water under the earth; you shall not bow down to them nor serve them. For I, the LORD your God, am a jealous God* (Exodus 20:4-5).

b. **He made it into a carved image and a molded image**: By his fallen nature, man wants to make God into *his* image. Many religious people carve their own concept of God and assume that this is the God of the Bible. It takes effort to understand and accept the God of the Bible.

i. The sense of this passage is that Micah did all this *easily*. It wasn't hard to have an idol made in Israel at that time. This shows how Israel's society was bent towards idolatry.

3. (5) Micah establishes elaborate worship.

The man Micah had a shrine, and made an ephod and household idols; and he consecrated one of his sons, who became his priest.

a. **Micah had a shrine**: Micah first sets up a **shrine**, sort of a small temple, a place where others came to worship these idols.

b. **And made an ephod**: Micah imitated the worship at the true tabernacle of God by making an **ephod**. This was a specific garment worn by priests of Israel.

c. **And household idols**: In addition to this first idol, Micah also made **household idols** – literally, *teraphim* – gods that were worshipped in the hope of gaining prosperity and guidance.

d. **He consecrated one of his sons, who became his priest**: Finally, Micah established an order of priesthood among his sons. By each of these actions, Micah did everything he could to set up a rival religion in Israel.

i. All of this came from Micah and not from God. This was a completely man-originated and man-centered religion. Therefore, the purpose of the shrine, the beautiful ephod, the attractive idols, and the established priesthood was to serve and please man, not God. This pattern of man-pleasing religion continues to be common with many religions and churches today.

4. (6) A summarization of the spiritual state of Israel during the time of the judges.

In those days *there was* no king in Israel; everyone did *what was* right in his own eyes.

a. **There was no king in Israel**: There was, in fact, a king in Israel – Israel should have recognized the LORD God as their King. But since Israel rejected God as King, they were without any good and effective leadership.

b. **Everyone did what was right in his own eyes**: This refers to the radical individualism that marked the time of the judges. People looked to *self* for their guide to morality and ethics. The people genuinely felt that they **did what was right**, but they measured it only by their **own eyes**.

i. This is very much like the modern, "follow-your-heart" or "let-your-heart-be-your-guide" thinking. Modern culture regards this as the ideal state of society. Yet the Bible and common sense tell us that this kind of moral, spiritual, and social anarchy brings nothing but destruction.

- It seemed **right** in the **eyes** of Adam and Eve to eat the forbidden fruit, but God said it was wrong.
- It seemed **right** in the **eyes** of the sons of Jacob to sell Joseph into slavery, but God said it was wrong.
- It seemed **right** in the **eyes** of Nadab and Abihu to offer strange fire before the LORD, but God said it was wrong.
- It seemed **right** in the **eyes** of King David to commit adultery with Bathsheba and cover it with murder, but God said it was wrong.
- It seemed **right** in the **eyes** of Judas to betray Jesus, but God said it was wrong.

ii. *There is a way that seems right to a man, but its end is the way of death* (Proverbs 14:12). When man follows his own instincts – apart from

142   Judges 17

the redeemed nature of the converted person – it leads to ruin. We need to follow God's way, not our own.

B. Micah hires an unscrupulous Levite.

1. (7-8) An opportunistic Levite looking for employment.

Now there was a young man from Bethlehem in Judah, of the family of Judah; he *was* a Levite, and was staying there. The man departed from the city of Bethlehem in Judah to stay wherever he could find *a place*. Then he came to the mountains of Ephraim, to the house of Micah, as he journeyed.

a. **There was a young man from Bethlehem**: This man, as a **Levite**, had cities to live in and a place established by God for him to minister. Instead, he wanted to do what was right in his own eyes and went about offering himself as a priest for hire, **wherever he could find a place**.

b. **Then he came to the mountains of Ephraim, to the house of Micah**: This explains how this particular Levite and the previously mentioned Micah crossed paths.

2. (9-11) Micah hires the Levite.

And Micah said to him, "Where do you come from?"

So he said to him, "I *am* a Levite from Bethlehem in Judah, and I am on my way to find *a place* to stay."

Micah said to him, "Dwell with me, and be a father and a priest to me, and I will give you ten *shekels* of silver per year, a suit of clothes, and your sustenance." So the Levite went in. Then the Levite was content to dwell with the man; and the young man became like one of his sons to him.

a. **Dwell with me, and be a father and a priest to me**: Micah wanted this Levite to stay with him and work as a **priest** for him. He did this because he wanted to legitimize his personal shrine by having an officially recognized priest serving there. Deep down he knew that his idolatry was false and meaningless, and he hoped that *this* would make it legitimate.

i. "Men crave for a priest.... Be my priest; say for me to God what I cannot say. The sacrifices offered by thy hands are more likely to avail with Him than those rendered by mine." (Meyer)

b. **I will give you ten shekels of silver per year, a suit of clothes, and your sustenance**: So, for **ten shekels** and a **suit of clothes**, the Levite hired himself out to the idolatry of Micah. The Levite was a perfect example of a hireling, someone who served God (or an idol) for what it could give him, instead of serving to glorify the LORD.

> i. There are many different ways that hirelings get what they want. The monetary hireling is obvious, but there are also emotional hirelings who get into the ministry because of their insecurities and their need for approval.

c. **Then the Levite was content to dwell with the man**: The arrangements seemed perfect to everyone, and Micah felt he had gained a son.

> i. "Micah was attempting to maintain his relationship with God by violating the commands of God. The Levite degenerated into an attempt to secure his own material comfort by compromise." (Morgan)

3. (12-13) False consecration and false confidence.

So Micah consecrated the Levite, and the young man became his priest, and lived in the house of Micah. Then Micah said, "Now I know that the LORD will be good to me, since I have a Levite as priest!"

a. **So Micah consecrated the Levite**: Micah's consecration meant nothing at all. He had no authority from God to declare a renegade Levite as set apart (**consecrated**) by God to the service of this idolatrous shrine.

> i. In this tragic account, each person is guilty of terrible sin. Yet we could say that the Levite was guiltier than Micah was. We can say this because the Levite was at least *supposed* to know the word of God.

b. **Now I know that the LORD will be good to me, since I have a Levite as priest**: Micah's confidence was just as false as his consecration was. They were both based on superstition, not on God's word.

> i. We can say Micah was utterly sincere – but totally wrong. Sincerity is nice but gets you nowhere if it is not coupled with truth. The person who sincerely thinks they can swim across the Pacific Ocean will drown just as surely as the person who isn't as sincere.

Judges 18 – Micah's Idolatry and the Migration of the Tribe of Dan

A. Dan spies out Laish.

1. (1-2) The tribe of Dan sends spies to look for land to take among the people of Israel.

In those days *there was* no king in Israel. And in those days the tribe of the Danites was seeking an inheritance for itself to dwell in; for until that day *their* inheritance among the tribes of Israel had not fallen to them. So the children of Dan sent five men of their family from their territory, men of valor from Zorah and Eshtaol, to spy out the land and search it. They said to them, "Go, search the land." So they went to the mountains of Ephraim, to the house of Micah, and lodged there.

> a. **For until that day their inheritance among the tribes of Israel had not fallen to them**: The tribe of Dan had land apportioned to them, but they found their own land too hard to conquer.
>
>> i. Judges 17 was the story of compromise and self-willed carnality in the lives of a few individuals. Judges 18 shows how these individual sins made entire tribes wicked and rebellious against God.
>
> b. **So they went to the mountains of Ephraim**: Looking for easier land to conquer and make their own, the Danites came to the land of the tribe of Ephraim and the house of Micah.

2. (3-6) The Danites meet with Micah's Levite.

While they *were* at the house of Micah, they recognized the voice of the young Levite. They turned aside and said to him, "Who brought you here? What are you doing in this *place*? What do you have here?"

He said to them, "Thus and so Micah did for me. He has hired me, and I have become his priest."

So they said to him, "Please inquire of God, that we may know whether the journey on which we go will be prosperous."

And the priest said to them, "Go in peace. The presence of the LORD *be* with you on your way."

a. **They recognized the voice of the young Levite**: It may be that the spies from the tribe of Dan knew the renegade Levite personally. It is also possible that they simply recognized his accent as being from the southern part of Judea.

b. **Please inquire of God, that we may know whether the journey on which we go will be prosperous**: This shows what a spiritually confused time this was in Israel. These Danites on a sinful mission met with a *sinful* Levite and wanted to know from a *righteous* God if their mission would be successful. Then the sinful Levite sent the sinning men on their way with God's blessing.

3. (7-10) The Danites choose a city for expansion: Laish.

So the five men departed and went to Laish. They saw the people who *were* there, how they dwelt safely, in the manner of the Sidonians, quiet and secure. *There were* no rulers in the land who might put *them* to shame for anything. They *were* far from the Sidonians, and they had no ties with anyone.

Then *the spies* came back to their brethren at Zorah and Eshtaol, and their brethren said to them, "What *is* your *report*?"

So they said, "Arise, let us go up against them. For we have seen the land, and indeed it *is* very good. *Would* you *do* nothing? Do not hesitate to go, *and* enter to possess the land. When you go, you will come to a secure people and a large land. For God has given it into your hands, a place where *there is* no lack of anything that *is* on the earth."

a. **They dwelt safely, in the manner of the Sidonians**: The Danites found a city nearby that was not occupied by Israelites, but by a colony of the **Sidonians**. This was a group that God told Israel to drive out of the land of Canaan (Joshua 13:4).

i. In his sermon titled *The Danger of Carnal Security*, Charles Spurgeon used the description of the Sidonians in Judges 18:7, 27-28 as a description of the false security of the carnal believer. They are, like the Sidonians:

- Free from all internal struggles or conflicts.
- Free from rulers such as the governor of conscience.

146 *Judges 18*

- Free from ties and concerns to other people.
- Free from the fear of invasion.

b. **For we have seen the land, and indeed it is very good**: Seeing that the land was good, and the city was not heavily defended, the Danites believed this would be a good city to conquer and take as their own territory.

4. (11-13) They assemble an army of 600 to take possession of Laish.

And six hundred men of the family of the Danites went from there, from Zorah and Eshtaol, armed with weapons of war. Then they went up and encamped in Kirjath Jearim in Judah. (Therefore they call that place Mahaneh Dan to this day. There *it is*, west of Kirjath Jearim.) And they passed from there to the mountains of Ephraim, and came to the house of Micah.

a. **Six hundred men...armed with weapons of war**: Curiously, they assembled an army of 600 men to fight for the city of Laish in the land of the tribe of Ephraim; yet they could not fight for the land of their own tribal allotment. For some reason (to them and often to us) a distant battle seemed easier than a close battle.

B. **The tribe of Dan adopts Micah's idolatry.**

1. (14-18) On their way to Laish, the army of 600 men take Micah's shrine for themselves.

Then the five men who had gone to spy out the country of Laish answered and said to their brethren, "Do you know that there are in these houses an ephod, household idols, a carved image, and a molded image? Now therefore, consider what you should do." So they turned aside there, and came to the house of the young Levite man—to the house of Micah—and greeted him. The six hundred men armed with their weapons of war, who *were* of the children of Dan, stood by the entrance of the gate. Then the five men who had gone to spy out the land went up. Entering there, they took the carved image, the ephod, the household idols, and the molded image. The priest stood at the entrance of the gate with the six hundred men *who were* armed with weapons of war.

When these went into Micah's house and took the carved image, the ephod, the household idols, and the molded image, the priest said to them, "What are you doing?"

a. **Entering there, they took the carved image, the ephod, the household idols, and the molded image**: This was a strange combination of low morality and strong religious feeling. It was as if someone really wanted to study the Bible – therefore they stole several Bibles.

i. There are many examples in history of people satisfying a religious impulse in a completely immoral way. In Europe in the 14th century, unemployed soldiers often became small armies of bandits and robbed and burned and killed and raped towns and villages all over Europe. These brutal criminals often negotiated with a town before attacking it. If the town agreed to give the brutes a large amount of money, the army left the city alone. If the town refused to give the money or could not give the money, they attacked. These arrangements were made with formal negotiations and contracts. They have discovered that when these horrible men came to a monastery, they insisted on money as well – but they also demanded that the priests of the monastery give them a written document saying that all their sins were forgiven.

b. Took the carved image, the ephod, the household idols, and the molded image: They used violence and theft to supposedly advance a religious cause, and **the priest** allowed them by standing aside as they did so.

2. (19-21) The Levite goes with the army from the tribe of Dan.

And they said to him, "Be quiet, put your hand over your mouth, and come with us; be a father and a priest to us. *Is it* better for you to be a priest to the household of one man, or that you be a priest to a tribe and a family in Israel?" So the priest's heart was glad; and he took the ephod, the household idols, and the carved image, and took his place among the people.

Then they turned and departed, and put the little ones, the livestock, and the goods in front of them.

a. **Put your hand over your mouth**: This was a threat. They commanded the Levite to stop objecting or be attacked.

b. **So the priest's heart was glad**: His **heart was glad** because he was filled with mercenary ambition. The Levite did not care about Micah, only for the pay and status that he might get by being the priest for a whole tribe instead of a mere family.

3. (22-24) Micah's foolish idolatry comes to nothing.

When they were a good way from the house of Micah, the men who *were* in the houses near Micah's house gathered together and overtook the children of Dan. And they called out to the children of Dan. So they turned around and said to Micah, "What ails you, that you have gathered such a company?"

So he said, "You have taken away my gods which I made, and the priest, and you have gone away. Now what more do I have? How can you say to me, 'What ails you?'"

> a. **You have taken away my gods which I made**: This is powerful irony. Micah had to rescue his own gods. Obviously, his gods should be able to care for themselves. We wonder if Micah saw the foolishness of this.
>
>> i. We each either worship a god of our own making or we worship the true God who made us. The idols themselves are of less value than we are. Idol worship can be just a way of worshipping ourselves.
>>
>> ii. **And the priest**: Micah was foolish enough to have a priest who could be taken away, and it reminds us of how wonderful it is to have a High Priest who cannot change, and who can never be taken away from us. As F.B. Meyer wrote, "Whatever can be taken from us has the mark and signature of man upon it." Yet Jesus Christ, our High Priest, can never change; will never leave us out of a concern for someone else; and our sins and failures cannot rob us of Him.
>
> b. **Now what more do I have?** This shows how empty Micah's idolatry was. His false gods didn't bring him any lasting good.

4. (25-26) The army of the tribe of Dan refuses to give Micah his gods back, so Micah goes home empty-handed.

And the children of Dan said to him, "Do not let your voice be heard among us, lest angry men fall upon you, and you lose your life, with the lives of your household!" Then the children of Dan went their way. And when Micah saw that they *were* too strong for him, he turned and went back to his house.

> a. **Lest angry men fall upon you, and you lose your life**: This event and these words illustrate the general lawlessness in Israel during this long period of the judges. The children of Dan stole Micah's idols simply upon the principle of "might makes right."
>
> b. **When Micah saw that they were too strong for him**: They were too strong for *both* Micah and his gods. One should never have a god that needs protection.

5. (27-29) The army from the tribe of Dan conquers the city of Laish and rename it Dan.

So they took *the things* Micah had made, and the priest who had belonged to him, and went to Laish, to a people quiet and secure; and they struck them with the edge of the sword and burned the city with fire. *There was* no deliverer, because it *was* far from Sidon, and they had

no ties with anyone. It was in the valley that belongs to Beth Rehob. So they rebuilt the city and dwelt there. And they called the name of the city Dan, after the name of Dan their father, who was born to Israel. However, the name of the city formerly *was* Laish.

> a. **To Laish, to a people quiet and secure.... There was no deliverer**: This is written in a way meant to make us at least a little sympathetic towards the people of Laish. The people of Israel were instructed to take the land from the Canaanites, but this seemed like an unprincipled attack from wicked men of the tribe of Dan.
>
> b. **And they called the name of the city Dan**: The city of **Dan** will become the most prominent northern city in Israel. The phrase "from Dan to Beersheba" (Judges 20:1, 1 Samuel 3:20) will become an expression meaning, "from the north to the south of Israel" indicating all of Israel.

6. (30-31) The tribe of Dan officially adopts the idolatry that began with Micah.

Then the children of Dan set up for themselves the carved image; and Jonathan the son of Gershom, the son of Manasseh, and his sons were priests to the tribe of Dan until the day of the captivity of the land. So they set up for themselves Micah's carved image which he made, all the time that the house of God was in Shiloh.

> a. **The children of Dan set up for themselves the carved image**: This was the beginning of *established* idolatry in Israel in the Promised Land. There was *individual* idolatry in Israel long before this, but this is *official* idolatry.
>
>> i. Through a strange chain of events, this began with a son stealing 1,100 shekels from his mother (Judges 17:1-2). It ended with an entire tribe of Israel led into established idolatry.
>
> b. **So they set up for themselves Micah's carved image**: We can suppose that Micah had no idea how far-reaching the effects of his sin would become. His personal idolatry became the idolatry of an entire tribe, setting up a rival center of worship to **the house of God** in **Shiloh**.
>
>> i. "Whether intentionally on the part of the writer or no, there is a touch of satire in this declaration. There, at Shiloh, was the true centre of the national life, the house of God.... Nevertheless, at Dan they gathered about the false, and rendered a worship which was destructive." (Morgan)

Judges 19 – Gibeah's Crime

A. The Levite and his concubine.

1. (1) A Levite takes a concubine.

And it came to pass in those days, when *there was* no king in Israel, that there was a certain Levite staying in the remote mountains of Ephraim. He took for himself a concubine from Bethlehem in Judah.

a. **There was no king in Israel**: This set the stage for the terrible story in the following chapters. **No king in Israel** meant more than the absence of a political monarch; it also meant that they refused to recognize *God's leadership* over them.

i. What unfolds in the rest of this chapter is so distasteful that the commentator F.B. Meyer recommended *not* reading it. Commenting on this first verse, he wrote: "It will be sufficient to ponder these words, which occur four times in the book, without reading further in this terrible chapter, which shows the depths of the depravity to which man may sink apart from the grace of God."

b. **He took for himself a concubine**: The Levite's **concubine** was recognized as his legal partner, but she did not have the same status in the home or in society as a wife.

i. In this sense a concubine was a legally recognized mistress. Many prominent men in the Old Testament had concubines. Examples include Abraham (Genesis 25:6), Jacob (Genesis 35:22), Caleb (1 Chronicles 2:46), Saul (2 Samuel 3:7), David (2 Samuel 5:13), Solomon (1 Kings 11:3 – 300 concubines), and Rehoboam (2 Chronicles 11:21). Significantly, we *never* see this kind of family life blessed by God.

ii. The New Testament makes it clear that from the beginning God's plan was one man and one woman to be one flesh forever (Matthew 19:4-6), and each man is to be a "one-woman man" (1 Timothy 3:2).

2. (2-4) The Levite reconciles with his concubine after she commits adultery.

But his concubine played the harlot against him, and went away from him to her father's house at Bethlehem in Judah, and was there four whole months. Then her husband arose and went after her, to speak kindly to her *and* bring her back, having his servant and a couple of donkeys with him. So she brought him into her father's house; and when the father of the young woman saw him, he was glad to meet him. Now his father-in-law, the young woman's father, detained him; and he stayed with him three days. So they ate and drank and lodged there.

a. **Went after her, to speak kindly to her and bring her back**: Here the Levite was an example of how an offended spouse should act when there is adultery. Though she broke the bond between them, he worked hard to bring the relationship back together and succeeded.

i. Jesus told us that divorce is never *commanded* when there is adultery (Matthew 19:8). If a partner in marriage is sinned against by adultery, they should still work to make the marriage survive and succeed, up to the best of their ability.

b. **When the father of the young woman saw him, he was glad to meet him**: Perhaps the father was glad to see the Levite and his daughter back together or perhaps the father was simply glad to have his daughter out of his house again.

3. (5-10) The father of the concubine extends the visit with a traditionally generous show of hospitality.

Then it came to pass on the fourth day that they arose early in the morning, and he stood to depart; but the young woman's father said to his son-in-law, "Refresh your heart with a morsel of bread, and afterward go your way."

So they sat down, and the two of them ate and drank together. Then the young woman's father said to the man, "Please be content to stay all night, and let your heart be merry." And when the man stood to depart, his father-in-law urged him; so he lodged there again. Then he arose early in the morning on the fifth day to depart, but the young woman's father said, "Please refresh your heart." So they delayed until afternoon; and both of them ate.

And when the man stood to depart—he and his concubine and his servant—his father-in-law, the young woman's father, said to him,

"Look, the day is now drawing toward evening; please spend the night. See, the day is coming

to an end; lodge here, that your heart may be merry. Tomorrow go your way early, so that you may get home."

However, the man was not willing to spend that night; so he rose and departed, and came to opposite Jebus (that *is*, Jerusalem). With him were the two saddled donkeys; his concubine *was* also with him.

> a. **It came to pass on the fourth day**: This portion explains why the Levite and his concubine were delayed in Bethlehem at the home of the concubine's father. He intended to leave on **the fourth day** but was persuaded to stay one more night.
>
> b. **So they delayed until afternoon**: This explains why they left late in the day instead of early in the morning, which would normally be a more sensible time to depart for a long journey.

4. (11-15) Returning home, the Levite and the concubine decide to spend the night in Gibeah.

They *were* near Jebus, and the day was far spent; and the servant said to his master, "Come, please, and let us turn aside into this city of the Jebusites and lodge in it."

But his master said to him, "We will not turn aside here into a city of foreigners, who *are* not of the children of Israel; we will go on to Gibeah." So he said to his servant, "Come, let us draw near to one of these places, and spend the night in Gibeah or in Ramah." And they passed by and went their way; and the sun went down on them near Gibeah, which belongs to Benjamin. They turned aside there to go in to lodge in Gibeah. And when he went in, he sat down in the open square of the city, for no one would take them into *his* house to spend the night.

> a. **We will not turn aside here into a city of foreigners**: The Levite and his concubine considered a pagan town too dangerous. They therefore went on to **Gibeah**, a city of Israel, because they thought they would be safer there.
>
> b. **No one would take them into his house to spend the night**: The Levite and his concubine found no hospitality in Gibeah. This reflects poorly on the people of Gibeah because God commanded such hospitality among the people of God (Leviticus 19:33-34, Leviticus 25:35, Matthew 25:35, Hebrews 13:2). There is something wrong when there is no such hospitality among God's people.

5. (16-21) Finally, a fellow Ephraimite finds them and extends hospitality.

Just then an old man came in from his work in the field at evening, who also *was* from the mountains of Ephraim; he was staying in Gibeah, whereas the men of the place *were* Benjamites. And when he raised his eyes, he saw the

traveler in the open square of the city; and the old man said, "Where are you going, and where do you come from?"

So he said to him, "We *are* passing from Bethlehem in Judah toward the remote mountains of Ephraim; I *am* from there. I went to Bethlehem in Judah; *now* I am going to the house of the Lord. But there *is* no one who will take me into his house, although we have both straw and fodder for our donkeys, and bread and wine for myself, for your female servant, and for the young man *who is* with your servant; *there is* no lack of anything."

And the old man said, "Peace *be* with you! However, *let* all your needs *be* my responsibility; only do not spend the night in the open square." So he brought him into his house, and gave fodder to the donkeys. And they washed their feet, and ate and drank.

> a. **Who also was from the mountains of Ephraim**: The only person to extend hospitality to the Levite and his concubine was a man from their own region. None of the native people of Gibeah cared for the strangers in their midst.
>
> b. **Now I am going to the house of the Lord**: We remember that the **house of the Lord** was not at Jerusalem, but at Shiloh (Judges 18:31).

B. The crime of Gibeah.

1. (22) Their perverted demand.

As they were enjoying themselves, suddenly certain men of the city, perverted men, surrounded the house *and* beat on the door. They spoke to the master of the house, the old man, saying, "Bring out the man who came to your house, that we may know him *carnally*!"

> a. **Surrounded the house and beat on the door**: The verb form of the term **beat on the door** indicates that there was an increasingly loud pounding on the door. This was in no way a polite or casual request.
>
> b. **Bring out the man who came to your house, that we may know him carnally**: Their request was the same made by the homosexuals who surrounded the house of Lot in Sodom (Genesis 19:5). The picture is clear: At times in the period of the judges, Israel was as bad as Sodom and Gomorrah.

2. (23-26) The wickedness and perversion of the men of Gibeah.

Judges 19

But the man, the master of the house, went out to them and said to them, "No, my brethren! I beg you, do not act *so* wickedly! Seeing this man has come into my house, do not commit this outrage. Look, *here is* my virgin daughter and *the man's* concubine; let me bring them out now. Humble

them, and do with them as you please; but to this man do not do such a vile thing!" But the men would not heed him. So the man took his concubine and brought *her* out to them. And they knew her and abused her all night until morning; and when the day began to break, they let her go.

Then the woman came as the day was dawning, and fell down at the door of the man's house where her master *was,* till it was light.

> a. **The man took his concubine and brought her out to them**: Though the perverted men of Gibeah were clearly guilty, so were the Levite and the host of the home. They clearly should have been willing to sacrifice themselves before their daughters and companions.
>
> > i. Each person in this sordid drama was guilty, except of course for the concubine herself.
> >
> > - The wicked men of Gibeah who were more like men of Sodom and Gomorrah than men of Israel.
> > - The master of the house who was willing to sacrifice his own daughter.
> > - The Levite who cared nothing for his concubine.
>
> b. **And they knew her and abused her**: When describing the full meaning of the original Hebrew, Adam Clarke, due to modesty, did not translate the meaning into English. He left it in Latin so only the learned could understand the full implications of the wickedness and perversion of the men of Gibeah.
>
> > i. "One can easily see why the concubine had left her husband in the first place. She was virtually sacrificed to save his skin as the men sexually abused her all night." (Wolf)
> >
> > ii. Clarke on Gibeah's sinful men: "Rascals and miscreants of the deepest dye; worse than brutes, being a compound of beast and devil inseparably blended."
> >
> > iii. Centuries later, Israel still remembered this crime at Gibeah, and used it as an example of wickedness. *They are deeply corrupted, as in the days of Gibeah* (Hosea 9:9); *O Israel, you have sinned from the days of Gibeah* (Hosea 10:9).

3. (27-30) The Levite discovers his dead concubine and issues a call for national judgment.

When her master arose in the morning, and opened the doors of the house and went out to go his way, there was his concubine, fallen *at* the door of the house with her hands on the threshold. And he said to her, "Get up and let us

be going." But there was no answer. So the man lifted her onto the donkey; and the man got up and went to his place.

When he entered his house he took a knife, laid hold of his concubine, and divided her into twelve pieces, limb by limb, and sent her throughout all the territory of Israel. And so it was that all who saw it said, "No such deed has been done or seen from the day that the children of Israel came up from the land of Egypt until this day. Consider it, confer, and speak up!"

> a. **Get up and let us be going**: This is a painfully clear demonstration of the heartlessness of the Levite towards his concubine.

> b. **Divided her into twelve pieces, limb by limb, and sent her throughout all the territory of Israel**: This was an obviously grotesque way to deliver a message, but the method worked. It was tragic that the Levite did not show this kind of concern for righteousness earlier.

Judges 20 – Israel's War with Benjamin and Gibeah

A. The nation gathers to judge Gibeah.

1. (1-2) The nation gathers at the Levite's request.

So all the children of Israel came out, from Dan to Beersheba, as well as from the land of Gilead, and the congregation gathered together as one man before the LORD at Mizpah. And the leaders of all the people, all the tribes of Israel, presented themselves in the assembly of the people of God, four hundred thousand foot soldiers who drew the sword.

> a. **So all the children of Israel came out**: It was a positive sign to see Israel gather for such a reason. This showed that they were willing to deal with the problem of sin in their midst.
>
>> i. "A great moral passion flamed out. Underneath all the degeneracy was a true stratum of religious conviction, which in the presence of the iniquity of the men of Gibeah sprang to life and action." (Morgan)
>>
>> ii. It seems that the crime of Gibeah shocked the conscience of Israel. Today it seems that the crime at Gibeah would be material for tabloid news, cable television, daytime talk shows, and talk radio – more than a national call to righteousness and repentance.
>
> b. **The leaders of all the people, all the tribes of Israel, presented themselves**: Deuteronomy 13:12-18 instructed Israel how to deal with such abominations among them. It said they must first test the truth of the accusations. If the charges were true, they must then utterly destroy those who committed such an abomination.

2. (3-7) The Levite describes the abuse and murder of his concubine.

(Now the children of Benjamin heard that the children of Israel had gone up to Mizpah.)

Then the children of Israel said, "Tell *us*, how did this wicked deed happen?"

So the Levite, the husband of the woman who was murdered, answered and said, "My concubine and I went into Gibeah, which belongs to Benjamin, to spend the night. And the men of Gibeah rose against me, and surrounded the house at night because of me. They intended to kill me, but instead they ravished my concubine so that she died. So I took hold of my concubine, cut her in pieces, and sent her throughout all the territory of the inheritance of Israel, because they committed lewdness and outrage in Israel. Look! All of you *are* children of Israel; give your advice and counsel here and now!"

    a. **Tell us, how did this wicked deed happen?** The children of Israel wanted to know, so they could *do* something about this outrage.

    b. **They intended to kill me, but instead ravished my concubine**: The Levite spun the story to his own advantage. What he said was true, but he *didn't* mention the cruel and callous way he abandoned his concubine to the mob.

3. (8-11) Preparations for war made.

So all the people arose as one man, saying, "None *of us* will go to his tent, nor will any turn back to his house; but now this *is* the thing which we will do to Gibeah: *We will go up* against it by lot. We will take ten men out of *every* hundred throughout all the tribes of Israel, a hundred out of *every* thousand, and a thousand out of *every* ten thousand, to make provisions for the people, that when they come to Gibeah in Benjamin, they may repay all the vileness that they have done in Israel." So all the men of Israel were gathered against the city, united together as one man.

    a. **So all the people arose as one man**: This was an encouraging response in a very dark time. They came together in unity and decided to bring justice to the people of Gibeah.

    b. **They may repay all the vileness that they have done in Israel**: This was extreme, but a valid and proper fulfillment of God's command to Israel Deuteronomy 13:12-18.

4. (12-17) Benjamin's help is sought but not given.

Then the tribes of Israel sent men through all the tribe of Benjamin, saying, "What *is* this wickedness that has occurred among you? Now therefore, deliver up the men, the perverted men who *are* in Gibeah, that we may put them to death and remove the evil from Israel!" But the children of Benjamin would not listen to the voice of their bretheren, the children of Israel. Instead, the children of Benjamin gathered together from their cities to Gibeah, to go to battle against the children of Israel. And from their cities at that time the children of Benjamin numbered twenty-six thousand men who drew the sword, besides the inhabitants of Gibeah, who numbered seven hundred select men. Among all this people *were* seven hundred select men *who were* left-handed; every one could sling a stone at a hair's *breadth* and not miss. Now besides Benjamin, the men of Israel numbered four hundred thousand men who drew the sword; all of these *were* men of war.

> a. **But the children of Benjamin would not listen to the voice of their brethren**: The other tribes of Israel did the right thing in asking the tribe of Benjamin to **deliver up the men** who committed this crime. They sought to justly resolve the crisis without full war. But the tribe of Benjamin committed a great sin by putting loyalty to their tribe before obedience to God's Law.
>
>> i. Modern followers of God can make the same mistake today when they put the interests of their own nation before the interests of the kingdom of God. It is important for Christians to remember that they are citizens of the kingdom of God first (Philippians 3:20).
>
> b. **Seven hundred select men who were left-handed; every one could sling a stone at a hair's breadth and not miss**: The tribe of Benjamin not only failed to support the just cause of the other tribes, they actively resisted the other tribes with an assembled army. The army included this division of **seven hundred select men**.
>
>> i. **And not miss**: The Hebrew word translated **miss** is literally *sin*. This illustrates the principle that the word "sin" literally means to "miss the mark" – whether missing by an inch or a yard.
>
> c. **Besides Benjamin, the men of Israel numbered four hundred thousand men**: The tribes of Israel prepared for a small civil war against the tribe of Benjamin. Israel was right in believing that the greatest good was not unity. Unity apart from justice and truth is unity not worth having.

B. The battle against Benjamin and Gibeah.

1. (18-21) The first day of battle – Israel is defeated before Benjamin.

Then the children of Israel arose and went up to the house of God to inquire of God. They said, "Which of us shall go up first to battle against the children of Benjamin?"

The Lord said, "Judah first!"

So the children of Israel rose in the morning and encamped against Gibeah. And the men of Israel went out to battle against Benjamin, and the men of Israel put themselves in battle array to fight against them at Gibeah. Then the children of Benjamin came out of Gibeah, and on that day cut down to the ground twenty-two thousand men of the Israelites.

a. **Went up to the house of God to inquire of God**: In the first battle, Israel sought the LORD – yet they were defeated. We can speculate that though they inquired of God, they still trusted in the might of their army and in the goodness of their cause, but not in the LORD.

b. **The children of Benjamin came out of Gibeah, and on that day cut down to the ground twenty-two thousand men of the Israelites**: This was a staggering, severe loss in the first battle of this small civil war. After this first day of battle, it seemed that the single tribe of Benjamin might successfully resist the other tribes of Israel.

i. Perhaps there was something wrong in the way that Israel sought the LORD before this battle. Or, it is also just as likely that this was simply part of God's plan to discipline and correct His disobedient nation.

ii. The American President, Abraham Lincoln, in his second inaugural address, spoke on this very theme in relation to the American Civil War:

Fondly do we hope, fervently do we pray, that this mighty scourge of war may speedily pass away. Yet, if God wills that it continue until all the wealth piled by the bondsman's two hundred and fifty years of unrequited toil shall be sunk, and until every drop of blood drawn with the lash shall be paid by another drawn with the sword, as was said three thousand years ago, so still it must be said "the judgments of the Lord are true and righteous altogether." (1865)

iii. Perhaps, something of the same dynamic was at work with Israel at this time – God correcting a disobedient nation through the tragic loss of 22,000 soldiers of Israel.

2. (22-23) Israel seeks God after the first defeat.

And the people, that is, the men of Israel, encouraged themselves and again formed the battle line at the place where they had put themselves in array on the first day. Then the children of Israel went up and wept before the LORD until evening, and asked counsel of the LORD, saying, "Shall I again draw near for battle against the children of my brother Benjamin?"

And the LORD said, "Go up against him."

Judges 20

> a. **The men of Israel, encouraged themselves and again formed the battle line**: This was a wonderful reaction amid such a dark event. These soldiers did not lose hope; like David in 1 Samuel 30:6, they strengthened themselves in the LORD and moved forward.
>
> b. **Then the children of Israel went up and wept before the LORD until evening**: To their credit, the children of Israel did not stop seeking the LORD after the first disaster in battle. They properly humbled themselves before God and sought Him regarding the next battle.

3. (24-25) On the second day of battle Israel is defeated before Benjamin again.

So the children of Israel approached the children of Benjamin on the second day. And Benjamin went out against them from Gibeah on the second day, and cut down to the ground eighteen thousand more of the children of Israel; all these drew the sword.

> a. **So the children of Israel approached the children of Benjamin on the second day**: This would not be an easy or a quick war. After the first day of heavy losses, the **children of Israel** were willing to keep fighting.
>
> b. **Cut down to the ground eighteen thousand more of the children of Israel**: The loss on the second day of battle was also severe. This shows that even though the tribes of Israel sought the LORD and fought in a just cause, it was still a very difficult struggle. There was a great cost for them to pay in doing what was right.

4. (26-28) Israel repents before God after the second defeat.

Then all the children of Israel, that is, all the people, went up and came to the house of God and wept. They sat there before the LORD and fasted that day until evening; and they offered burnt offerings and peace offerings before the LORD. So the children of Israel inquired of the LORD (the ark of the covenant of God *was* there in those days, and Phinehas the son of Eleazar, the son of Aaron, stood before it in those days), saying, "Shall I yet again go out to battle against the children of my brother Benjamin, or shall I cease?"

And the LORD said, "Go up, for tomorrow I will deliver them into your hand."

> a. **Went up and came to the house of God and wept. They sat there before the LORD and fasted that day until evening**: God allowed the two days of defeat for the purpose of bringing Israel low. They needed to be humbled, and these days of defeat compelled them to humble themselves.
>
>> i. God used this to humble the whole nation. They had to understand that the horror of the crime at Gibeah was not merely the result of

the sin of one group of men, or one city, or even one tribe. The whole nation had to be humbled because they first thought that the sin problem was only in Benjamin. Israel had to see that the nation as a whole had a sin problem.

ii. After the first failure, Israel was sorry and wept. But it was only after the second failure that they put their repentance into action by fasting and making a sacrifice for sins. Sorrow and weeping are not enough if they are not matched by real repentance and taking care of the sin problem through sacrifice – the sacrifice of the cross.

iii. Part of their demonstration of humility was in *fasting*. In 1827, Adam Clarke wrote about fasting: "At present it is but little used; a strong proof that *self-denial* is wearing out of fashion." Clarke thought this was true of his day; he would probably think it all the truer of modern times.

iv. The mention of Phinehas as high priest means that this was early in the days of the judges (Numbers 25:7, 25:11).

b. **Go up, for tomorrow I will deliver them into your hand**: God didn't want the two days of humbling to make Israel think that they could never win. They were encouraged to go out **tomorrow** and trust God's promise.

5. (29-48) Third day of battle – victory for Israel over Benjamin and Gibeah.

Then Israel set men in ambush all around Gibeah. And the children of Israel went up against the children of Benjamin on the third day, and put themselves in battle array against Gibeah as at the other times. So the children of Benjamin went out against the people, *and* were drawn away from the city. They began to strike down *and* kill some of the people, as at the other times, in the highways (one of which goes up to Bethel and the other to Gibeah) and in the field, about thirty men of Israel. And the children of Benjamin said, "They *are* defeated before us, as at first."

But the children of Israel said, "Let us flee and draw them away from the city to the highways." So all the men of Israel rose from their place and put themselves in battle array at Baal Tamar. Then Israel's men in ambush burst forth from their position in the plain of Geba. And ten thousand select men from all Israel came against Gibeah, and the battle was fierce. But *the Benjamites* did not know that disaster *was* upon them. The LORD defeated Benjamin before Israel. And the children of Israel destroyed that day twenty-five thousand one hundred Benjamites; all these drew the sword.

So the children of Benjamin saw that they were defeated. The men of Israel had given ground to the Benjamites, because they relied on the men in ambush whom they had set against Gibeah. And the men in ambush quickly rushed upon Gibeah; the men in ambush spread out and struck the whole city with the edge of the sword. Now the appointed signal between the men of Israel and the men in ambush was that they would make a great cloud of smoke rise up from the city, whereupon the men of Israel would turn in battle. Now Benjamin had begun to strike *and* kill about thirty of the men of Israel. For they said, "Surely they are defeated before us, as *in* the first battle." But when the cloud began to rise from the city in a column of smoke,

the Benjamites looked behind them, and there was the whole city going up *in smoke* to heaven. And when the men of Israel turned back, the men of Benjamin panicked, for they saw that disaster had come upon them. Therefore they turned *their backs* before the men of Israel in the direction of the wilderness; but the battle overtook them, and whoever *came* out of the cities they destroyed in their midst. They surrounded the Benjamites, chased them, *and* easily trampled them down as far as the front of Gibeah toward the east. And eighteen thousand men of Benjamin fell; all these *were* men of valor. Then they turned and fled toward the wilderness to the rock of Rimmon; and they cut down five thousand of them on the highways. Then they pursued them relentlessly up to Gidom, and killed two thousand of them. So all who fell of Benjamin that day were twenty-five thousand men who drew the sword; all these *were* men of valor.

But six hundred men turned and fled toward the wilderness to the rock of Rimmon, and they stayed at the rock of Rimmon for four months. And the men of Israel turned back against the children of Benjamin, and struck them down with the edge of the sword—from *every* city, men and beasts, all who were found. They also set fire to all the cities they came to.

> a. **Let us flee and draw them away from the city to the highways**: The strategy used by the tribes of Israel against Gibeah was remarkably similar to the strategy used at Ai (Joshua 8). Perhaps they got this strategy by reading the writings of Joshua and Moses; this may reflect that they returned to God's word in the course of their repentance.
>
> > i. **The LORD defeated Benjamin before Israel**: "These words briefly recall the real meaning of the awful judgment that fell upon Benjamin. It was the stroke of God." (Morgan)

b. **Six hundred men turned and fled toward the wilderness**: The two days of defeat made the tribes of Israel ruthless towards the tribe of Benjamin, and they killed thousands of the men of Benjamin. As a result of the battle, there remained only a 600-man remnant from the tribe of Benjamin.

c. **The men of Israel turned back against the children of Benjamin, and struck them down with the edge of the sword; from every city, men and beasts, all who were found**: The tribe of Benjamin was undeniably guilty, but there was no need for the complete slaughter as described here. This too-severe judgment against the tribe of Benjamin would soon be regretted by Israel.

> i. "Uninstructed zeal, even in the cause of righteousness, often goes beyond its proper limits." (Morgan)

Judges 21 – Wives for the Remnant of Benjamin

A. A foolish oath.

1. (1) At Mizpah, a curse is laid on anyone who gives their daughter as a wife for the tribe of Benjamin.

Now the men of Israel had sworn an oath at Mizpah, saying, "None of us shall give his daughter to Benjamin as a wife."

> a. **None of us shall give his daughter to Benjamin**: Considering their anger against Benjamin, this probably seemed like the right thing to do. But this foolish oath had unforeseen consequences. Justice not only brings punishment to evildoers, but it also guards against punishment that is too harsh.

2. (2-3) Israel realizes that a whole tribe is in danger of extinction.

Then the people came to the house of God, and remained there before God till evening. They lifted up their voices and wept bitterly, and said, "O Lord God of Israel, why has this come to pass in Israel, that today there should be one tribe *missing* in Israel?"

> a. **Why has this come to pass in Israel, that today there should be one tribe missing in Israel?** They cried out to God, almost as if it was *His* responsibility that the tribe of Benjamin was on the edge of extinction. The question, **"Why has this come to pass?"** was easily answered: Because of the excessive vengeance of the tribes of Israel against the tribe of Benjamin.

> b. **One tribe missing**: Down to almost only 400 men – and those men unable to marry because of the curse pronounced in Judges 21:1 – the tribe of Benjamin was almost extinct.

B. Solutions to the problem of the foolish oath.

1. (4-15) Destroying the city of Jabesh Gilead and taking their young women.

So it was, on the next morning, that the people rose early and built an altar there, and offered burnt offerings and peace offerings. The children of Israel said, "Who *is there* among all the tribes of Israel who did not come up with the assembly to the LORD?" For they had made a great oath concerning anyone who had not come up to the LORD at Mizpah, saying, "He shall surely be put to death." And the children of Israel grieved for Benjamin their brother, and said, "One tribe is cut off from Israel today. What shall we do for wives for those who remain, seeing we have sworn by the LORD that we will not give them our daughters as wives?"

And they said, "What one *is there* from the tribes of Israel who did not come up to Mizpah to the LORD?" And, in fact, no one had come to the camp from Jabesh Gilead to the assembly. For when the people were counted, indeed, not one of the inhabitants of Jabesh Gilead *was* there. So the congregation sent out there twelve thousand of their most valiant men, and commanded them, saying, "Go and strike the inhabitants of Jabesh Gilead with the edge of the sword, including the women and children. And this *is* the thing that you shall do: You shall utterly destroy every male, and every woman who has known a man intimately." So they found among the inhabitants of Jabesh Gilead four hundred young virgins who had not known a man intimately; and they brought them to the camp at Shiloh, which is in the land of Canaan.

Then the whole congregation sent *word* to the children of Benjamin who *were* at the rock of Rimmon, and announced peace to them. So Benjamin came back at that time, and they gave them the women whom they had saved alive of the women of Jabesh Gilead; and yet they had not found enough for them.

And the people grieved for Benjamin, because the LORD had made a void in the tribes of Israel.

> a. **Who is there among all the tribes of Israel who did not come up with the assembly to the LORD?** Here again, Israel did something that seemed right at the time but was instead a horror. In declaring, **he shall surely be put to death**, they decided to slaughter a whole city of Israel, a city that refused to join with Israel in the fight against Benjamin.
>
>> i. This was doing one bad thing to make up for another. Israel instead should have repented of their foolish oath made at Mizpah, and they should have agreed to give their daughters as wives to the men of the tribe of Benjamin, renouncing the foolish vow of Judges 21:1.
>
> b. **They found among the inhabitants of Jabesh Gilead four hundred young virgins**: In the ungodly massacre at Jabesh Gilead, they killed all

but 400 young virgins. Still, this was not enough: **yet they had not found enough for them.**

2. (16-24) A scheme to give the remaining men of Benjamin an opportunity to take wives.

Then the elders of the congregation said, "What shall we do for wives for those who remain, since the women of Benjamin have been destroyed?" And they said, *"There must be* **an inheritance for the survivors of Benjamin, that a tribe may not be destroyed from Israel. However, we cannot give them wives from our daughters, for the children of Israel have sworn an oath, saying, 'Cursed** *be* **the one who gives a wife to Benjamin.'" Then they said, "In fact,** *there is* **a yearly feast of the LORD in Shiloh, which** *is* **north of Bethel, on the east side of the highway that goes up from Bethel to Shechem, and south of Lebonah."**

Therefore they instructed the children of Benjamin, saying, "Go, lie in wait in the vineyards, and watch; and just when the daughters of Shiloh come out to perform their dances, then come out from the vineyards, and every man catch a wife for himself from the daughters of Shiloh; then go to the land of Benjamin. Then it shall be, when their fathers or their brothers come to us to complain, that we will say to them, 'Be kind to them for our sakes, because we did not take a wife for any of them in the war; for *it is* **not** *as though* **you have given the** *women* **to them at this time, making yourselves guilty of your oath.'"**

And the children of Benjamin did so; they took enough wives for their number from those who danced, whom they caught. Then they went and returned to their inheritance, and they rebuilt the cities and dwelt in them. So the children of Israel departed from there at that time, every man to his tribe and family; they went out from there, every man to his inheritance.

a. **Every man catch a wife for himself from the daughters of Shiloh**: They answered the problem of wives for the remaining Benjaminites by creating a little drama where the Benjaminites were allowed to "kidnap" women (who were no doubt willing), so that the marriages could be arranged without "official" approval.

i. Rather than go through this charade, they should have simply confessed their sin of making a foolish oath and done the right thing instead of trying to make two wrongs equal a right.

b. **Then they went and returned to their inheritance, and they rebuilt the cities and dwelt in them**: In this, the tribe of Benjamin was sufficiently restored to provide Israel with its first king (Saul).

3. (25) The summary observation of the times of Israel.

In those days *there was* no king in Israel; everyone did *what was* right in his own eyes.

    a. **There was no king in Israel**: This kind of moral, political, social, and spiritual chaos could only happen where there was no recognized king over Israel – and where people forgot about God as their King.

    b. **Everyone did what was right in his own eyes**: Generally, the 400-year period of the judges was marked by this radical individualism. They rejected the standard of God's word and accepted the individual standard of **what was right** in their **own eyes**.

        i. "It is impossible to read this appendix to the Book of Judges, and especially the closing part of it, without being impressed with how sad is the condition of any people who act without some definitely fixed principle. Passion moves to purpose only as it is governed by principle." (Morgan)

Ruth 1 – Ruth's Journey

A. Background: Elimelech and his sons.

1. (1) A sojourn in Moab.

Now it came to pass, in the days when the judges ruled, that there was a famine in the land. And a certain man of Bethlehem, Judah, went to dwell in the country of Moab, he and his wife and his two sons.

> a. **In the days when the judges ruled**: This account begins in the closing days of the judges, a 400-year period of general anarchy and oppression when the Israelites were not ruled by kings, but by periodic deliverers whom God raised up when the nation sought Him again.
>
>> i. Notable among the judges were Gideon, Samson, and Deborah. Each of these was raised up by God, not to rule as kings, but to lead Israel during a specific challenge, and then to go back to obscurity.
>>
>> ii. The **days when the judges ruled** were dark days for Israel; the period was characterized by the phrase *everyone did what was right in his own eyes* (Judges 17:6, 21:25).
>
> b. **A certain man of Bethlehem**: In these days, a man from **Bethlehem** left the land of Israel to **dwell in the country of Moab**, because of famine. Bethlehem was a rich agricultural area (the city name means "House of Bread"), but times were tough, so he went to the pagan land of Moab.
>
>> i. To do so, he had to hike through the desolate Jericho pass, through the Judean wilderness near the Dead Sea, going across the Jordan River, into the land of Moab. This was a definite departure from the Promised Land of Israel, and a return to the wilderness from which God had delivered Israel hundreds of years before. These were clearly steps in the *wrong* direction.
>
> c. **A famine in the land**: God specifically promised there would always be plenty in the land if Israel was obedient. Therefore, **a famine in the land**

meant that Israel, as a nation, was not obedient to the LORD (Deuteronomy 11:13-17).

d. **Went to dwell**: This means to leave with the intention to return. The next verse tells us the name of the man was *Elimelech* and his intention of a short visit turned into ten, tragedy-filled years – and Elimelech never returned to Israel. The name *Elimelech* means "God is King" – but he didn't live as if God was his king.

2. (2-5) Tragedy in Moab.

The name of the man *was* Elimelech, the name of his wife *was* Naomi, and the names of his two sons *were* Mahlon and Chilion—Ephrathites of Bethlehem, Judah. And they went to the country of Moab and remained there. Then Elimelech, Naomi's husband, died; and she was left, and her two sons. Now they took wives of the women of Moab: the name of the one *was* Orpah, and the name of the other Ruth. And they dwelt there about ten years. Then both Mahlon and Chilion also died; so the woman survived her two sons and her husband.

a. **Then Elimelech, Naomi's husband, died**: When Elimelech and his family came to Moab, they did not find life easier. Elimelech soon died, and his wife Naomi was left to care for their two boys, Mahlon and Chilion.

i. It is hard to say that this was the direct hand of God's judgment against them. It is sometimes difficult to discern why tragic things happen. What is certain is that the change of scenery didn't make things better.

ii. We sometimes think we can move away from our problems, but find we just bring them with us. No matter where you go, you bring yourself with you – so the same problems can continue in a different place.

b. **Now they took wives of the women of Moab**: Mahlon and Chilion grew, and took wives among the Moabite women, named Orpah and Ruth. Again, this was not in obedience to God; God commanded the Israelites to not marry among the pagan nations surrounding them.

c. **Both Mahlon and Chilion died**: As time went on (**about ten years**) Naomi's sons died. So now there were three childless widows – Naomi and her two daughters-in-law, Orpah and Ruth.

i. To be a childless widow was to be among the lowest, most disadvantaged classes in the ancient world. There was no one to support you, and you had to live on the generosity of strangers. Naomi had no family in Moab, and no one else to help her. It was a desperate situation.

B. The return to Judah.

1. (6-7) The three widows head back to Judah.

Then she arose with her daughters-in-law that she might return from the country of Moab, for she had heard in the country of Moab that the LORD had visited His people by giving them bread. Therefore she went out from the place where she was, and her two daughters-in-law with her; and they went on the way to return to the land of Judah.

> a. **She had heard in the country of Moab that the LORD had visited His people**: From distant Moab, Naomi heard that God was doing good things back in Israel. She wanted to be part of the good things that God was doing.
>
>> i. Our life with God should make others want to come back to the LORD just by looking at our lives. Our walk with the LORD should be something that makes others say, "I want some of that also!"
>
> b. **She went out from the place where she was**: This set Naomi apart from many other people. Many hear of the good things God is doing in the lives of others, and only *wish* they could have some of it – instead of actually setting out to receive it. Naomi could have stayed in Moab all of her life wishing things were different, but she did something to receive what God had to give her.

2. (8-9) Naomi petitions her daughters-in-law to go back to Moab.

And Naomi said to her two daughters-in-law, "Go, return each to her mother's house. The LORD deal kindly with you, as you have dealt with the dead and with me. The LORD grant that you may find rest, each in the house of her husband."

So she kissed them, and they lifted up their voices and wept.

> a. **Go, return each to her mother's house**: By all common sense, this was the wise thing to do. Orpah and Ruth had stronger family ties in Moab than they did with Naomi, so it made sense for them to stay in Moab instead of going to a new land – Israel – with Naomi.
>
> b. **The LORD deal kindly with you.... The LORD grant that you may find rest**: With these words Naomi freely blessed them. She prayed that they would remarry (**each in the house of her husband**).
>
>> i. **Deal kindly** is the ancient Hebrew word *hesed*. "*Hesed* encompasses deeds of mercy performed by a more powerful party for the benefit of the weaker one." (Huey)
>
>> ii. In Ruth 1:9, Naomi described marriage as a place of **rest**: **The LORD grant that you may find rest, each in the house of her husband.**

God intends that each marriage be a place and source, of rest, peace, and refreshment in life.

c. **She kissed them…they lifted up their voices and wept**: The emotion shown is evidence of the real relationship of love between Naomi and her daughters-in-law.

3. (10-13) Naomi pleads with her daughters-in-law to stay in Moab.

And they said to her, "Surely we will return with you to your people."

But Naomi said, "Turn back, my daughters; why will you go with me? *Are* there still sons in my womb, that they may be your husbands? Turn back, my daughters, go—for I am too old to have a husband. If I should say I have hope, *if* I should have a husband tonight and should also bear sons, would you wait for them till they were grown? Would you restrain yourselves from having husbands? No, my daughters; for it grieves me very much for your sakes that the hand of the LORD has gone out against me!"

a. **Are there still sons in my womb**: According to the laws of ancient Israel, if a young woman was left widowed, without having had a son, then one of her deceased husband's brothers was responsible for being a "surrogate father" and providing her with a son. Naomi here says that she has no other sons to give either Orpah or Ruth.

i. Trapp on **if I should have a husband tonight and should also bear sons**: "Without having a husband, she doth not once think of having children, as many wantons and light-skirts do; making themselves whores, and their children bastards, and all for satisfying the rage of present lust, though after they repent with grief and shame."

b. **The hand of the LORD has gone out against me**: This obviously weighed heavily on Naomi's heart and mind. She felt that the calamity which came upon her family came because they were disobedient, probably in leaving the Promised Land of Israel and marrying their sons to Moabite women.

i. Perhaps Naomi felt a particular guilt; perhaps she was the one who pushed to move out of Israel, and who pushed to marry off the sons.

c. **The hand of the LORD has gone out against me**: Despite this feeling, Naomi is going back to the land of Israel – and going back to her God. Though she felt that the **hand of the LORD has gone out against me**, she did not grow bitter against God. She returned to Him in repentance, knowing that the answer is drawing *closer to* Him, not going *further from* Him.

> i. Naomi didn't accuse God of doing something wrong against her. She acknowledged His total control over all circumstances. It was actually an expression of trust in Him.
>
> ii. If Naomi was bitter or angry against God, she probably would have gone another way – *further* from the God of Israel, rather than back to Him. Instead, she showed that she trusted in the sovereignty of God, and knew that despite her personal calamities, He is a good God who blesses.
>
> iii. What Naomi could not see is that the hand of the Lord would go out *for* her shortly! There is never a reason for us to despair if we believe **the hand of the Lord has gone out against me**. If we will return to Him, His hand will go out *for us* again! Naomi had no idea – not the slightest – of how greatly God was going to bless her in a short time.

4. (14) Orpah stays in Moab; Ruth continues on with Naomi.

Then they lifted up their voices and wept again; and Orpah kissed her mother-in-law, but Ruth clung to her.

> a. **They lifted up their voices and wept again**: Both Orpah and Ruth felt deeply; both loved Naomi; both were anxious about the future. But a choice had to be made, and Orpah chose to stay in Moab, while Ruth **clung** *to* Naomi.
>
> b. **Orpah kissed her mother-in-law, but Ruth clung to her**: There comes a place in our following after God where it comes down to *doing*. Ruth and Orpah both felt the same feelings, but Ruth *acted* differently than Orpah.
>
> > i. Some are content with feeling Christian feelings – with feeling love for God, with feeling love for His word, with feeling love for His people. But what will you *do*? We are glad that God didn't just feel His love for us; instead, *For God so loved the world, that He <u>gave</u> His only begotten Son.* (John 3:16)
>
> c. **Orpah kissed her mother-in-law**: What happened to Orpah? Of course, we don't know. But men have always concocted traditions to make up for what they don't know. Jewish traditions say this request of Naomi came four miles outside of Moab; and that Orpah shed only four tears over the thought of parting from her mother-in-law Naomi. But the rabbis go on to say that in recompense for the four miles that she went with Naomi, Orpah gave birth to four sons – Goliath and his three brothers.

5. (15-18) Ruth's eloquent statement of faith.

And she said, "Look, your sister-in-law has gone back to her people and to her gods; return after your sister-in-law."

But Ruth said:

"Entreat me not to leave you,
Or to turn back from following after you;
For wherever you go, I will go;
And wherever you lodge, I will lodge;
Your people *shall be* my people,
And your God, my God.
Where you die, I will die,
And there will I be buried.
The LORD do so to me, and more also,
If *anything but* death parts you and me."

When she saw that she was determined to go with her, she stopped speaking to her.

    a. **Look, your sister-in-law has gone**: Naomi did what she could to discourage Ruth from coming with her back to Israel. It wasn't that Naomi didn't want Ruth to come, but she didn't want a fair-weather friend either.

    b. **Wherever you go, I will go; and wherever you lodge, I will lodge; your people shall be my people**: This was a noble – even outstanding – friend-to-friend commitment. But Ruth's commitment to Naomi went even further: **And your God, [will be] my God**.

        i. This was more than a change of address. Ruth was willing to forsake the Moabite gods she grew up with and embrace the God of Israel. She was deciding to follow the LORD. This Gentile woman, once far from God, had drawn near to Him.

        ii. **And your God**, [will be] **my God** meant that Naomi's relationship with God made an impact on Ruth. This is striking because Naomi did not have an easy life. She had been widowed, had lost both her sons and believed that she had caused each calamity by her disobedience. Yet she still honored and loved the LORD.

        iii. People should be able to look at your life, just as Ruth looked at Naomi's, and say "I want your God to be my God." Your trust in God, and turning towards Him in *tough* times, will often be the thing that draws others to the LORD.

    c. **Your God, my God**: Ten years of Naomi's compromise in Moab never made Ruth confess her allegiance to the God of Israel. Yet as soon as Naomi stood and said, "I'm going back to the God of Israel, I'll put my fate in His hands" Ruth stood with her. If you think you will persuade your friends or relatives to follow Jesus by your compromise, you are mistaken. Perhaps you are sincere, but you are mistaken. Only a bold stand for Jesus will really do it.

> i. "Ah! You will never win any soul to the right by a compromise with the wrong. It is decision for Christ and his truth that has the greatest power in the family, and the greatest power in the world, too." (Spurgeon)

d. **The LORD do so to me, and more also, if anything but death parts you and me**: Ruth had little knowledge of the true God, the God of Israel – but she knew He was a God of fairness and justice, so He could be called upon to hold Ruth accountable to this promise.

6. (19-21) Naomi and Ruth return to Bethlehem.

Now the two of them went until they came to Bethlehem. And it happened, when they had come to Bethlehem, that all the city was excited because of them; and the women said, "*Is* this Naomi?"

But she said to them, "Do not call me Naomi; call me Mara, for the Almighty has dealt very bitterly with me. I went out full, and the LORD has brought me home again empty. Why do you call me Naomi, since the LORD has testified against me, and the Almighty has afflicted me?"

a. **The two of them went until they came to Bethlehem**: It was a long walk from Moab to Bethlehem, and the trip was mostly uphill. We can imagine along the way, Ruth asking her mother-in-law Naomi all about the God of Israel and the land of Israel.

b. **All the city was excited because of them**: Bethlehem was just a large village; everyone in the village would have known everyone else and remembered those who had left years ago.

c. **Do not call me Naomi; call me Mara**: The name **Naomi** means "pleasant"; the name **Mara** means "bitter." Naomi used this to tell the people of Bethlehem that her time away from Israel, her time away from the God of Israel, had not been pleasant – it was bitter.

> i. Naomi didn't put on a false face. She wasn't going to go home, pretend everything was fine, and be "pleasant." She was honest and said, "Here I am and my life has been bitter."

d. **The Almighty has dealt very bitterly with me...the LORD has brought me home again empty.... the LORD has testified against me**: Naomi was not afraid to see the hand of God in all her calamity.

> i. Naomi knew that the tragedy that came into her life was not because of fate, chance, or blind fortune. She felt the tragedies were an example of God's affliction because she could not see the end of His plan. But

she knew there was a sovereign God of heaven and didn't think she had just run into a string of "bad luck."

ii. Yet, in the midst of all these bitter circumstances, Naomi was *not* bitter against the LORD. We can imagine one of the villagers asking, "Naomi, if God has dealt very bitterly with you, if the LORD has brought you home empty, if the LORD has testified against you, then why have you come back?" And she would have said, "Because I want to get right with Him again. Things have been terrible, and the answer isn't in going further from God, but in drawing closer to Him."

iii. Not everyone reacts to trials in the way Naomi did. "Many are humbled, but not humble; low, but not lowly. These have lost the fruit of their afflictions…and are therefore most miserable." (Trapp)

7. (22) Naomi's return.

So Naomi returned, and Ruth the Moabitess her daughter-in-law with her, who returned from the country of Moab. Now they came to Bethlehem at the beginning of barley harvest.

a. **So Naomi returned**: Naomi came back repentant and honest. She has felt that *the Almighty has afflicted me*. But in the coming chapters, it will be shown the Almighty will bless her. If only she could see it!

b. **Now they came to Bethlehem**: It would have been easy for Naomi to focus on what she had lost. She had lost a husband, two sons, and one daughter-in-law. She had lost all kinds of material possessions. All she had left was one daughter-in-law, Ruth. But through that one thing she had left, God was going to bring unbelievable blessing into her life.

i. All the good that happens in the future chapters begins here: With Naomi's godly repentance and honesty. It will make a difference not only in her life, but in the life of her daughter-in-law Ruth, and in the destiny of the nation Israel, and in your eternal salvation.

ii. It is possible for God to accomplish amazing things both for now and eternity, if we will turn towards Him today, not only in our feelings but also in our actions.

Ruth 2 – Ruth's Work as a Gleaner

A. Ruth gleans in Boaz's field.

1. (1) Naomi's kinsman: Boaz.

There was a relative of Naomi's husband, a man of great wealth, of the family of Elimelech. His name *was* Boaz.

a. **There was a relative of Naomi's husband**: Naomi was related to this man Boaz through her deceased husband, Elimelech. We don't know exactly how he was related, but he was.

b. **A man of great wealth**: During the time of famine, when Elimelech, Naomi, and their whole family had left the Promised Land and gone to Moab, Boaz had stayed behind – and God provided for him. In fact, God made Boaz **a man of great wealth**.

i. Ten years before, Naomi and her family made a choice, and it was a choice made in a hard time – a time of famine. But they didn't *have* to make the wrong choice that they did. The people of Bethlehem had not perished from hunger. They were still there. And they were blessed more than Naomi's family.

ii. Sometimes we justify wrong choices because of difficult circumstances. But God will strengthen us, and bless us, to make the right choice, even in difficult circumstances.

iii. "The exact expression rendered *a mighty man of wealth* is elsewhere translated 'a mighty man of valour' (*e.g.*, Jdg. 11:1). We perhaps get the force of it by thinking of our word 'knight.'" (Morris)

c. **A relative**: This particular **relative** will be revealed (Ruth 3:8-9) as a kinsman, a *goel* for Ruth and Naomi. This was more than merely a family relation. It will be seen that Boaz was a special family representative. He was a chieftain in the family.

2. (2-3) Ruth happens upon Boaz's field.

So Ruth the Moabitess said to Naomi, "Please let me go to the field, and glean heads of grain after *him* in whose sight I may find favor."

And she said to her, "Go, my daughter."

Then she left, and went and gleaned in the field after the reapers. And she happened to come to the part of the field *belonging* to Boaz, who *was* of the family of Elimelech.

> a. **Please, let me go to the field, and glean heads of grain**: Leviticus 19:9-10 commanded farmers in Israel that they should not completely harvest their fields. They were commanded to "cut corners" in harvesting, and always leave some behind. Also, if they happened to drop a bundle of grain, they were commanded to leave it on the ground and not pick it up.
>
>> i. This was one of the social assistance programs in Israel. Farmers were not to completely harvest their fields, so the poor and needy could come and glean the remains for themselves.
>>
>> ii. This was a wonderful way of helping the poor. It commanded the farmers to have a generous heart, and it commanded the poor to be active and work for their food. It was a way for them to provide for their own needs with dignity.
>
> b. **Then she left**: So, Ruth, on her own initiative, set out to glean in the fields to support her and her mother-in-law, Naomi. This showed a wonderful hard-working spirit in Ruth, and it was spiritual also – she would not have been more spiritual to sit back at home and pray for food.
>
> c. **She happened to come to the part of the field belonging to Boaz**: It says that Ruth **happened** to come to that place and certainly, that is how it seemed to her. But it was not how it actually came to pass. Ruth came to that field because God was guiding her.
>
>> i. This shows us some of the wonderful ways that the invisible hand of God works. If Ruth would have stayed home and waited for a "spiritual" feeling, she might have waited a long time – and still probably would have gone to the wrong field. Instead, Ruth experienced the very *natural* moving of the *supernatural* hand of God.
>>
>> ii. Many times when we are walking in the Spirit, we can only see the invisible hand of God as we look back. If we spend too much time trying to look for His hand ahead of us, we can make problems for ourselves.

3. (4-7) Boaz learns of Ruth.

Now behold, Boaz came from Bethlehem, and said to the reapers, "The LORD *be* with you!"

And they answered him, "The LORD bless you!"

Then Boaz said to his servant who was in charge of the reapers, "Whose young woman *is* this?"

So the servant who was in charge of the reapers answered and said, "It *is* the young Moabite woman who came back with Naomi from the country of Moab. And she said, 'Please let me glean and gather after the reapers among the sheaves.' So she came and has continued from morning until now, though she rested a little in the house."

> a. **The LORD be with you**: This shows us something of the heart and character of Boaz. Apparently, his workers loved him and had a good relationship with him. You can often tell the real character of a man in authority by seeing how he relates to his staff and by what they think of him.
>
> b. **And she said, "Please let me glean and gather"**: As the supervisor reported to Boaz, he told of Ruth's submissive attitude. There is a sense in which the gleaning was hers by *right* – after all, she could have quoted Leviticus 19:9-10 back at him. But she kindly and properly asked for the right to gather in his field.
>
> c. **So she came and has continued from morning until now**: Ruth may not have known it, but she was under inspection. The supervisor was looking at what kind of job she did and he was impressed that she did a good job. And the fact that she did a good job was important because it made a good impression on Boaz.
>
>> i. We are under inspection also. At times when we don't know it, we are being watched by others to see how we will walk with God. And what they see will make a *difference*.

4. (8-9) Boaz speaks kindly to Ruth.

Then Boaz said to Ruth, "You will listen, my daughter, will you not? Do not go to glean in another field, nor go from here, but stay close by my young women. *Let* your eyes *be* on the field which they reap, and go after them. Have I not commanded the young men not to touch you? And when you are thirsty, go to the vessels and drink from what the young men have drawn."

> a. **Stay close by my young women**: These were Boaz's female field workers, who tied together the cut stalks of grain. Boaz told Ruth to stay close to them, so she would be well taken care of.

b. **Do not go to glean in another field**: God was blessing Ruth already and all because He guided her to Boaz's field. Boaz knew that if Ruth stayed in his fields, she would be blessed.

- In Boaz's field, Ruth would find *companionship* (among the **young women**).
- In Boaz's field, Ruth would find *protection* (**Have I not commanded the young men not to touch you?**).
- In Boaz's field, Ruth would find *refreshment* (**when you are thirsty**).

   i. The *kindness* of Boaz was wonderful. At this time, we have no indication of a romantic attraction between Boaz and Ruth and we have no idea how Ruth looked (even if she was pretty, she was probably pretty ragged from a whole day of hard work). Yet Boaz extended this kindness to her.

   ii. We often find it easy to be kind to others when we can see a potential return from the investment of our kindness. Yet true kindness is shown when we extend ourselves to others who, as far as we can see, have nothing to give us.

5. (10-13) Ruth thanks Boaz for his kindness.

So she fell on her face, bowed down to the ground, and said to him, "Why have I found favor in your eyes, that you should take notice of me, since I *am* a foreigner?"

And Boaz answered and said to her, "It has been fully reported to me, all that you have done for your mother-in-law since the death of your husband, and *how* you have left your father and your mother and the land of your birth, and have come to a people whom you did not know before. The LORD repay your work, and a full reward be given you by the LORD God of Israel, under whose wings you have come for refuge."

Then she said, "Let me find favor in your sight, my lord; for you have comforted me, and have spoken kindly to your maidservant, though I am not like one of your maidservants."

   a. **Why have I found favor in your eyes**: Ruth's attitude was wonderful. Some of us would have said, "Well it's about time someone noticed! I've been working hard all day. Now God will give me the blessings that I deserve."

   i. We never see Ruth asking why all the *hard things* have come upon her in life. Instead, she asks why this *good thing* has come. This is a significant difference in attitude.

b. **Since I am a foreigner**: This was constantly on Ruth's mind. She was a Moabitess, and not an Israelite. She knew that on the basis of her national background, she didn't belong. This made Boaz's kindness to her all the more precious.

> i. The Bible says that we should be kind to the strangers among us, but this also applies on another level. Since our society is no longer structured around the *family*, for many people, their most important circle of association is their *friends*. Sociologists call this "tribalization" – we become part of a little "tribe," a little circle of friends. The command to love the stranger means that we should not only associate with those of our own tribe, and that we should always welcome those outside of our tribe.

c. **It has been fully reported to me**: This is a dynamic of small-town life; everybody knows everybody else's business. Yet it also shows that Ruth's devotion to Naomi mattered – it was noticed.

d. **The LORD repay your work and a full reward be given you by the LORD God of Israel**: Fittingly, Boaz encouraged Ruth as if she were a new convert to the God of Israel. In many ways, Ruth stands as an example of a new believer.

- She put her trust in the God of Israel.
- She had left her former associates.
- She had come in among strangers.
- She was very low in her own eyes.
- She found protection under the wings of God.

> i. In the same way, older Christians should be like Boaz to younger Christians who are like Ruth. "Observe that he saluted her with words of tender encouragement; for this is precisely what I want all the elder Christians among you to do to those who are the counterparts of Ruth.... I want you to make a point of looking out the young converts, and speaking to them goodly words, and comfortable words, whereby they may be cheered and strengthened." (Spurgeon)

> ii. Significantly, though these words were said to Ruth, they were also *a prayer to God for Ruth*. Christians should pray for one another, and in particular, older Christians should pray for new converts.

e. **The LORD God of Israel, under whose wings you have come for refuge**: Boaz especially knew of Ruth's commitment to the God of Israel. This was his way of showing kindness and encouragement to a young believer in the LORD.

i. **Under whose wings**: This is a beautiful picture. "The imagery is probably that of a tiny bird snuggling under the wings of a foster-mother. It gives a picture of trust and security (*cf.* Ps. 17:8; 36:7; 63:7)." (Morris)

f. **Let me find favor in your sight**: This was a very polite way of saying "thank you" to Boaz. Ruth was almost overwhelmed by his kindness, and was polite enough to say, "Thank you."

6. (14-16) Boaz continues to show great favor to Ruth.

Now Boaz said to her at mealtime, "Come here, and eat of the bread, and dip your piece of bread in the vinegar." So she sat beside the reapers, and he passed parched *grain* to her; and she ate and was satisfied, and kept some back. And when she rose up to glean, Boaz commanded his young men, saying, "Let her glean even among the sheaves, and do not reproach her. Also let *grain* from the bundles fall purposely for her; leave *it* that she may glean, and do not rebuke her."

a. **Dip your piece of bread in the vinegar**: Perhaps now, we see the first hint of a romance. Boaz showed great kindness and favor to Ruth at mealtime. It would be enough to have just invited her, but he also invited her to share fully in the meal, even the privileged dipping.

b. **She ate and was satisfied, and kept some back**: Ruth also may be awakening to some romance towards Boaz; she **kept some back**. She did not eat all that was offered to her, meaning that she didn't want to seem like a greedy eater in front of Boaz, and that she was sensible enough to take some home to Naomi.

i. Ruth was satisfied because she answered the generous invitation of Boaz. She was not one of the reapers, but **she sat beside the reapers** and ate as if she was one of them and **she ate and was satisfied**. In the same way, those outside the kingdom of God and its promises can sit among the reapers, at the invitation of Jesus, and by faith they can eat and be **satisfied**.

ii. "'She did eat, and was satisfied.' Your *head* shall be satisfied with the precious truth which Christ reveals; your *heart* shall be content with Jesus, as the altogether lovely object of affection; your *hope* shall be satisfied, for whom have you in heaven but Christ? Your *desire* shall be satiated, for what can even the hunger of your desire wish for more than 'to know Christ, and to be found in him.' You shall find Jesus fill your *conscience*, till it is at perfect peace; he shall fill your *judgment*, till you know the certainty of his teachings; he shall fill your *memory* with recollections of what he did, and fill your *imagination* with the prospects of what he is yet to do. You shall be 'satisfied.'" (Spurgeon)

c. **Let her glean even among the sheaves**: This was more generous than the command in Leviticus 19:9-10. Boaz would allow Ruth to take some from among the already gathered sheaves of grain.

d. **Let grain from the bundles fall purposefully for her**: This was also beautiful. Boaz wanted to bless Ruth, but he didn't want to dishonor her dignity by making her a charity case. So, he allowed some grain to fall, supposedly by accident, so that she could pick it up.

B. Ruth reports the day's events to Naomi.

1. (17-18) She brings home the day's fruits to Naomi.

So she gleaned in the field until evening, and beat out what she had gleaned, and it was about an ephah of barley. Then she took *it* up and went into the city, and her mother-in-law saw what she had gleaned. So she brought out and gave to her what she had kept back after she had been satisfied.

a. **She gleaned in the field until evening, and beat out what she had gleaned**: Yes, God blessed Ruth. Yes, people were generous to her. At the same time, she did work hard. This was a sun-up to sun-down day, and Ruth worked hard all day long.

i. We should use Ruth's example to glean everything we can from the word of God:

- Ruth worked hard.
- Ruth had to stoop to gather every grain.
- Ruth could only pick up one grain at a time.
- Ruth had to hold on to each grain, and not immediately drop it.
- Ruth took the grain home and threshed it.
- Ruth took the threshed grain and winnowed it.
- Ruth was nourished by the grain.

b. **It was about an ephah of barley**: This was about a five-and-one-half gallon tub (22 liters) of barley – a wonderful day's earnings to people who had nothing.

c. **Gave to her what she had kept back**: Besides all the barley grain, Ruth brought Naomi the food left over from the meal with Boaz. This was obviously a blessing for Naomi.

2. (19-23) Naomi praises God for His goodness to her and Ruth.

And her mother-in-law said to her, "Where have you gleaned today? And where did you work? Blessed be the one who took notice of you."

So she told her mother-in-law with whom she had worked, and said, "The man's name with whom I worked today *is* Boaz."

Then Naomi said to her daughter-in-law, "Blessed *be* he of the Lord, who has not forsaken His kindness to the living and the dead!" And Naomi said to her, "This man *is* a relation of ours, one of our close relatives."

Ruth the Moabitess said, "He also said to me, 'You shall stay close by my young men until they have finished all my harvest.'"

And Naomi said to Ruth her daughter-in-law, *"It is* good, my daughter, that you go out with his young women, and that people do not meet you in any other field." So she stayed close by the young women of Boaz, to glean until the end of barley harvest and wheat harvest; and she dwelt with her mother-in-law.

a. **Blessed be he of the Lord, who has not forsaken His kindness to the living and the dead**: Is this the same woman who came into town saying, *call me Mara, for the Almighty has dealt very bitterly with me* (Ruth 1:20)? Is this the same woman who said, *the Almighty has afflicted me* (Ruth 1:21)? Of course, it is! Now she sees more of God's plan unfolding, so she can see better how all things are working together for good for those who love God.

b. **It is good, my daughter**: Of course, Naomi told Ruth, "Stay with this man Boaz!" Not only was he generous, but he was also **one of** their **near kinsmen** – the importance of which will be unfolded in the coming chapters.

Ruth 3 – Ruth Makes an Appeal

A. Naomi's instructions to Ruth.

1. (1-2a) Security for Ruth through a kinsman.

Then Naomi her mother-in-law said to her, "My daughter, shall I not seek security for you, that it may be well with you? Now Boaz, whose young women you were with, *is he* not our relative?

> a. **Then Naomi her mother-in-law said**: The time of the harvest was over, and certainly Ruth and Boaz had been around each other much in the weeks covering the barley and the wheat harvests (Ruth 2:23). They had many opportunity to get to know each other.
>
>> i. However, according to the customs of the day, we can't say that Ruth and Boaz were "dating" in the way we think of "dating" in our modern culture. They were not paired off as a couple with one-on-one time with each other; rather, they spent their time together in the context of a group – the men and women who worked for Boaz in the harvest.
>>
>> ii. From God's perspective, there is much in the "dating game" that works against forming healthy, lasting relationships. For many people, dating means the continual making and breaking of casual romantic relationships -- patterns that teach us more about how to end relationships than how to make them last.
>>
>> iii. Additionally, dating can be a relatively superficial way to get to know someone. Each person in a dating relationship tends to put on a mask for the other. For example, many women have been deceived into thinking a man is a good, nice man because he is nice to them in a dating relationship. Of course, he is! Often, he's nice because he wants something in that dating relationship. A better gauge to measure the man or the woman is to see how they act towards others in a group

setting – because sooner or later, that is how they are going to treat you.

iv. So over the period of the harvests, Ruth and Boaz got to know each other pretty well – by seeing what kind of person the other was around a larger group.

b. **Shall I not seek security for you**: Naomi knew that Ruth could best be taken care of if she was married, so she suggested that she appeal to Boaz for marriage.

i. The Hebrew word for **security** in verse one is the same word for *rest* in Ruth 1:9, where Naomi hoped that her daughters-in-law would find rest and security in the home of a new husband. This Hebrew word (*manowach*) speaks of what a home should be – a place of rest and security.

c. **Now Boaz…is he not our relative?** One might easily think that it was inappropriately forward of Naomi to suggest this to Ruth. It is possible to think that Naomi plotted with Ruth to make her a man-trap, to go out and hunt down a reluctant Boaz for marriage. Not at all; Naomi's suggestion to Ruth was rooted in a peculiar custom in ancient Israel – the meaning behind the Hebrew word *goel*.

i. This was the point in Naomi's question about Boaz: **Is he not our relative?** She reminded Ruth that Boaz was their family *goel*.

ii. The *goel* – sometimes translated *kinsman-redeemer* – had a specifically defined role in Israel's family life.

- The kinsman-redeemer was responsible for buying a fellow Israelite out of slavery (Leviticus 25:48).
- He was responsible for being the "avenger of blood" to make sure the murderer of a family member answered to the crime (Numbers 35:19).
- He was responsible for buying back family land that had been forfeited (Leviticus 25:25).
- He was responsible for carrying on the family name by marrying a childless widow (Deuteronomy 25:5-10).

iii. In this, we see that the *goel*, the kinsman-redeemer, was responsible for safeguarding the *persons*, the *property*, and the *posterity* of the family. "Words from the root *g'l* are used with a variety of meanings in the Old Testament, but the fundamental idea is that of fulfilling one's obligations as a kinsman." (Morris)

d. **Is he not our relative?** Since Boaz was a recognized *goel* for the family of Elimelech – the deceased husband of Naomi and father-in-law of Ruth – Ruth could appeal to him to safeguard the posterity of Elimelech's family and take her in marriage. It may seem forward to us, but it was regarded as proper in that day.

i. If Boaz did not fulfill this duty towards Elimelech (though he was now deceased), then the direct family and name of Elimelech would perish. Perpetuating the family name of Elimelech (and every man in Israel) was thought to be an important duty. These protections showed how important it was to God to preserve the institution of the family in Israel – and that it is also important to Him today.

2. (2b-5) Naomi instructs Ruth as to how to petition Boaz to exercise his responsibilities as her *goel*.

In fact, he is winnowing barley tonight at the threshing floor. Therefore wash yourself and anoint yourself, put on your *best* garment and go down to the threshing floor; *but* do not make yourself known to the man until he has finished eating and drinking. Then it shall be, when he lies down, that you shall notice the place where he lies; and you shall go in, uncover his feet, and lie down; and he will tell you what you should do."

And she said to her, "All that you say to me I will do."

a. **Therefore wash yourself:** Naomi, in her advice to Ruth, showed a keen knowledge of male behavior. She instructed Ruth to make herself pretty and fragrant (**anoint yourself, put on your best garment**), and to leave Boaz alone while he ate (**do not make yourself known to the man until he has finished eating and drinking**).

b. **Uncover his feet, and lie down:** Naomi instructed Ruth to **go in, uncover his feet, and lie down** at the appropriate time. Some might think this was a provocative gesture, as if Ruth was told to offer herself sexually to Boaz. This was not how this gesture was understood in that day. In the culture of that day, this was understood as an act of *total submission*.

i. In that day, this was understood to be the role of a servant – to lay at their master's feet and be ready for any command of the master. So, when Naomi told Ruth to **lie down** at Boaz's feet, she told her to come to him in a totally humble, submissive way.

ii. Don't lose sight of the larger picture: Ruth came to claim a right. Boaz was her *goel*, her kinsman-redeemer, and she had the *right* to expect him to marry her and raise up a family to perpetuate the name of Elimelech. But Naomi wisely counseled Ruth to not come as a victim demanding her rights, but as a humble servant, trusting in the goodness of her kinsman-redeemer. She said to Boaz, "I respect you, I trust you, and I put my fate in your hands."

c. **He will tell you what you should do**: Of course, this was a situation that had the potential for disaster if Boaz should mistreat Ruth in some way. But Naomi and Ruth had the chance to get to know Boaz, and they knew what kind of man he was – a good man, a godly man, one to whom Ruth could confidently submit.

i. In the marriage relationship, many husbands wish they had a wife who submitted to them the way Ruth is being told to here. But do they provide the kind of godly leadership, care, and concern that Boaz showed towards Ruth and others?

ii. In the marriage relationship, many wives wish they had a husband who loved, cared, and treated them the way Boaz did Ruth. But do they show the same kind of humble submission and respect Ruth showed to Boaz?

d. **All that you say to me I will do**: Ruth humbly and wisely received the counsel of her mother-in-law Naomi.

i. "On the whole, we must say, had not Boaz been a person of extraordinary piety, prudence, and continence, this experiment might have been fatal to Ruth. We cannot easily account for this transaction; probably Naomi knew more than she revealed to her daughter-in-law. The experiment however was dangerous, and should in no sense be imitated." (Clarke)

ii. "Let none be encouraged hereby to enter into God's ordinance through the devil's portal, lest they smart and smoke for it." (Trapp)

B. Ruth and Boaz at the threshing floor.

1. (6-7) Ruth lays down at Boaz's feet.

So she went down to the threshing floor and did according to all that her mother-in-law instructed her. And after Boaz had eaten and drunk, and his heart was cheerful, he went to lie down at the end of the heap of grain; and she came softly, uncovered his feet, and lay down.

a. **He went to lie down at the end of the heap of grain**: There was a good reason why Boaz slept at the **threshing floor**. These were the days of the judges when there was much political and social instability in Israel. It wasn't unusual for gangs of thieves to come and steal all the hard-earned grain a farmer had grown. Boaz slept at the threshing floor to guard his crop against the kind of attacks described in 1 Samuel 23:1.

b. **She came softly**: Ruth did just as her mother-in-law Naomi had recommended. She heard the advice, she said she would do it, and she did it.

2. (8-9) Ruth's request.

Now it happened at midnight that the man was startled, and turned himself; and there, a woman was lying at his feet. And he said, "Who *are* you?"

So she answered, "I *am* Ruth, your maidservant. Take your maidservant under your wing, for you are a close relative."

a. **It happened at midnight that the man was startled**: This was an amazing scene. We can well imagine that Boaz was indeed **startled**, waking up in the night as he turned in his sleep, knowing that someone was out there but not being able to see clearly because of the darkness and the sleep in his eyes.

i. Since Boaz had been there to protect against thieves, it must have given him quite a shock to wake up and know someone was there. But his shock quickly turned to wondering when he found out the visitor was a woman.

b. **Take your maidservant under your wing, for you are a close relative**: Ruth identified herself and made a simple request. In beginning with the words "**take your maidservant**," Ruth again showed great humility and submission. She presented herself as Boaz's servant.

c. **Under your wing**: Here, she boldly asked Boaz to take her in marriage. The phrase can also be translated as "*spread the corner of your garment over me.*" This was a culturally relevant way to say, "I am a widow, take me as your wife."

i. "The spreading of a skirt over a widow as a way of claiming her as a wife is attested among Arabs of early days, and Jouon says it still exists among some modern Arabs." (Morris)

ii. "Even to the present day, when a Jew marries a woman, *he throws the skirt or end of his talith over her*, to signify that he has taken her under his protection." (Clarke)

iii. In Ezekiel 16:8, God uses the same terminology in relation to Israel: *I spread My wing over you and covered your nakedness. Yes, I swore an oath to you and entered into a covenant with you and you became Mine, says the LORD God.*

d. **For you are a close relative**: This shows that this was not an inappropriate thing for Ruth to do towards Boaz. It was bold, but not inappropriate.

Ruth understood this as she identified Boaz as her **close relative** (literally, *you are a goel*, a kinsman-redeemer).

> i. Though deceased, Elimelech had the right to have his family name carried on and as *goel*, Boaz had the responsibility to do this for Elimelech. This could only happen through Boaz marrying Ruth and providing children to carry on the name of Elimelech. Ruth boldly, yet humbly and properly, sought her rights.

3. (10-11) Boaz's response.

Then he said, "Blessed *are* you of the Lord, my daughter! For you have shown more kindness at the end than at the beginning, in that you did not go after young men, whether poor or rich. And now, my daughter, do not fear. I will do for you all that you request, for all the people of my town know that you *are* a virtuous woman."

> a. **Blessed are you of the Lord, my daughter.... you did not go after young men**: Apparently, there was a considerable age difference between Ruth and Boaz. It also seems that because of this, Boaz considered himself unattractive to Ruth and had therefore ruled out any idea of a romance between them.
>
>> i. This shows something else wonderful about Boaz. He had the right to force himself upon Ruth as her *goel*, but he did not. He wasn't going to just say, "There's a woman I want, and I have her by right." He was kind enough to not act as *goel* towards Ruth unless *she* desired it.
>>
>> ii. It also shows something else wonderful about Ruth: She based her attraction to Boaz more on *respect* than on image or appearance. Tragically, many people fall in love with an image or an appearance, rather than with a person worthy of respect.
>
> b. **I will do for you all that you request**: Boaz made Naomi look brilliant in her advice to Ruth. The plan worked perfectly.
>
> c. **All the people of my town know that you are a virtuous woman**: Boaz was also attracted to Ruth because of her character. We don't know how Ruth looked, but we do know that she was a woman of godly character.
>
>> i. Literally, Boaz called Ruth a *hah-yil* woman. The basic meaning behind this Hebrew word is "strength; moral strength, good quality, integrity, virtue." This same word is used in a term for heroes in the Bible: *A mighty man of valor*. Just as courage and strength make a man a hero, so Ruth's courage and strength, shown in her virtue – make her a hero, in the Proverbs 31 kind of definition of a woman of virtue.

4. (12-13) A potential problem: A nearer kinsman.

Now it is true that I *am* a close relative; however, there is a relative closer than I. Stay this night, and in the morning it shall be *that* if he will perform the duty of a close relative for you—good; let him do it. But if he does not want to perform the duty for you, then I will perform the duty for you, *as* the LORD lives! Lie down until morning."

> a. **There is a relative closer than I**: Apparently, though Boaz was a recognized *goel* towards Ruth, there was another *goel* closer in relation to her deceased father-in-law Elimelech. So, Boaz could not exercise his right as kinsman-redeemer unless this closer kinsman-redeemer relinquished his rights towards Ruth.
>
> b. **If he does not want to perform the duty for you, then I will perform the duty for you**: Wonderfully, Boaz wasn't willing to cut corners. He would do God's will God's way. He knew that if it was really of the LORD, then it could be done in an orderly and proper way.

C. Ruth goes home.

1. (14-15) Boaz sends Ruth home.

So she lay at his feet until morning, and she arose before one could recognize another. Then he said, "Do not let it be known that the woman came to the threshing floor." Also he said, "Bring the shawl that *is* on you and hold it." And when she held it, he measured six *ephahs* of barley, and laid *it* on her. Then she went into the city.

> a. **Do not let it be known**: Boaz and Ruth were not trying to hide anything scandalous; it was just that Boaz didn't want this nearer kinsman to learn that Ruth was now demanding her right to marriage to a *goel* before Boaz could tell him personally.
>
> b. **He measured six ephahs of barley**: As a proper gentleman, Boaz did not send Ruth home empty-handed. Not having any chocolates, he gave her six handfuls of grain. The added word *ephahs* is almost certainly incorrect; that would be more than thirty-three gallons (120 liters) of grain, more than Ruth could carry home in her shawl.
>
>> i. Jewish traditions say that the six measures of barley given as a gift to Ruth were a sign of six pious men who would descend from her, endowed with six spiritual gifts: David, Daniel, Hananiah, Mishael, Azariah, and the Messiah.

2. (16-18) Ruth tells her mother-in-law Naomi all that happened.

When she came to her mother-in-law, she said, "*Is* that you, my daughter?"

Then she told her all that the man had done for her. And she said, "These six

ephahs of barley he gave me; for he said to me, 'Do not go empty-handed to your mother-in-law.'"

Then she said, "Sit still, my daughter, until you know how the matter will turn out; for the man will not rest until he has concluded the matter this day."

> a. **Sit still, my daughter...the man will not rest until he has concluded the matter this day**: This was a time of considerable anxiety for Ruth. She had claimed her right to marriage and would be married. The only question was to *whom* would she be married? Would it be to Boaz, or to the nearer *goel*? The issue would be decided that very day.

Ruth 4 – The Marriage of Boaz and Ruth

A. The nearer kinsman declines his right of redemption.

1. (1-2) Boaz meets the nearer kinsman at the city gates.

Now Boaz went up to the gate and sat down there; and behold, the close relative of whom Boaz had spoken came by. So Boaz said, "Come aside, friend, sit down here." So he came aside and sat down. And he took ten men of the elders of the city, and said, "Sit down here." So they sat down.

> a. **Now Boaz went**: The previous chapter left us at a dramatic point. Ruth and Boaz seemed to be in love and wanted to get married, with Boaz exercising the right of the *goel* – the kinsman-redeemer. Yet, there was a kinsman closer to Ruth and he had priority. Would *he* claim the right of kinsman-redeemer towards Ruth, and keep her and Boaz from coming together?
>
> b. **Boaz went up to the gate**: The **gate** of the city was always the place where the esteemed and honorable men of the city sat. For an ancient city in Israel it was a combination of a city council chamber and a courtroom.
>
>> i. The city gate was "A kind of outdoor court, the place where judicial matters were resolved by the elders and those who had earned the confidence and respect of the people…a place for business and as a kind of forum or public meeting place." (Huey)
>
> c. **The close relative of whom Boaz had spoken came by**: Boaz surprised Ruth in Ruth 3:12 by telling her there was a nearer kinsman than himself. Now this man came by the city gates as Boaz sat there.
>
>> i. Because Ruth had quietly gone back home at Boaz's instruction, after being at the threshing floor, (Ruth 3:14), Boaz's approach to this nearer kinsman was planned as a complete surprise to the other man. Clearly, this was a tactical advantage to Boaz.

d. **Come aside, friend, sit down here**: Literally, in the ancient Hebrew, when Boaz greeted the nearer kinsman he called him "Mr. So-and-so." The writer of Ruth never identified the name of the nearer kinsman because he was not worthy of the honor. He declined to fulfill his obligations as the nearer kinsman to Ruth.

> i. "Doubtless Boaz both knew his name, and called him by it; but it is omitted by the holy writer, partly because it was unnecessary to know it; and principally in way of contempt, as is usual, and a just punishment upon him, that he who would not preserve his brother's name might lose his own, and lie buried in the grave of perpetual oblivion." (Poole)

2. (3-4) Boaz asks the nearer kinsman to redeem the land of Naomi (and Elimelech).

Then he said to the close relative, "Naomi, who has come back from the country of Moab, sold the piece of land which *belonged* to our brother Elimelech. And I thought to inform you, saying, 'Buy *it* back in the presence of the inhabitants and the elders of my people. If you will redeem *it*, redeem *it*; but if you will not redeem *it*, *then* tell me, that I may know; for *there is* no one but you to redeem *it*, and I *am* next after you.'"

And he said, "I will redeem *it*."

a. **Naomi…sold the piece of land**: The duty of the *goel* – the kinsman-redeemer – was more than the duty to preserve the family name of his brother in Israel. It was also to keep land allotted to members of the clan within the clan.

> i. When Israel came into the Promised Land during the days of Joshua, the land was divided among the tribes and then among the family groups. God intended that the land stay within those tribes and family groups, so the land could never permanently be sold. Every fifty years, it had to be returned to the original family group (Leviticus 25:8-17).

> ii. But fifty years is a long time. So, God made provision for land that was "sold," that it might be redeemed back to the family by the kinsman-redeemer.

> iii. Again, the kinsman-redeemer had the responsibility to protect the *persons*, *property*, and *posterity* of the larger family – and all of these duties went together.

b. **The piece of land**: When Boaz brought the matter up to the nearer kinsman, he brought it up as a matter regarding *property* – something any man would be interested in. Anyone would want to buy back a piece of property and keep it in the family name by keeping it for one's self.

c. If you will redeem it, redeem it: When Boaz put it in terms of purely a land transaction, there was no hesitation on the nearer kinsman's part. Of course, he said, "**I will redeem it**."

i. Certainly Ruth and Naomi were watching and listening. How their hearts must have sunk when they heard the nearer kinsman say, "**I will redeem it**." They heard from his own lips that he would exercise his right as kinsman-redeemer, and that meant that he would gain not only the property in question, but also marry Ruth – in the place of Boaz. But Boaz knew exactly what he was doing, and he had the situation under control.

3. (5) Boaz informs the nearer kinsman of his duty to redeem the *posterity* of Elimelech if he will redeem the *property* of Elimelech.

Then Boaz said, "On the day you buy the field from the hand of Naomi, you must also buy *it* from Ruth the Moabitess, the wife of the dead, to perpetuate the name of the dead through his inheritance."

a. **On the day you buy the field from the hand of Naomi, you must also buy it from Ruth the Moabitess**: Boaz surprised the nearer kinsman. He told him that he wasn't only dealing with Naomi and the property of Elimelech, he also had to deal with Ruth.

i. Because Naomi was older and beyond the years of bearing children, the nearer kinsman was not expected to marry Naomi and raise up children to the family name of her deceased husband Elimelech. But Ruth was another matter – she *was* able to marry and bear children.

b. **Buy it from Ruth the Moabitess, the wife of the dead, to perpetuate the name of the dead through his inheritance**: Boaz explained what everyone knew – that this was a package deal. If someone was going to exercise the right of kinsman-redeemer towards the deceased Elimelech, he had to fulfill the duty in regard to *both* the property and the posterity.

i. Because of Boaz's wise (perhaps shrewd) way of framing the occasion, this was the first time that the nearer kinsman considered this, and it was a pretty big question to take in all at once. When it was just a matter of property, it was easy to decide on; but if he must take Ruth as a wife, that was another matter.

4. (6) The nearer kinsman declines his right of redemption of the property and posterity of Elimelech.

And the close relative said, "I cannot redeem *it* for myself, lest I ruin my own inheritance. You redeem my right of redemption for yourself, for I cannot redeem *it*."

> a. **I cannot redeem it for myself**: Though it would be great to receive the property associated with Ruth, the nearer kinsman knew that taking her into his home and raising up her children would **ruin** his **own inheritance**.
>
> b. **Lest I ruin my own inheritance**: Probably, the man had grown sons that had already received their inheritance of lands. The problem of dividing that inheritance among future children he would have with Ruth was more than he wanted to deal with.
>
>> i. Also, no doubt, the man was married – and knew it would be awkward (at best!) to bring home Ruth as wife number two.
>
> c. **You redeem my right of redemption for yourself, for I cannot redeem it**: These were glorious words in the ears of Ruth and Naomi. A moment before, all seemed lost when the nearer kinsman had said, "**I will redeem it**." But Boaz's plan had a surprise and an unexpected wisdom to it. And it worked!
>
>> i. Some might have thought Boaz's plan was foolish: to gain Ruth by offering her and her land to the nearer kinsman. How could that work? But the seemingly foolish plan did work.

B. The ceremony to document the proceedings.

1. (7-8) The custom of the sandal in transactions.

Now this *was the custom* in former times in Israel concerning redeeming and exchanging, to confirm anything: one man took off his sandal and gave *it* to the other, and this *was* a confirmation in Israel.

Therefore the close relative said to Boaz, "Buy *it* for yourself." So he took off his sandal.

> a. **This was the custom in former times in Israel**: Deuteronomy 25:5-10 describes the ceremony conducted when a kinsman declined his responsibility. The one declining removed a sandal and the woman he declined to honor spat in his face. But in this case, because there was not a lack of honor involved, they just did the part of the ceremony involving the sandal.
>
> b. **Buy it for yourself**: The nearer kinsman said, "The land is yours to redeem, because you are also willing to redeem the posterity of Elimelech by taking Ruth as his wife, something I am not willing to do."

2. (9-10) Boaz's announcement to the elders and the people.

And Boaz said to the elders and all the people, "You *are* witnesses this day that I have bought all that was Elimelech's, and all that *was* Chilion's and Mahlon's, from the hand of Naomi. Moreover, Ruth the Moabitess,

the widow of Mahlon, I have acquired as my wife, to perpetuate the name of the dead through his inheritance, that the name of the dead may not be cut off from among his brethren and from his position at the gate. You *are* witnesses this day."

> a. **Boaz said to the elders and all the people**: Boaz joyfully proclaimed – legally sealing the transaction – that he would redeem both the property and the posterity of Elimelech, and (best of all!) take Ruth, the woman he loved, as his wife.
>
>> i. **That the name of the dead may not be cut off from among his brethren and from his position at the gate** is a good description of the idea of preserving the posterity of the deceased.
>
> b. **Ruth...I have acquired as my wife**: Back in chapter one, Ruth seemed to be giving up on her best chance of marriage by leaving her native land of Moab and giving her heart and life to the God of Israel. But as Ruth put God first, He brought her together in a relationship greater than she could have imagined. Today, God will bless those wanting to get married in the same way if they will only put Him first.
>
> c. **You are witnesses this day**: This explains why a marriage ceremony is important, and why it should be recognized by the civil authorities. Boaz had a love for Ruth that was public, a love that wanted to be publicly witnessed and registered.
>
>> i. Sometimes, people wonder why a marriage ceremony or a marriage license is important. "Can't we just be married before God?" But there is something severely lacking in a love that doesn't want to proclaim itself; that does not want witnesses, and that does not want the bond to be recognized by the civil authorities. That love falls short of true marital love.
>
>> ii. So, those who say "Well, if we were on a desert island and no one was there to marry us, could we still be married before God?" need to hear the answer: "Yes – on a desert island. But you aren't on a desert island. There are witnesses and civil authorities for you to proclaim your commitment of marital love to. God wants you to do it."

3. (11-12) The blessing of the witnesses to the wedding.

And all the people who *were* at the gate, and the elders, said, *"We are witnesses. The* L*ord* *make the woman who is coming to your house like Rachel and Leah, the two who built the house of Israel; and may you prosper in Ephrathah and be famous in Bethlehem. May your house be like the house of Perez, whom Tamar bore to Judah, because of the offspring which the* L*ord* *will give you from this young woman."*

    a. **All the people who were at the gate, and the elders, said, "We are witnesses"**: No doubt, the crowd cheered! The men thought Ruth was beautiful and the women thought Boaz was handsome. Everybody could see what a romantic, loving occasion this was.

    b. **Like Rachel and Leah**: These two had thirteen children between them and were the "mothers" of the whole nation of Israel. This was a big blessing to put on Boaz and Ruth.

    c. **Like the house of Perez**: What was so special about Perez? The story of his birth is in Genesis 38:27-30.

        i. Trapp on **May your house be like the house of Perez**: "That breach-maker, as the midwife called him, because he would needs be born before his brother, and carried away the first birthright: and afterwards became happy in a numerous and honourable posterity."

        ii. "Indeed, it seems that Pharez was the ancestor of the Bethlehemites in general (1 Ch. 2:5, 18, 50f.). Moreover, Pharez gave his name to the section of the tribe of Judah that was descended from him (Num. 26:20)." (Morris)

C. Happily ever after.

1. (13) Ruth and Boaz have their first child.

So Boaz took Ruth and she became his wife; and when he went in to her, the L*ord* *gave her conception, and she bore a son.*

    a. **The** L**ord** **gave her conception**: The gift of children was never taken for granted in Israel. The fact that Boaz and Ruth were able to raise up a son to the deceased Elimelech was evidence of God's blessing.

2. (14-16) The blessed life of Naomi.

Then the women said to Naomi, "Blessed be the L*ord,* *who has not left you this day without a close relative; and may his name be famous in Israel! And may he be to you a restorer of life and a nourisher of your old age; for your daughter-in-law, who loves you, who is better to you than seven sons, has borne him." Then Naomi took the child and laid him on her bosom, and became a nurse to him.*

Ruth 4

    a. **Blessed be the Lord**: Look at blessed Naomi! She now had a grandson; she was now **famous in Israel**; and she got to be a nurse to her own grandson.

    b. **Who has not left you this day without a close relative**: It was fitting that these blessings in the life of Naomi be given so much attention at the end of the book. Naomi was the one whose original returning to the Lord began all this great work of God. If Naomi had not decided to go back to Bethlehem, the land of Israel, and the God of Israel, none of this would have happened.

        i. This is a marvelous demonstration of what God can do through one poor woman who gets right with Him.

        ii. It is also fitting because Naomi was the one who said in chapter one, *the Almighty has dealt very bitterly with me.... the Lord has brought me home again empty.... the Lord has testified against me* (Ruth 1:20-21). If only Naomi could have seen *then* how greatly the Lord would bless her at the end!

        iii. We can't blame Naomi – we certainly do the same kind of thing. But we should also learn from what she learned. We should learn that God's plan is perfect and filled with love, and even when we can't understand what He is doing and it all seems so desperate, He still knows what He is doing. We should learn that *all things work together for good to those who love God, to those who are the called according to His purpose* (Romans 8:28).

3. (17-22) Ruth and Boaz: Great-grandparents to David, king of Israel.

Also the neighbor women gave him a name, saying, "There is a son born to Naomi." And they called his name Obed. He *is* the father of Jesse, the father of David. Now this *is* the genealogy of Perez: Perez begot Hezron; Hezron begot Ram, and Ram begot Amminadab; Amminadab begot Nahshon, and Nahshon begot Salmon; Salmon begot Boaz, and Boaz begot Obed; Obed begot Jesse, and Jesse begot David.

    a. **There is a son born to Naomi**: The son of Ruth and Boaz was named **Obed**. He had a son named **Jesse**. He had a son named **David** and David had a descendant named *Jesus*.

        i. "God's hand is all over history. God works out His purpose, generation after generation. Limited as we are to one lifetime, each of us sees so little of what happens. A genealogy is a striking way of bringing before us the continuity of God's purpose through the ages. The process of history is not haphazard. There is a purpose in it all. And the purpose is the purpose of God." (Morris)

b. **The father of David**: Naomi's return to Bethlehem, and the roots of David in Bethlehem, going back to Ruth and Boaz, are why Joseph and Mary had to go to Bethlehem to register in the census of Augustus (Luke 2:1-5). Ruth and Boaz are the reason why Jesus was born in Bethlehem!

i. But the consideration of Jesus in this book of Ruth doesn't begin with the mention of King David; Jesus has been through the whole book, pictured by Boaz and the office of the kinsman-redeemer.

- The kinsman-redeemer had to be a family member; Jesus added humanity to His eternal deity, so He could be our kinsman and save us.
- The kinsman-redeemer had the duty of buying family members out of slavery; Jesus redeemed us from slavery to sin and death.
- The kinsman-redeemer had the duty of buying back land that had been forfeited; Jesus will redeem the earth that mankind "sold" over to Satan.
- Boaz, as kinsman-redeemer to Ruth, was not motivated by self-interest, but motivated by love for Ruth. Jesus' motivation for redeeming us is His great love for us.
- Boaz, as kinsman-redeemer to Ruth, had to have a plan to redeem Ruth himself – and some might have thought the plan to be foolish. Jesus has a plan to redeem us, and some might think the plan foolish (saving men by dying for them on a cruel cross?), yet the plan works and is glorious.
- Boaz, as kinsman-redeemer to Ruth, took her as his bride; the people Jesus has redeemed are collectively called His bride (Ephesians 5:31-32; Revelation 21:9).
- Boaz, as kinsman-redeemer to Ruth, provided a glorious destiny for Ruth. Jesus, as our redeemer, provides a glorious destiny for us.

ii. But it all comes back to the idea of Jesus as our *kinsman-redeemer*; this is why He became a man. God might have sent an angel to save us, but the angel would not have been our *kinsman*. Jesus, in His eternal glory, without the addition of humanity to His divine nature might have saved us, but He would not have been our *kinsman*. A great prophet or priest would be our kinsman, but his own sin would have disqualified him as our *redeemer*. Only Jesus, the eternal God who added humanity to His eternal deity, can be both the *kinsman* and the *redeemer* for mankind!

iii. Isaiah 54:4-8 describes the beautiful ministry of the LORD as our *goel* – our kinsman-redeemer: *Do not fear, for you will not be…disgraced, for you will not be put to shame…. your* [Kinsman] *Redeemer is the Holy One of Israel…. For the LORD has called you like a woman forsaken and grieved in spirit…. with everlasting kindness I will have mercy on you, says the LORD, your* [Kinsman] *Redeemer.*

iv. From eternity, God planned to bring Ruth and Boaz together, and thus make Bethlehem His entrance point for the coming of Jesus as our true Kinsman-Redeemer, fully God and fully man. In a real-life spiritual sense, all must to come to Bethlehem for the redemption that only Jesus can provide.

Bibiliography

Judges

Clarke, Adam *The Holy Bible, Containing the Old and New Testaments, with A Commentary and Critical Notes, Volume II – Joshua to Esther* (New York: Eaton and Mains, 1827?)

Cundall, Arthur E. "Judges," in *Judges and Ruth, an Introduction and Commentary* (Nottingham, England: Intervarsity Press, 1968)

Ginzberg, Louis *The Legends of the Jews, Volumes 1-7* (Philadelphia: The Jewish Publication Society of America, 1968)

Meyer, F.B. *Joshua and the Land of Promise* (Fort Washington, Pennsylvania: Christian Literature Crusade, 1977)

Meyer, F.B. *Our Daily Homily* (Westwood, New Jersey: Revell, 1966)

Morgan, G. Campbell *Searchlights from the Word* (New York: Revell, 1926)

Morgan, G. Campbell *An Exposition of the Whole Bible* (Old Tappan, New Jersey: Revell, 1959)

Poole, Matthew *A Commentary on the Holy Bible, Volume 1* (London, Banner of Truth Trust, 1968)

Spurgeon, Charles Haddon *The New Park Street Pulpit, Volumes 1-6* and *The Metropolitan Tabernacle Pulpit, Volumes 7-63* (Pasadena, Texas: Pilgrim Publications, 1990)

Trapp, John *A Commentary on the Old and New Testaments, Volume 1 – Genesis to Second Chronicles* (Eureka, California: Tanski Publications, 1997)

Wolf, Herbert "Judges," in *The Expositor's Bible Commentary: Deuteronomy, Joshua, Judges, Ruth, 1 & 2 Samuel*, ed. Frank E. Gaebelein, vol. 3 (Grand Rapids, MI: Zondervan Publishing House, 1992)

Wood, Leon *Distressing Days of the Judges* (Grand Rapids, Michigan: Zondervan, 1975)

Ruth

Clarke, Adam *The Holy Bible, Containing the Old and New Testaments, with A Commentary and Critical Notes, Volume II – Joshua to Esther* (New York: Eaton and Mains, 1827?)

Huey, F.B. Jr. "Ruth," in *The Expositor's Bible Commentary: Deuteronomy, Joshua, Judges, Ruth, 1 & 2 Samuel*, ed. Frank E. Gaebelein, vol. 3 (Grand Rapids, MI: Zondervan Publishing House, 1992)

Meyer, F.B. *Our Daily Homily* (Westwood, New Jersey: Revell, 1966)

Morgan, G. Campbell *Searchlights from the Word* (New York: Revell, 1926)

Morgan, G. Campbell *An Exposition of the Whole Bible* (Old Tappan, New Jersey: Revell, 1959)

Morris, Leon "Ruth," in *Judges and Ruth, an Introduction and Commentary* (Nottingham, England: Intervarsity Press, 1968)

Poole, Matthew *A Commentary on the Holy Bible, Volume 1* (London, Banner of Truth Trust, 1968)

Spurgeon, Charles Haddon *The New Park Street Pulpit, Volumes 1-6* and *The Metropolitan Tabernacle Pulpit, Volumes 7-63*(Pasadena, Texas: Pilgrim Publications, 1990)

Trapp, John *A Commentary on the Old and New Testaments, Volume 1 – Genesis to Second Chronicles* (Eureka, California: Tanski Publications, 1997)

Author's Remarks

As the years pass I love the work of studying, learning, and teaching the Bible more than ever. I'm so grateful that God is faithful to meet me in His Word.

For another time I am tremendously grateful to Alison Turner for her proofreading and editorial suggestions, especially with a challenging manuscript. Alison, thank you so much!

Thanks to Brian Procedo for the cover design and the graphics work.

Most especially, thanks to my wife Inga-Lill. She is my loved and valued partner in life and in service to God and His people.

David Guzik

David Guzik's Bible commentary is regularly used and trusted by many thousands who want to know the Bible better. Pastors, teachers, class leaders, and everyday Christians find his commentary helpful for their own understanding and explanation of the Bible. David and his wife Inga-Lill live in Santa Barbara, California.

You can email David at
david@enduringword.com

For more resources by David Guzik,
go to www.enduringword.com